Russian Regional Journalism

This book is part of the Peter Lang Media and Communication list.
Every volume is peer reviewed and meets
the highest quality standards for content and production.

PETER LANG
New York • Bern • Berlin
Brussels • Vienna • Oxford • Warsaw

Elina Erzikova and Wilson Lowrey

Russian Regional Journalism

Struggle and Survival in the Heartland

PETER LANG
New York • Bern • Berlin
Brussels • Vienna • Oxford • Warsaw

Library of Congress Cataloging-in-Publication Data

Names: Erzikova, Elina, author. | Lowrey, Wilson, author.
Title: Russian regional journalism: struggle and survival in the heartland / Elina Erzikova, Wilson Lowrey.
Description: New York: Peter Lang, 2020.
Includes bibliographical references and index.
Identifiers: LCCN 2020025757 (print) | LCCN 2020025758 (ebook)
ISBN 978-1-4331-7133-8 (hardback) | ISBN 978-1-4331-7134-5 (paperback)
ISBN 978-1-4331-7135-2 (ebook pdf)
ISBN 978-1-4331-7136-9 (epub) | ISBN 978-1-4331-7137-6 (mobi)
Subjects: LCSH: Journalism, Regional—Russia (Federation)—History—21st century. | Journalists—Russia (Federation) | Journalism—Social aspects—Russia (Federation)—History—21st century. | Journalism—Political aspects—Russia (Federation)—History—21st century. | Press and politics—Russia (Federation)—History—21st century.
Classification: LCC PN5277.R44 E79 2020 (print) | LCC PN5277.R44 (ebook) | DDC 070.4/33—dc23
LC record available at https://lccn.loc.gov/2020025757
LC ebook record available at https://lccn.loc.gov/2020025758
DOI 10.3726/b15828

Bibliographic information published by **Die Deutsche Nationalbibliothek**.
Die Deutsche Nationalbibliothek lists this publication in the "Deutsche Nationalbibliografie"; detailed bibliographic data are available on the Internet at http://dnb.d-nb.de/.

© 2020 Peter Lang Publishing, Inc., New York
80 Broad Street, 5th floor, New York, NY 10004
www.peterlang.com

All rights reserved.
Reprint or reproduction, even partially, in all forms such as microfilm, xerography, microfiche, microcard, and offset strictly prohibited.

Elina: *To Tom and Region Wright, former newspaper editors of* The Decatur Daily, *Decatur, AL*
Wilson: *To Mary Loyd, Perrin and Wes*

Table of Contents

Acknowledgments ix

Section I: Russian Regional Journalism and Its Contexts
Chapter One: Introduction 3
Chapter Two: Russia's Regions and Regional Journalism: The Current Context 25
Chapter Three: Local Russian Journalism as a Social Space: Field and Ecology
    Perspectives 47

Section II: Findings: The Three Regions, Their Journalism, Journalists and
    Communities
Chapter Four: Russian Regional Journalism and Its Environments 69
Chapter Five: Regional Journalists: Scarcity, Divisiveness and Persistence 89
Chapter Six: Russian Regional Journalists in a Digital Era 109
Chapter Seven: Journalists' Shifting, Versatile Roles 131
Chapter Eight: Cracks in the System: Journalists' Pursuit of Autonomy 153
Chapter Nine: Conclusions: Daunting Challenges and Ways Forward 173

Appendix: Methodology 191
Index 201

Acknowledgments

First and foremost, both of us—Elina and Wilson—thank those whom we cannot name. We promised anonymity to 124 individuals—newspaper editors, reporters, advertising managers and proofreaders—who welcomed our research into their newsrooms and lives making this project possible. These individuals never said they feared being identified. The reason was, as one reporter put it, "Nothing left to lose." But we were (and are) still cautious.

For more than thirteen years, Elina religiously traveled to Russia every year, taking part in journalistic communities in three Russian districts or regions. Besides conducting interviews, focus groups and observations, she did what everyone was supposed to do while in Russia: drank a lot of tea and ate uncounted boxes of chocolate (not just ballet and hockey are great in Russia). Participants shared anger, joy, secrets, disagreements, values, Instagram photos, bad/good days, passion for writing, love of art and appreciation of humor.

Meanwhile, Wilson stayed put, but not idle, working on the project's scaffolding—helping fashion the frameworks of our inquiry and the words through which we shared them—while always staying in touch, at a distance, with Elina's lively and lived experiences in the regions.

Of course, our participants had an agenda. They felt their work as regional journalists is a largely untold story, and this is why many conversations started with them saying, "Tell the West."

And we do.

The West, listen up. Russian regional journalists, overlooked and even looked down upon and having little chance competing for scholars' interests with their colleagues from the national capital, want you to know that … well, it's all in the book.

Many scholars helped us assure this book accurately represents Russia and its journalism, today and in the past. We are grateful to Sergei Samoilenko, Svetlana Pasti, Vera Slavtcheva-Petkova, Michael Alexeev, Ilya Kiriya and anonymous reviewers for what Russians call конструктивная критика (constructive criticism) and insightful comments. Of course, any errors are entirely our own.

We appreciate care and guidance of the Peter Lang Publishing, Inc.'s editorial team—Erika Hendrix and Liam McLean.

We thank our families for helping us power through. Your unconditional love and faith that this book would eventually be completed inspired us every day (if not every hour). A special thanks to Perrin for his careful work in checking references.

Elina and Wilson,
May 7, 2020

SECTION I

RUSSIAN REGIONAL JOURNALISM AND ITS CONTEXTS

CHAPTER ONE

Introduction

In 2012, a reporter for the Government newspaper, the oldest local paper in its region, received a phone call from an employee of a local factory in a remote village. The factory's owner had refused to pay salaries and threatened to close the factory, the employee said—a move that would cripple the small community. The reporter followed up, asking regional government officials to comment. Officials listened but warned the reporter off the story. The factory owner was a "nut case from Moscow," they said, and he would hurt people if the story were published. The reporter decided to kill her story, as she "did not want to aggravate" the delicate situation and risk a factory shutdown. In the past month, six of her investigations had withered on the vine, all discouraged by officials, and the reporter was frustrated. But she was philosophical. She had come to believe it was more important to help people in need than to publish a story that might do them damage. She said that in the 1990s "reporters would have thrown stories like bombs into a crowd," but today, reporters are being careful. No reporter, she said, wants her story to be the "last straw"—the story that leads to disaster.

Local Russian journalists[1] have a history of connecting personally with the citizens who read their stories. Local Russian citizens have a history of reaching out to journalists, often in desperation. We see evidence of both in the anecdote above, told to us by a reporter interviewed for our study of journalism in Russia's regions.

For the citizens in the regions we studied, often burdened by poverty and neglected by government, the press could be a final hope, and journalists sometimes have pushed officials to help citizens. Yet, local journalists themselves have been threatened by poverty and some news outlets threatened with closure. The COVID-19 pandemic, spreading around the world as we complete this book, is surely making these hard times worse. And so, often, journalists have not pushed officials, as journalists' vulnerability and dependence on government have grown. With meager revenue and diminished autonomy, regional journalists who seek to serve both citizens and local elite face a steep, risky challenge.

Today, political engagement by journalists and citizens at Russia's regional levels is as important as ever. Russia's national regime draws critical support from the regional "heartland," despite the fact that, historically, these areas have been subsumed within national-level governance, and obscured by the wealth, power and cultural dominance of "the capitals," Moscow and St. Petersburg.

National Russian policy, from the reign of Catherine the Great through the Soviet era and on to today, has often discouraged the notion that the *regions*—Peter the Great's *provintsiia*[2]—are individually distinctive. The regions have been portrayed as uniform, a vague backdrop to the country's vibrant capital cities and distinctive ethnic areas. The regions' journalism and other cultural forms have tended to be overlooked as well.

Of course, Russia's regions are not uniform. They are diverse, in geography, resources and economic fabric, ethnicities, religion and culture. Differences across a country enhance the chances for change, and cultural, political and economic diversity should encourage diversity in journalism content. No doubt, the journalism of Russia's regions shows significant conformity to Russia's uniform national governance and culture, but in our research, we also found journalism norms, values and practices that are shaped by other important contexts, including both local and occupational communities.

Mixed contexts suggest questions. What are the varying characteristics of the challenging environments within which local journalists live and work? How do these characteristics constrain and shape their journalism and notions about its purposes? How have these characteristics and their influences changed (or not changed) across the Putin era? Can local journalists truly reflect their regions and the needs of regional citizens? Can local journalists connect with both government and citizen and bridge the two? If so, how?

We explore these questions through qualitative case studies of local newspaper journalism in Russia, conducted each year from 2007 to 2019. We studied journalists, their work and their perceptions at newspapers in three regions. Newspapers in one region, our primary region of study, were examined across all 13 years, while newspapers in the other two regions were studied over the last half of that period.

The primary regional case, which we call Region A, is a small, fairly typical region suffering through economic adversity. The two other regions, Region B and Region C, are explored less thoroughly, but they offer valuable comparison as they are larger and relatively wealthier and more stable. Theories of social fields and ecologies serve as lenses for analysis, and we provide detail on our conceptual framework below and in Chapter 3.

This book follows a number of recent studies that have also looked at subsections of Russia's news media, including studies of journalism in particular regions (Romanovich, 2006; Roudakova, 2017; Verkhovskya, 2006) and several overviews of regional journalism (Pasti, 2005; Pasti & Pietiläinen, 2008; Pietiläinen, 2002). Other recent studies have focused on news media niches, such as journalism in smaller, more liberal outlets (Slavtcheva-Petkova, 2018) and online digital media (Oates, 2013). Our book contributes to this increasingly varied literature on Russian journalism by providing analysis of a regional social space, offering comparison across multiple regions, across multiple news outlets of different ownership types, and across time, from the post-perestroika period forward.

Russian Regional Journalism as Local Journalism

Not all the troubles of regional Russian journalists are unique to Russia. Both the scholarly literatures on Russia's regional journalism and the general literature on local journalism—in Europe, the U.S. and elsewhere—suggest local journalists across the world struggle to connect the intimate space of people's everyday lives with the space of local governance and the broad space of national governance.

Several challenges derive from small scale, a quality shared generally by local communities and their news sources. One common challenge is the unified power of local elites, which constrains media and limits the diversity of viewpoints in smaller social environments (Tichenor, Olien & Donohue, 1980; Nah & Armstrong, 2011; Rankine et al., 2011). Dependence on the local elite was certainly evident among the papers in our research. One editor noted the small "pool of information" in his region: "You upset a few press secretaries, and next you don't know where to go to gather information."

Local news organizations and communities also generally have fewer human and financial resources than do national-level news organizations in the largest cities (Culver, 2014; Fink & Anderson, 2015; Zion et al., 2016). Resource scarcity was evident at most papers we studied. Over the last decade, one paper shrank from 12 to three reporters, all desperately trying to fill a growing news hole due to declining advertising. The limiting effects of resource scarcity on the reach, depth and general quality of news have been common across media systems (Berkowitz,

2007; Franklin, 2006), and smaller staffs tend to rely more heavily on media releases from government agencies and businesses.

A third common condition is the close quarters between journalists and residents, and the shared trust between the two that this proximity fosters. Research indicates that journalists who identify authentically with their community encourage trust—i.e., when a journalist perceives the community as "my home," residents perceive the journalist as "one of our own" (Chernov & Ivanova, 2013; Hatcher & Haavik, 2014; Matthews, 2017; Thomson et al., 2015). Such identification is important but increasingly hard to come by, given news staff turnover. We also note that strong bonds between journalists and communities can bring dysfunction, encouraging insularity and boosterism, which can hinder social change (Gutsche, 2015).

We discuss these common traits and challenges of local-level journalism in more depth in Chapter 3. However, we won't take the universal comparison too far. Russian local journalists enact their work within distinct cultural and political-economic contexts and dynamics. These contexts and dynamics shape the analytical field of this book's case studies, and we need to understand their origins. Later in the book, we look at the contexts of the three regions we studied. However, all regions in Russia's heartland share some common history, and we explore this history next, as knowing where you've been is important to understanding where you are.

Russian Journalism at Russia's "Sub-National" Levels: A Brief History

No country's journalism follows a single course over time. Russia's local journalism has not, though in Russia's case, the perception of a single course is somewhat understandable, as the nation state has dominated Russia's regions, politically, economically and culturally. Journalism's history in the "capital cities" of Moscow and St. Petersburg has received much more attention than Russia's less urban regions (Beumers, Hutchings, & Rulyova, 2009), and research on the politics, economics and culture of Russia's sub-national level has been less common than research on the nation-state. However, there has been an active vein of research on sub-national Russia, and it informs the following brief historical account of Russia's local journalism.

Pre-Soviet and Soviet Eras

As early as the 1830s, local Russian journalism could be seen as the product of two very different kinds of storytellers. One was the local "chronicler." Chroniclers were clergy who kept the village archive as one of their clerical responsibilities. Archives included accounts of cultural and religious events, prominent residents and momentous occasions, and publication of these accounts had a wide-ranging audience, including nobles and merchants, as well as peasants. The second was the government, producing stories driven by political and economic need. Regional newspapers were established by law in 1837 as part of an effort to spur economic growth across Russia, a rationalist response to growing global trade. These newspapers reported information from the regions on prices, descriptions of factories, and the like. The expectation that regional resources would serve national need was not invented in 1837—it preceded the 1800s and continues today as part of the identity of the provinces (Smith-Peter, 2018). As an afterthought, economic newspapers also included histories of the local area, supplementing the parish chronicles. Though not priority, these accounts were ambitious, with local editors filling pages "with their archival and ethnographic findings, ultimately constructing a kaleidoscope of regional histories" (Evtuhov, 2018, p. 283). These two threads of local journalism—service to government, and cultivation of communal culture and everyday life—would interlace, tangle and diverge across the decades.

During and before the 17th Century, regions developed a spiritual, mystical identity suffused with accounts of "sacred groves and springs, and the regional lives of saints" (Smith-Peter, 2018, p. 19). However, the rationalizing enlightenment era discouraged non-rational regional distinctiveness and encouraged the view that regions were empty spaces that needed centralized planning (Smith-Peter, 2018). While there were occasional efforts to strengthen regional power and identity during the 1800s (see Smith-Peter, 2018), regions' identities were shaped by powerful accounts from beyond their borders, including the cultural intelligentsia of Moscow and St. Petersburg. "The provinces can only be imagined within the 'capital/provinces' binary," according to Parts (2016, p. 201). Low literacy rates in non-urban areas contributed to perceptions that the regions were nondescript backwaters and to the confinement of Russia's public sphere to the large cities (Stepin, 2015). Prominent writers and thinkers from the capitals dismissed Russian regions as homogenous and characterless—they are "the same, the same, the same," declared 19th Century writer Vladimir Sollogub (Lounsbery, 2018, p. 45). Characterizations of "sameness" are consistent with a homogenizing 19th Century national policy for urban development, which required each provincial city to model its planning on the nearest more successful city, all the way up to Moscow and St. Petersburg (Lounsbery, 2018).

The early Soviet era saw some modest decentralizing. A political example is Soviet Federalism's loose rein on neighboring republics (e.g., Georgia, Armenia, etc.) (Forestier-Peyrat, 2017). Also, efforts were made early in the Soviet era to bring the common people into the country's information processes through the establishment of the *rabselkory*, or worker-peasant correspondents, who provided provincial voices through grassroots reports on their local workplaces or villages. Though censored by central administrators who sought to infuse the accounts with educational value, this effort contributed to a tradition of horizontal communication among everyday people at local levels (Hopkins, 1970; Kelly, 2002). The 1920s also produced a movement to study and recognize regional cultures. Such efforts were suppressed during the Stalin era but rose again in the 1960s, a counter to the general centralizing policies of the Soviet state (Smith-Peter, 2018).

Centralization strongly shaped journalism during the Soviet era. Yet, "small differences in press coverage [were] encouraged by the party/state in order to appeal to audiences of different regions, educational levels and occupations" (Becker, 2014, p. 194). Local journalists experienced meaningful feelings of obligation to both professional community and local community, encouraged by an ideological mission that has been missing in today's Russia (Roudakova, 2017). But, there is still evidence of these feelings. As a reporter with a commercial newspaper told us: "We—reporters and ordinary folks—are on one side of the barricade and bureaucrats are on the other."

The Perestroika Era

The final decades of the Soviet era brought modest shifts in political-economic power from the national to the sub-national level. As costs of centralization grew, regional officials gained some influence over taxing and distributing income, functions that had been controlled by the nation state (Gel'man, 2010). Following the demise of the Soviet Union, the Federation Treaty of 1992 and Russian Constitution in 1993 provided greater autonomy to the republics and provinces (Kirkow, 1998; Moses, 2004). These "centrifugal tendencies" in post-Soviet Russia "enhanced the autonomy and importance of the provincial media" (Davis, Hammond, & Nizamova, 1998, p. 77). Perestroika enabled a broad, if poorly defined, press freedom (Kirkow, 1998; Ledeneva, 2006; Von Seth, 2012), a level of autonomy not seen before or since. A "golden age" of Russian journalism had dawned, according to many of our interview respondents, who valued the right to question officials as well as the freedom to produce their own journalism and write in personal, reflective ways. A few journalists we interviewed owned a regional newspaper in the '90s that published relatively independent reporting. Early on, their newspaper circulation grew "like a mushroom after a heavy rain," as a former editor said, and local bureaucrats started their day by reading the paper to find out if "they were scolded there."

However, dawn turned to dusk as problems emerged for the regions and for local journalism. Weak and ambiguous laws and judiciary (Sheftelevich, 2009), ineffective planning, lax federal law enforcement, and a harsh financial climate undermined the regions' political and economic liberalization (Kirkow, 1998). Difficult financial times challenged liberalization as well, including continuing problems from the collapse of the Soviet Union such as the demise of Soviet-era artificial cities—once built around particular resource needs of the USSR, they fell into crisis, failing to adjust to new markets (Kiriya & Kachkaeva, 2011).

To avoid rigid Soviet-style centralization, Boris Yeltsin, past president of the Russian Soviet Federal Socialist Republic, encouraged federal subjects to "take as much sovereignty as you can swallow" ("Берите столько суверенитета, сколько сможете проглотить") (Yeltsin Center, 2015), encouraging regional elites to ignore federal law (Smith, 2003). Provincial populations suffered in poverty and grew more dependent on the resources of local authorities, who controlled local businesses and criminal groups in exchange for their "support of the status quo" (Gel'man, 2010, p. 9). The "absence of strong institutionalized political parties" (Ross, 2002, p. 49), the lax judicial oversight, and the fragmented local legislatures produced a "loosening of institutional coherence" (Kirkow, 1998, p. 3) that allowed wealthy, powerful business owners and politicians to assert monopolistic control, despite regular regional elections. This depressed citizen activism and weakened press autonomy (Ross, 2006). In short, the withdrawal of central state control was double-edged for local news media. Though it loosened constraints, it left unprepared and cash-strapped journalists vulnerable to chaotic markets and opportunistic oligarchs (Soldner, 2008). This eroded their professional autonomy and principles. As one of our research participants said, "The power that feels unsecure began producing journalists who were similar to the power."

Political power swung back toward the nation state, as a recessionary economy in the '90s made life in the regions increasingly grim, and dependency on the central government grew. Wages fell as immigrant population surged, rates for divorce and single-parent households increased, mortality rates rose, and birthrates fell (Kirkow, 1998; White, 2004). Salaries "were spent within a week, so that the rest of the month was spent borrowing from relatives and friends" (White, 2004, pp. 97–98). Many who sought opportunities in a freer market had no business experience and lacked connections with "the right people" in their areas. In her ethnographic study of the regions, White (2004) recounts one poorly connected resident who tried to start a business with her husband: "They forced us to shut down" she said, and she "ended up as a poorly paid journalist instead" (p. 122).

A wide range of problems ended the perestroika era's "golden age" for local journalists. New press laws allowed more journalistic autonomy, but the lack of legal detail undermined press freedom (Soldner, 2008). Weak federal-level oversight, a creeping economic recession in poor regions, an unsustainable explosion of new publications, lack of business experience among local journalists, an absence of strong political parties and organized movements, and a growing plutocracy of opportunistic local political and business leaders—all these undermined journalists' independence.

The corrosive practice of publishing "kompromat"—politically compromising material—spread after laws emerged that allowed the reporting of revelatory information about officials. Compromising materials were often paid for by one powerful figure to use against a rival, including some newspapers in our study, and local news outlets desperately needed this money. While kompromat could reveal socially important information, its rampant use tainted journalism's image, and citizens wearied of it (Ledeneva, 2006). Professional journalistic principles such as accountability and transparency lost their luster, becoming linked in the popular mind with cut-throat competition among self-serving elites (Ledeneva, 2006). A reporter interviewed for our study recalled this era's "oppositional papers" as plagued by "pathology" and full of "poison that was spilling over." It seemed these methods were not helping to make public opinion "constructive and useful for the system" (Pietiläinen, 2002, p. 454).

So, just as regional journalists thought they had found a path to independence, they lost their way. In a country where "business is politics" (de Smaele, 2009, p. 58), local political-economic strongmen were pitted against one another, and the journalistic community splintered as well, amid harsh financial circumstances, venomous competition, stories produced for the "highest bidder," and accusations of falsehoods. The news turned nasty. The sense that "journalists and readers were 'in it together'" was eroding (Roudakova, 2017, pp. 23–24). Fewer local residents felt that local journalism was important to their lives: There were "better sources of information, such as phone calls to friends" (White, 2004, p. 194). Further, as dependence on government increased, journalists' influence with officials and journalists' role in local political life weakened. As a journalist we interviewed noted, local officials, who in the past had been responsive to reported problems, declared that officials have one month to respond to local media criticism, despite federal law requiring response within seven days. Local journalists were losing the threads that connected them to both government and the lives of everyday people.

Post-Perestroika

Citizens, leaders and many journalists craved order, fairness and an end to governmental caprice (Ross, 2010), and the regions were fertile for the rise of a strong national leader (Zubarevich, 2010). Vladimir Putin promised the country order while taking advantage of perestroika-era disorder and corruption (Gel'man, 2010;

Ross, 2010; Zubarevich, 2010). Over the post-perestroika years of the late '90s and early 2000s, Kremlin control over the regions gradually tightened, though early control took the form of loose co-optation. Local elite were still powerful, and Moscow left them nominally in charge (Gel'man, 2010; Zubarevich, 2010). Putin also pursued cultural co-optation of the regions by encouraging pride in an imagined "heartland" and by fueling the regions' age-old distrust of the West and of Russia's Europe-facing capitals. Local points of pride in the regions, often with historical connections to Russian Orthodoxy, were co-opted as emblems of "the true" national core (Lounsbery, 2018). Regions lost the authority to fund their own unique cultural agendas, and, according to Donovan (2018), local heroes and myths were being embedded within "a state-backed mythology that corresponded with the patriotic politics of the Putinist era" (p. 88).

Economic control joined political and cultural control in subduing provincial media. Enabled by both economic growth in the 2000s and Kremlin support, national business conglomerates broke down barriers to local markets (Gel'man, 2010; Zubarevich, 2002), buying up local media and strengthening central control over these outlets. National media have also spread into the regions, offering mostly entertainment, indicating "no interest in local issues [or in] the unique interests of the citizens" (Kasyutin, 2011, p. 87). One of our study participants shared her impressions of a prominent TV personality who "came to journalism from the street, and the street entered the profession with him." As a result, she said, "we got *popsa* [low-brow entertainment]."

The mechanisms of national-level control have tended to be fairly indirect. There was an understanding that overt, iron-fisted control over the regions, such as the removal of "regional barons," could backfire on the Kremlin. As Ottaway (2003) noted, "semi-authoritarian" regimes "leave enough political space for political parties and organizations of civil society to form, for an independent press to function to some extent, and for some political debate to take place" (p. 3). Though these relatively light-handed strategies have resulted in effective control, pluralism in media ownership and "the absence of a highly developed ideology" in national governance cracked the door a bit, allowing for some hopes for societal change and civic liberties, given the right moment (Becker, 2014, p. 204). Where there is regional variation, governmental change and civic regeneration is more thinkable (Hobsawn & Ranger, 1983; Liikanen, 2008).

Yet the government's grip over media production—especially TV—tightened over the years (Becker, 2014). A long-time journalist we interviewed said she has never experienced less autonomy as a journalist: "Censorship is tougher today than it was during Yeltsin's time and much tougher than it was in [Soviet Premier] Brezhnev's time." Slim hopes for media freedom confront the unforgiving realities of harsh economic times and dependence on government, weakened professional commitment, and the people's disenchantment over journalists' political role. In addition, journalist's safety is increasingly threatened. Practicing political journalism in the outer regions has become particularly dangerous, one journalist noted (Felgengauer, in Slavtcheva-Petkova, 2018).

The financial situation for most local journalists has grown more desperate and the workload heavier over the last decade. In the past five years, more than 12,000 periodic publications, most of them regional or local, have gone bankrupt (Press Market Report, 2018). According to a 2012 national survey of Russian journalists, a third said their news outlet staffs had shrunk during the five years before the survey, and around 20% reported holding additional jobs to make ends meet (Nygren, 2015). Along with financial struggles, we have seen strong dependence on local officials and weakened ethical standards. More than two-thirds of journalists surveyed in a 2017 report said payment to sources for confidential information was justified at least "on occasion," and over a quarter said accepting money from sources was justified, at least on occasion (Anikina, Frost & Hanitzsch, 2017, p. 3).

The Promise of Russian Local Journalism

Across our 13 years of research, political-economic elites and structures have, in many ways, dominated the practice of local journalism in the regions we studied. This finding is consistent with a history of subordination to national and regional powers and of struggles during harsh economic times. And, the finding is not surprising in a society that does not "consider itself as something autonomous and independent from the state" (Vartanova, 2012, p. 131).

However, we found the situation to be more complex. Journalists sometimes defied or negotiated with local power in latent ways, with an eye on helping community residents. Journalists also sought to connect personally with citizens, producing content that addressed their apolitical needs, from daily, mundane problems to spiritual inspiration. Though the citizen-journalist relationship has been strained, many research participants thought citizens still viewed them as "one of their own." According to one participant, a journalism that gives no voice to citizens is not journalism:

> Journalism as a phenomenon can exist only if it reflects points of view of citizens. If journalism is not able to do this, journalism ends, and something else—PR—starts.

Our findings suggest the age-old threads connecting local journalists with both powerful elite and common citizens are not frayed through. But it's a difficult task to weave these threads together—to encourage and enable meaningful communication between haves and have-nots, and between officials and everyday people. This task would be formidable enough without journalists' own financial hardships and their weakened, fragmented journalistic community.

The brief history above suggests a number of reasons we need to understand local Russian journalism. One, variability and pluralism across regions indicate potential for change. Two, citizens' identification with the local is strong. In 2011, Kasyutin described Russia as "a large loose space" where "local identity is intensively developing, reinforced by the opposition to the onslaught of information globalization" (p. 89). Recent surveys show that while national identity remains solid, Russians identify with their local city more than they identify with their federal region (Savoskul, 2017). Three, PR efforts by the national regime suggest an understanding of the power of local-level identity. The regime nurtures support within Russia's "heartland," adopting rhetoric that connects rural regions with a militaristic patriotism and pits the regions against liberal urban areas. We see the tendency toward an urban-rural divide around the world. The rural areas, towns and small cities—the overlooked heartlands, hinterlands and "flyover" areas—are staking out opposition to globally networked urban corridors (Castells, 2011), demanding to be heard and understood (Algan, Guriev, Papaioannou & Passari, 2017; Mounk, 2018). While the Kremlin's narrative that real Russian patriotism derives from the provincial heartland seems to be resonating, it seems unlikely that top-down national policies can fully address the needs of such a large, diverse population. Finally, a better understanding of the local Russian journalism space provides another lens for the research on local journalism globally, a growing and increasingly important area of journalism studies. In Chapter 3, we explore the broader literature on local journalism and its recent struggles, and we revisit this context in our discussion of findings.

What are the political and societal futures of the regions and their journalism? Is there hope that local journalists and their news outlets will gain the autonomy needed to link political space with personal space in their regions, and aid citizens in meaningful ways? What might such linkages look like, and what factors may make them more or less likely?

Our Case Studies: The Regions and Newspapers

Our book sheds light on these questions through an analysis of 13 years of qualitative case studies of newspaper organizations in three Russian regions. Local newspapers are important in the study of local Russian journalism, as many rural areas are not covered by regional TV stations (Beumers, Rulyova & Hutchings,

2009) and internet can be prohibitively expensive: One month of internet access is roughly equal to a six-month weekly newspaper subscription.

Though the histories, cultures and political-economic conditions of the three regions differ, national-level control across the centuries has encouraged similarities. Demographically and politically, these regions are fairly typical. They vary most notably in their size and economic situations. Region A, which receives the most attention in this book, ranks among the poorer regions in Russia. Region B, is more populous and somewhat wealthier, and Region C is the wealthiest of the three, with abundant natural resources. We provide general information on these regions and their papers in subsequent chapters.

Region A takes center stage. We studied the processes and content of three newspapers in this region for the study's duration, from 2007 to 2019, and a fourth from 2007 to 2013. For comparison's sake, in 2012 we added one newspaper from Region B, and in 2013 we added three newspapers from Region C. All newspapers are regional in scope and are published regularly; all are socio-political or "quality" publications; and at the time of their selection, all had weekly circulations of at least 10,000 and had operated for at least 10 years. These newspapers differ by ownership type and business model, with some owned and funded entirely by the government and others privately owned and supported by both commercial revenue and government revenue.

As the reader has noticed, pseudonyms are used for regions' names. We also use pseudonyms for the Region A newspapers. The *Government* newspaper is the oldest and is the official organ of the regional government. The *Private* newspaper is privately owned by a local businessman who has multiple media holdings, and among the region's papers, it has had the most success gaining ad revenue. The *Traditional* newspaper was launched by the city administration during perestroika to counter regional media controlled by the governor; the mayor was defeated and today the paper struggles financially, though it receives some funding from the regional government. The fourth publication, the *Regional Branch* newspaper, was owned by a Moscow-based media company and was dropped from the study in 2013 when it became an advertising vehicle. Appendix A provides more detail about the study's newspapers and our methods.

Our research is based on in-depth interviews and focus group sessions with more than 100 individuals, including newspaper staff and management, government officials, and PR practitioners, as well as observation of news-work practices. Most interview data were collected in person at the newspapers during summers; however, year-round email and Skype conversations informed these data. Appendix A offers additional information on data collection.

We have promised our respondents anonymity, and we use pseudonyms for newspapers and regions. We identify individuals only by roles, level of experience (e.g., a vice-editor, a young reporter, a long-time owner, a media department official) and gender. We provide relevant, key information on each region, but we also avoid some detail. We made these decisions because of these journalists' tenuous employment situation and an increasingly fraught political environment. For our research purposes, the identity of specific regions and papers is not at issue, as we focus mostly on our research participants' perceptions of political, economic and cultural contexts and factors. Anonymity protects the respondents and papers. It also helped us gain access to these news outlets and journalists, and we believe it also encouraged more authentic responses.

We discuss our conceptual approach in detail in Chapter 3 but provide a thumbnail explanation here. Our regional cases exist in a social space, situated at a "meso-level." Various social actors—journalists, managers, media department officials, PR operatives, and citizens—engage in collective processes within this space. Their interactions and actions are constrained and enabled by macro-level political-economic contexts, by community contexts, and by a number of guiding "logics," which are broad ways of thinking that organize and govern the local journalism space. Journalists often respond or bend to government pressure and economic hardships in predictable ways, but they can also respond in indirect and surprising ways, pulled on by different community contexts and channeled by various logics. Logics shape perceptions of roles and guide practices (Scott, 2014), and a repertoire of multiple logics guide the regions' journalists: For example, a perestroika-era logic encourages or affords a role of confronting officials and revealing hidden information, and a "moral education" logic encourages or affords a role of instructing and inspiring readers. Through the various forces, logics, roles and actions, both structure and agency are important. Individual journalists play a part in making the history of their regions' journalism, though, assuredly, given the strong constraints, "they do not make it as they please" (Marx, 1974 [1852], p. 143).

Where appropriate, we adopt aspects of two particular meso-level approaches—the field theory approach, informed by the theory of sociologist Pierre Bourdieu (1993, [1992]1996), and the social ecology approach. These two approaches are often used in sociology and journalism studies (e.g., Liu & Emirbayer, 2016; Lowrey & Sherrill, 2019) and have been helpful in studying local journalism. Field theory is useful for explaining the struggle for autonomy in the context of power. Ecology approaches helps explain journalists' varied, surprising and sometimes unintentional adaptations to complex environments, as they seek to survive.

In short, we seek to shed light on the structures, connections and logics that hinder, channel and encourage journalists as they imagine their work roles, interact, and do their work. We also explore how all of this changed, or not, over the 13 years of study. A number of research questions guided our research, and they guide our book's analysis:

- What are the defining political-economic structures and governing logics of journalism's social space in these regions? How have they changed or remained unchanged over time?
- How are journalists' role conceptions and practices shaped by the various structures and logics of the social space?
- What is the nature of the occupational community of these local Russian journalists, and how and why has it changed or remained unchanged?
- What is the nature of journalists' connections with their local community, and how and why has this changed or remained unchanged? To what degree are local journalists bridging local citizens' needs with official responses, and in what ways?
- To what degree are journalists' pursuing autonomy relative to local power, and to what degree are they mostly trying to adapt and survive?

Outline of the Book

The first part of this book, chapters 1–3, establishes background and conceptual context for research findings. Chapters offer brief historical background of Russian regions and their journalism, an exploration of recent literatures on both Russia's regional journalism and local journalism broadly, and explanation of our conceptual approach. We detail the study's methods in Appendix A. The book's second part, chapters 4–8, presents results on our regional case studies. In Chapter 9 we discuss results and conclusions. We provide context for the regions' shifting governmental and economic power, logics and capital, but primarily we focus on the journalists themselves: their perceptions, role conceptions, decisions and practices, and how these change or remain the same across time.

Chapter 1 has provided an overview of the book's aims and scope, as well as brief historical context on Russia's regions and regional journalism.

Chapter 2 provides a contemporary political and economic context for our analysis of Russian local journalism, including a statistical overview of Russia's regions and regional journalism, and a general overview of the three regions under study. The chapter also provides a look at recent relevant research literature on Russia's local journalism and its current political, economic and social challenges.

Chapter 3 positions the study conceptually. We discuss "meso-level" spaces and their usefulness for our research purposes, and we detail field and social ecology approaches, explaining their relevance for our study. We also situate our conceptual approach within the broader research literature on local and community journalism, which is gaining scholarly attention worldwide.

We present findings on key contexts of our newspaper cases in Chapter 4. The chapter maps relationships that significantly shape the daily work of local journalists in the three regions: relationships between news outlets and local elite; between journalists and their news managers, and between journalists and the region's people and audience. We explore the various types of capital that accrue around these relationships and the constraints and opportunities this landscape presents to journalists and their news outlets.

We move inside the newsrooms in Chapter 5, and we stay there through Chapter 8. Chapter 5 focuses on the local journalists themselves, exploring their perceptions and practices, as well as their personal challenges. The chapter provides basic demographic and financial information about the journalists across the regions. The chapter also provides background on the weakening of local journalists' "occupational community," including its splintering along organizational lines, and a generation gap between perestroika-era journalists and younger journalists. We also look at journalists' perceptions of problems in journalism education and the quality of the local journalism labor force.

Consistent with worldwide trends, local journalists and journalism in Russia have been challenged by emerging digital online technologies, and Chapter 6 explores these challenges and their contexts. Regional newspapers' use of online media ranges from active use of social media and tracking of audience traffic numbers in the wealthier regions to news outlets that have no online presence in less wealthy regions. Government's increasing involvement in online media is found across the regions. The chapter discusses the ways journalists and administrators are still sorting out best practices for digital online media, the relatively scarce experimentation and innovation with new media forms, and pervasive ethical problems.

Chapter 7 explores the growing fragmentation in the local journalists' occupational community, and in the various logics, roles and purposes that have guided journalists' practices across the 13 years of study. The chapter examines journalists' differing and changing responses, to deteriorating political and economic conditions, shifting logics, and changing relationships with their local communities. The chapter maps out the various havens journalists have sought out amid these changes, as they find ways to reposition their professional purposes so they may adapt and survive.

Despite oppressive constraints, some local journalists have found ways to "take positions" in opposition to authority, often in latent and surprising ways. The "cracks" in the system that allow this position taking are explored in Chapter 8.

The chapter examines the modest leverage that news outlets gain from uncertain or fraught relationships between Moscow and the regions, journalists' promises of self-censorship in return for officials fixing community problems, personal expression in the online space, and journalists' small acts of subterfuge.

Chapter 9 synthesizes the book's findings, and explores variability across regions and news outlets, and across time, in order to address the original research questions: How do the challenging political-economic environments constrain and guide journalists' role conceptions and practices? What are the dominant logics of the local journalism space, and how have they influenced the ways journalists do their work? Do local journalists have the autonomy to connect meaningfully with both everyday citizens and local political-economic elite, and bridge the two? To what degree are journalists seeking autonomy vs. mere survival—i.e., does field theory or social ecology explain local journalism better? What is local Russian journalism's place within the global context of local journalism, and what do our findings tell us about the contexts, purposes and practices of local journalism, generally? Finally, we discuss possible ways forward, both bleak and promising.

Notes

1. We use the term "local journalism" throughout the text to refer to non-national journalism, as it is commonly used in journalism studies scholarship. In the Russian context, this means media outside of Moscow – regional, city and local (county) newspapers – though our analytical focus in the book is primarily on regional journalism.
2. Peter the Great used the term *provintsiaa* to refer to Russia's administrative units, which he remade to increase state power over these areas. Catherine the Great abolished *provintsiia* as an administrative unit, and the word acquired a new meaning, referring to territories outside the capitals (Kirichenko, 2010). Parts (2016) argues that while *region* is the preferred term of "historians and sociologists" (p. 200), the concept of the *province* continues to have negotiated meaning as a "symbolic locale" (p. 201). Throughout the book, we default to the term *region*, but we recognize that the terms *region* and *province* are often interchangeable in scholarly and popular usage, and we ourselves use *province* occasionally, when a local area's identity is at issue.

References

Algan, Y., Guriev, S., Papaioannou, E., & Passari, E. (2017). The European trust crisis and the rise of populism. *Brookings papers on economic activities*. Fall, *48*(2), 309–400.

Anikina, M., Frost, L., & Hanitzsch, T. (2017). Journalists in Russia. *Worlds of Journalism*. Retrieved April 30, 2020, from https://epub.ub.uni-muenchen.de/35063/1/Country_report_Russia.pdf

Becker, J. (2014). Russia and the new authoritarians. *Demokratizatsiya: The Journal of Post-Soviet Democratization, 22*(2), 191–206. http://demokratizatsiya.pub/archives/22_2_F1T0164470351334.pdf

Berkowitz, D. (2007). Professional views, community news: Investigative reporting in small US dailies. *Journalism, 8*(5), 551–558. https://doi.org/10.1177%2F1464884907081051

Beumers, B., Rulyova, N., & Hutchings, S. (2009). *The post-Soviet Russian media: Conflicting signals*. London: Routledge.

Bourdieu, P. (1993). The field of cultural production, or: The economic world reversed. In P. Bourdieu (Ed.), *The field of cultural production: Essays on art and literature* (pp 29–73). New York: Columbia University Press.

Bourdieu, P. ([1992] 1996). *The rules of art: Genesis and structure of the literary field*. Translated by S. Emanuel. Stanford, CA: Stanford University Press.

Castells, M. (2011). *The rise of the network society: The information age: Economy, society, and culture* (2nd ed. Vol. 1). Malden, MA: Wiley-Blackwell.

Chernov, A. V., & Ivanova, E. M. (2013). Regional media systems as a subject of discursive research. *Bulletin of the Novgorod State University, 73*, 37–41.

Culver, K. B. (2014). Advocacy and infrastructure: Community newspapers, ethics and information needs. *Journalism Practice, 8*(2), 137–148. https://doi.org/10.1080/17512786.2013.859826

Davis, H., Hammond, P., & Nizamova, L. (1998). Changing identities and practices in post-Soviet journalism. The case of Tatarstan. *European Journal of Communication, 13*(1), 77–97. https://doi.org/10.1177%2F0267323198013001004

De Smaele, H. (2009). In search of a label of the Russian media system. In B. Dobek-Ostrowska, M. Glowacki & K. Jakubowicz (Eds.), *Comparative media systems: European and global perspectives* (pp. 41–62). Central European University Press.

Donovan, V. (2018). Militarized memory: Patriotic re-branding in post-Soviet Pskov. In E. W. Clowes, G. Erbslöh & A. Kokobobo (Eds.), *Russia's regional identities: The power of the provinces* (pp. 73–95). London: Routledge.

Evtuhov, C. (2018). Afterword: The power of the provinces. In E. W. Clowes, G. Erbslöh & A. Kokobobo (Eds.), *Russia's regional identities: The power of the provinces* (pp. 278–288). London: Routledge.

Fink, K., & Anderson, C. W. (2015). Data journalism in the United States: Beyond the "usual suspects." *Journalism Studies, 16*(4), 467–481. https://doi.org/10.1080/1461670X.2014.939852

Forestier-Peyrat, E. (2017). Soviet federalism at work: Lessons from the history of the Transcaucasian Federation, 1922–1936. *Jahrbücher für Geschichte Osteuropas, 65*(4), 529–559. www.jstor.org/stable/44646088

Franklin, B. (2006). *Local journalism and local media: Making the local news*. London: Routledge.

Gel'man, V. (2010). The dynamics of sub-national authoritarianism: Russia in comparative perspective. In V. Gel'man & C. Ross (Eds.), *The politics of sub-national authoritarianism in Russia* (pp. 1–18). Farnham: Ashgate.

Gutsche, R. E., Jr. (2015). Boosterism as banishment: Identifying the power function of local, business news and coverage of city spaces. *Journalism Studies, 16*(4), 497–512. https://doi.org/10.1080/1461670X.2014.924730

Hatcher, J., & Haavik, E. (2014). "We write with our hearts": How community identity shapes Norwegian community journalists' news values. *Journalism Practice, 8*(2), 149–163. https://doi.org/10.1080/17512786.2013.859828

Hobsawn, E., & Ranger, T. (1983). *The invention of tradition*. Cambridge: Cambridge University Press.

Hopkins, M. W. (1970). *Mass media in the Soviet Union*. New York: Pegasus.

Kasyutin, V. L. (2011). A new policy in regulating the Russian regional press. Vestnik Moscowskogo Universiteta, *Journalism, 5*, 85–92. http://vestnik.journ.msu.ru/upload/iblock/2f7/2011-5-85-92.pdf

Kelly, C. (2002). 'A laboratory for the manufacture of proletarian writers': The *stengazeta* (wall newspaper), *kul'turnost'* and the language of politics in the early Soviet period. *Europe-Asia Studies, 54*(4), 573–602. https://doi.org/10.1080/09668130220139172

Kirichenko, E. I. (2010). *Gradostroitelstvo Rossii seredinu XIX—nachala XX veka. Kniga 3. Stolitsy i provinciia* [Urban development in Russia in the mid-19th–early 20th century. Book 3. Capital and province]. Progress-Traditsiyu.

Kiriya, I., & Kachkaeva, A. (2011). Economical forms of state pressure in Russian regional media. *Romanian Journal of Journalism and Communication, 6*(2), 5–11.

Kirkow, P. (1998). *Russia's provinces: Authoritarian transformation versus local autonomy?* London: Macmillan Press Ltd.

Ledeneva, A. V. (2006). *How Russia really works: The informal practices that shaped post-Soviet politics and business*. Ithaca, NY: Cornell University Press.

Liikanen, I. (2008). Civil society and the reconstitution of Russian political space: the case of the Republic of Karelia. In S. White (Ed.), *Media, culture and society in Putin's Russia* (pp. 7–36). New York: Palgrave Macmillan.

Liu, S., & Emirbayer, M. (2016). Field and ecology. *Sociological Theory, 34*(1), 62–79.

Lounsbery, A. (2018). Provinces, regions, circles, grids: How literature has shaped Russian geographical identity. In E. W. Clowes, G. Erbslöh & A. Kokobobo (Eds.), *Russia's regional identities: The power of the provinces* (pp. 44–69). London: Routledge.

Lowrey, W. & Sherrill, L. (2019). Fields and ecologies: Meso-level spatial approaches and the study of journalistic change. *Communication Theory*. Retrieved August 19, 2020 from https://doi.org/10.1093/ct/qtz003

Marx, K. (1974 [1852]). The eighteenth Brumaire of Louis Bonaparte. In D. Fernbach (Ed.), *Karl Marx: Surveys from exile* (pp. 143–249). New York: Vintage Books.

Matthews, J. (2017). The role of a local newspaper after disaster: An intrinsic case study of Ishinomaki, Japan. *Asian Journal of Communication, 27*(5), 464–479. https://doi.org/10.1080/01292986.2017.1280065

Moses, J. C. (2004). The politics of Kaliningrad Oblast: A borderland of the Russian Federation. *The Russian Review, 63*(1), 107–129. https://doi.org/10.1111/j.1467-9434.2004.00306.x

Mounk, Y. (2018) Germany's return of the repressed: The country's far-right wants to revive ethnic nationalism. The left must come up with its own alternative. *Foreign Policy*, Fall, 80–83. Retrieved August 19, 2020, from https://foreignpolicy.com/2018/09/05/germanys-return-of-the-repressed-mounk-review/

Nah, S., & Armstrong, C. L. (2011). Structural pluralism in journalism and media studies: A concept explication and theory construction. *Mass Communication and Society, 14*(6), 857–878. https://doi.org/10.1080/15205436.2011.615446

Nygren, G. (2015). Media development and professional autonomy. In G. Nygren & B. Dobek-Ostrowska (Eds.), *Journalism in change: Journalistic culture in Poland, Russia and Sweden* (pp. 119–152). Frankfurt am main: Peter Lang.

Oates, S. (2013). *Revolution stalled: The political limits of the internet in the post-Soviet sphere*. Oxford: Oxford University Press.

Ottaway, M. (2003). *Democracy challenged: The rise of semi-authoritarianism*. Carnegie Endowment for International Peace.

Parts, L. (2016). The Russian provinces as a Cultural Myth. *Studies in Russian and Soviet Cinema, 10*(3), 200–205. https://doi.org/10.1080/17503132.2016.1218624

Pasti, S. (2005). Return to media serving the state: Journalists in Karelia. In H. Melin (Ed.), *Social structure, public space and civil society* (pp. 117–144). Helsinki: Kikimora.

Pasti, S., & Pietiläinen, J. (2008). Journalists in the Russian regions: How different generations view their professional roles. In S. White (Ed.), *Media, Culture and Society in Putin's Russia* (pp. 109–132). New York: Palgrave Macmillan.

Pietiläinen, J. (2002). *The regional newspaper in post-Soviet Russia: Society, press and journalism in the Republic of Karelia 1985–2001*. Tampere: Tampere University Press.

Postanovlenie Sovmina RSFSR ot 23.07. 1965 № 882 "Ob organizatsii Vserossiyskogo dobrovolnogo obshestva okhrany pamyatnikov istorii I kultury." [Resolution of the Council of Ministers of the RSFSR of July 23, 1965 No. 882 "On the organization of the All-Russian Voluntary Society for the Protection of Historical and Cultural Monuments."] Retrieved from http://www.libussr.ru/doc_ussr/usr_6273.htm

Rankine, J., Barnes, A. M., Borell, B., McCreanor, T., Nairn, R., & Gregory, A. (2011). Suburban Newspapers' reporting of Māori news. *Pacific Journalism Review, 17*(2), 50–71. https://doi.org/10.24135/pjr.v17i2.351

Romanovich, N. A. (2006). Regionalnye SMI: Vozmozhnosti i problemy [Regional media: Capabilities and problems]. *Sociologicheskie Issledovaniya, 4*, 77–84. https://www.isras.ru/files/File/Socis/1-6-2006/romanovic.pdf

Ross, C. (2002). Political parties and regional democracy. In C. Ross (Ed.), *Regional politics in Russia* (pp. 37–56). Manchester: Manchester University Press.

Ross, C. (2006). Local government reform in the Russian Federation: A tortuous and twisted path. *Local Government Studies, 32*(5), 638–658. https://doi.org/10.1080/03003930600896251

Ross, C. (2010). Sub-national elections and the development of semi-authoritarian regimes. In V. Gel'man & C. Ross (Eds.), *The politics of sub-national authoritarianism in Russia* (pp. 171–190). Farnham: Ashgate.

Roudakova, N. (2017). *Losing Pravda: Ethics and the Press in Post-Truth Russia*. Cambridge: Cambridge University Press.

Savoskul, S. S. (2017). Lokalnoe samosoznanie lichnosti (avtobiograficheskii aspekt) [Local identity of the personality (autobiographical aspect)]. In T.B. Shchepanskaya (Ed.), *Russkii Sever: Identichnost, pamyat, biograficehskii tekst. K 95-letiyu so dnya rozhdeniya K.V. Chistova: sbornik naychnykh statei*. [*Russian North: Identities, Memory, Biographical Text. To the 95th anniversary of the birth of K.V. Chistova: collection of scientific articles*], pp. 289–299. MAE RAN SPb.

Scott, W. R. (2014). *Institutions and organizations: Ideas, interests and identities* (4th ed.). Los Angeles, Sage.

Sheftelevich, Y. (2009). The state of the media law in the Russian federation: A difficult past, an interesting present, an uncertain future. *Touro International Law Review, 12*, 88–106. https://www.tourolaw.edu/ILR/uploads/articles/V12/Sheftel.pdf

Slavtcheva-Petkova, V. (2018). *Russia's liberal media: Handcuffed but free*. Routledge.

Smith, M. (2003). Putin: An end to centrifugalism? In G. Herd & A. Aldis (Eds.), *Russian regions and regionalism: Strength through weakness* (pp. 19–37). Routledge Curson.

Smith-Peter, S. (2018). The six waves of Russian regionalism in European context, 1830–2000. In E. W. Clowes, G. Erbslöh & A. Kokobobo (Eds.), *Russia's regional identities: The power of the provinces* (pp. 15–43). London: Routledge.

Soldner, M. (2008). Political capitalism and the Russian media. In S. White (Ed.), *Media, culture and society in Putin's Russia* (pp. 154–177). New York: Palgrave Macmillan.

Stepin, V. S. (2015). Economics and culture. The Russian mentality and market reforms. *Russian Studies in Philosophy, 53*(2), 181–190. https://doi.org/10.1080/10611967.2015.1096703

Thomson, C., Bennett, D., Johnston, M., & Mason, B. (2015). Why the where matters: A Sense of place imperative for teaching better indigenous affairs reporting. *Pacific Journalism Review, 21*(2), 141–161. https://doi.org/10.24135/pjr.v21i2.125

Tichenor, P. J., Donohue, G. A., & Olien, C. N. (1980). *Community conflict & the press*. Sage.

Vartanova, E. (2012). The Russian media model in the context of post-Soviet dynamics. In D. C. Hallin & P. Mancini (Eds.), *Comparing media systems beyond the western world* (pp. 119–142). Cambridge: Cambridge University Press.

Verkhovskya, A. I. (2006). Socialnue aspekty vzaimootnoshenii SMI i biznesa v sovremennoi obshestvennoi situacii [Social aspects of media business relationships in modern social situations]. *Vestnik Moskovskogo Universiteta, 1*, 47–70.

Von Seth, R. (2012). The language of the press in Soviet and post-Soviet Russia: Creation of the citizen role through newspaper discourse. *Journalism: Theory, Practice and Criticism, 13*(1), 53–70. https://doi.org/10.1177%2F1464884911400844

White, A. (2004). *Small-town Russia: Postcommunist livelihoods and identities: A portrait of the intelligentsia in Achit, Bednodemyanovsk and Zubtsov, 1999–2000*. Routledge Curzon.

Yeltsin Center. (2015, August 6). Борис Ельцин: "Берите столько суверенитета, сколько сможете проглотить" [Boris Yeltsin: "Take as much sovereignty as you can swallow"]. https://yeltsin.ru/news/boris-elcin-berite-stolko-suverineteta-skolko-smozhete-proglotit/

Zion, L., Sherwood, M., O'Donnell, P., Dodd, A., Ricketson, M., & Marjoribanks, T. (2016). "It has a bleak future": The effects of job loss on regional and rural journalism in Australia. *Australian Journalism Review 38*(2), 115–127.

Zubarevich, N. (2002). Prishel, uvidel, pobedil? (Krupnyi biznes I regionalnaia vlast). *Pro et Contra, 7*(1), 107–119.

Zubarevich, N. (2010). State-business relations in Russia's regions. In V. Gel'man & C. Ross (Eds.), *The politics of sub-national authoritarianism in Russia* (pp. 211–226). Farnham: Ashgate.

CHAPTER TWO

Russia's Regions and Regional Journalism: The Current Context

The late Soviet and post-Soviet eras saw a fluctuating tension between national unity and local-level diversity. Today, the Kremlin has tightened its grip, and Russia is "one of the more centralized federal countries in the world" (Alexeev, Avxentyev, Mamedov & Sinelnikov-Murylev, 2018, p. 688). Yet, some diversity persists at the sub-national level, and regional power can shift over time. In this chapter we outline the current demographic, economic, cultural and media characteristics of Russia's regions, in comparison with Russia's national center, as well as characteristics of the three regions we studied. We also explore recent scholarly research on news media in the regions. This scholarship introduces complexities in relationships among journalists, officials and citizens that suggest some unconventional roles for journalists and pathways for agency.

Regionalism and Nationalism in Russia

Russia is extraordinarily complex. 147 million people live in 85 regions or constituent entities: 22 republics, nine territories, 46 *oblasts* (regions or provinces), three cities of federal significance, one autonomous oblast, and four autonomous *okrugs*.[1] Each of the 85 regions has its own head, parliament, set of cultural traditions and regional media, and despite Russia's centralizing tendencies, diversity in governance, culture and media are evident.

With over 190 ethnic groups speaking over 150 languages (Chislennost i razmeshchenie naseleniya, 2010), Russia is one of the most ethnically diverse countries in the world. The English word "Russians" has two different translations – the russkie (ethnic Russians, or those belonging to an East Slavic ethnic group) and the rossiyane—all of Russia's people. The russkie are the largest ethnic group, at 80% of the population. Six other nationalities consist of at least one million residents: Tatars, Ukrainians, Bashkirs, Chuvashs, Chechens and Armenians (Rossiya v tsifrakh, 2018). The population is unevenly distributed across 11 time zones: Around 75% of Russians live in the European part of the country, a fifth of the country geographically. The least populous region is Nenets Autonomous okrug, at about 44,000. The most populous is Moscow oblast with over 7 million residents.

For decades, Moscow has been the center of economic, political, scientific and cultural life, attracting the most ambitious and talented from across the country. Regional citizens typically admire Moscow, but many resent Muscovites, who are seen as living the good life at the expense of the provinces. Around 12% of the Russian population live in the capitals, Moscow and St. Petersburg, which attract workers because of higher pay: approximately 2 to 2.5 times more than the regions, with the same average workloads (Gorshkov & Tikhonova, 2018). Tax revenue from oil and gas production accounts for much of Moscow's wealth: Around half of the revenue goes to Moscow, and only about 15% goes to the provinces where the oil and gas are produced (Zubarevich, 2019b). The 2017 average monthly salary in Moscow was 73,812 rubles (around 1,200 USD). Compare this with a typical province: 300 miles away in the Tambov region the average monthly salary in 2017 was only 24,253 rubles (around 400 USD), and average consumer spending and cost of living as percent of salary were much higher than Moscow. Yet, in the post-perestroika era, Moscow has lost some luster, increasingly viewed, from the regions' perspective, as a haven for poor survivors from the provinces as much as a destination for ambitious dream-seekers (Shlapentokh, Levita, & Loiberg, 1997). A participant of our study shared a story about a provincial teacher who received a prestigious Putin stipend but was forced to sweep Moscow streets in the summer to make ends meet.

As discussed in Chapter 1, hard feelings between the regions and the capital cities have a history that predates the Soviet era. During perestroika, while residents of Moscow and Leningrad protested the 1991 anti-democrats' coup, the provinces remained silent, and many provincial citizens even sympathized with coup leaders. By 1994–1995, feelings of mutual alienation between Moscow and the rest of Russia had risen to new heights (Shlapentokh, Levita, & Loiberg, 1997), and since, the Putin government has stoked provincial citizens' distrust of the capitals (Beumers, Hutchings & Rulyova, 2009; Lounsbery, 2018). During the COVID-19 pandemic, Putin's officials initially blamed wealthy Muscovites for the spread of the virus: "A suitcase of viruses was brought from Courchevel," said Moscow's mayor, referring to a posh French ski resort (Coronavirus in Russia, 2020). The papers and journalists we studied echoed this story: A reporter in Region C blamed "all of these rich Muscovites doing weekend shopping in Europe."

Putin ascended to the presidency in 2000 with a promise of rebuilding a centralized Russian state and reforming relations between the center and the regions (Smith, 2003). He divided the country into seven federal districts and appointed envoys (*polpredy*) who ensured regions implemented federal-level decisions (Goode, 2011). Putin embraced a "managed democracy" approach, which emphasized social order and prevention of "mob rule and anarchy," while centralizing control and resources. Nominally, this system was to be a way station on the road to full democracy. However, the system gained permanence (Dunn, 2009, p. 50). Putin's concept of a top-down, centralized "power vertical" included instruments of control and coercion as well as incentives to ensure regional elites would follow the federal agenda (Berg-Nordlie, Holm-Hansen, & Kropp, 2018).

In 2000, Putin pushed through a law removing regional governors from parliament, and in 2004, he canceled the direct election of governors (Kiriya & Kachkaeva, 2011). Direct governor elections were reintroduced in 2012 following mass protests of the State Duma election (Goode, 2013), but the president may still fire governors and appoint interims, who then typically win the elections (Reuter, 2017). Often, governors native to their regions were left in office because their wide personal networks helped them ensure success of United Russia, Putin's political party. However, recently, Putin has been more likely to replace local politicians with political allies (Reuter, 2017).

Often, newly installed governors have been outsiders to their regions who are more concerned with "rent seeking" than with developing wealth within their regions (Sidorkin & Vorobyev, 2018). Or, as a regional citizen might put it, at least "with the 'old guy' who 'наворовался' [stole enough]," there was hope he would eventually aid his region. According to sociologist and former Kremlin aide Simon Kordonsky, revenue kickbacks to governors did not exceed 10% during the Stalin era: "Now kickbacks might reach 70%," a corrupt practice that undermines economic development (Kordonsky & Molyarenko, 2018, p. 21). In 2018, the Corruption Perceptions Index ranked Russia among the most corrupt, in terms of perceptions by experts and public opinion, with a score of 28/100 (0=highly corrupt, 100=very clean), and according to one study, corruption in Russia's regions accounted for 15% of the underinvestment in fixed capital in 2013 alone (Zakharov, 2019).

Differences across the Regions

Some parts of Russia are better positioned than others to tolerate challenges such as corruption, global sanctions, and rapidly changing industries, markets and technologies. According to Zubarevich (2016), Russia's center-periphery structure has led to the existence of four "Russias," differentiated by level of development and industry type. In this taxonomy, *Russia One* includes large cities with at least half a million residents and accounts for about a third of Russia's population, but Russia One is not homogeneous. While its leading cities (e.g., Moscow, St. Petersburg, Yekaterinburg, and Novosibirsk) are highly developed economically, other million-strong cities such as Omsk, Ufa, and Volgograd, which have maintained their Soviet-era industrial specialization rather than adjust to new markets, have progressed slowly. Cities in which our research participants live and work fall within the lower end of the Russia One category, with average-at-best economic development. Less than 30% of Russians live in *Russia Two*, which includes "rust-belt" industrial areas that are state-supported. Liberal ideas of modernization are unpopular in Russia Two, and a paternalistic state and large-scale social policy are valued. The residents of the industry-oriented Russia Two view themselves as Russia's "providers," and the Kremlin tends to pit them against residents of Russia One who, in the language of official propaganda, "wag their tongues and produce nothing" (Zubarevich, 2016, par. 15). *Russia Three* is the rural agricultural heartland, with towns and villages of less than 20,000. About a third of Russia's population live in Russia Three, which is characterized by informal employment (irregular work without a contract, usually small-scale and non-taxpaying), support of incumbent authorities, and depopulation. *Russia Four* includes republics of the North Caucasus, which account for 5% of Russia's population, and South Siberia, with less than 1% of the population. These areas tend to be under the control of large national companies.

Regions have also been categorized by levels of economic disparity—by "cheap" and "expensive" regions, for example (Zubarevich, 2019a). Nominal incomes in some regions may be 10 times the incomes in other regions, and some regions' poverty rates may be four times that of others—in the Tuva republic, for example, the poverty rate once exceeded 70% (Kolenikov & Shorrocks, 2005). Relative remoteness of regions contributes to financial inequality across the country (Perevyshin, Sinelnikov-Murylev, & Trunin, 2019): In 2018, the national average price of a basket of goods was 14,789, but prices ranged from 12,345 rubles in the western region of Ingushetia to roughly twice that in Kamchatka, at the distant eastern edge of Russia (Rossiya v tsifrakh, 2018).

Depending on whether a region receives дотации на выравнивание (alignment subsidies) from the federal budget, Russian regions have also been divided into *donor* regions and *recipient* regions. Most regions (85%) are economically unstable recipients (Utsyna, 2019), and these poorer recipient regions are associated with growing rates of informal employment (irregular work). Nationally, these informal employment rates grew from 12.5% in 2001 to 21.2% in 2016, resulting in fiscal loss of between 1 and 2.3% of Russia's Gross Domestic Product (World Bank Group, 2019). Kordonsky and Molyarenko (2018) noted that 33 million Russians—just a little less than half of the working age population—are self-employed. Nearly all of these Russians work in the "shadow" economy (Sidorkin & Vorobyev, 2018).

Differences and Similarities in the Regions under Study

While the journalists in our study live and work in regional capitals, their audiences include residents living across these three Russias. The regions' capital cities fall within Russia One, medium-sized cities and small towns fall within Russia Two, and the regions' small rural villages fall within Russia Three. Below, we provide rough economic, political, demographic and cultural descriptions of the three regions.[2]

Economics. During the period of study, these three regions, as with two-thirds of Russian territories, had an average gross regional product per capita that fell below the national average of 472,161.9 rubles (Regionalnaya Statistika, 2019). Among the three, Region C is the most economically developed, and Region A, our primary region of focus, is the least developed. The average poverty level in Russia is 13%, and this level is higher than the poverty levels in our regions A and C, but lower than the poverty level in Region B (despite B generally being more economically developed than A). In 2019, the average monthly salary for the nation was 47,600 rubles, or around 730 USD, and the mode (most common) salary was around 24,000 rubles a month (around 370 USD), received by about 20% of workers (Khachaturov & Kozlova, 2019). Average salaries for all three regions fell below the national average.

Political affiliation. The pro-Kremlin United Russia Party was formed in 2001 and became the dominant party by the middle of the 2000s (Panov & Ross, 2019). According to election data, United Russia's support has varied somewhat across the country, but in the three studied regions, United Russia has had the most success by far, with the Communist Party a distant second. This is to be expected: The strong hand of regional rulers controls political volatility and ensures votes for United Russia through the control of regional elites, which leads to pressure on voters (Panov & Ross, 2019).

Still, it is a challenge to measure regional popular support of United Russia with accuracy. Statistical analysis by Kobak, Shpilkin and Pshenichnikov (2016) indicates that in some regions, results of federal elections held between 2004 and 2012 were forged. Kynev (2014) documented approaches used in the forging: refusal to use a ballot-processing system and video cameras; refusal to allow election observers in polling places, and physical force used by police. Research participants from all three regions said they are aware of these practices being used in their regions.

Demographics. Region A is the smallest region in territory and population, and Region C is the largest. Region B falls between these two in terms of size, and it has the densest population of the three. As with many of Russia's regions, all three regions saw a population decline between the 2002 and 2010 censuses. In Russia's regions, population size tends to correlate with volume of economic activity (Shlapentokh, Levita, & Loiberg, 1997). Most residents in all three regions live in cities[3] rather than rural areas. Region C is closest to the national percent (74.66%) living in cities, and the percent of residents living in rural areas is higher in regions A and B than in Region C.

The three regions are consistent with the national proportion of men (46%) to women (54%). Their ethnic composition is similar to the nation's: More than 80% in all three regions are Russians (*russkie*). The regions' age breakdown is similar to the nation's as well: Nationally, 17% are under the working age of 16, 58% are working age (16–65), and 25% are older than working age.

Religion and culture. Religion plays an important role in the lives of the regions' citizens, as the collapse of the Soviet Union led to a search for ideology and identity. Between 1991 and 2015, the share of Russian adults identifying as Orthodox Christian grew from 37% to 71% (Lipka & Sahgal, 2017). More than 30,000 religious organizations were registered in Russia in 2018, with most being Russian Orthodox (60%) and Islamic (19%) (Rossiya v tsifrakh, 2018). Breakdowns in our regions were largely consistent with these statistics, and those identifying as Russian Orthodox tend to be older, female and university educated ("Russians return to religion," 2014). All three regions have seen religious revival, for example, through the restoration of Orthodox cathedrals and the construction of new churches and mosques in regions' capitals, small towns and villages.

All three region's capitals are cultural hubs for their regions: Each capital is home to a few theaters, concert halls, art galleries, museums and libraries. The capitals also have a number of state and private universities and community colleges. The three regions take pride in being "motherlands" of thinkers, writers, actors, and artists, many known across Russia and abroad.

Media consumption. Media use across these regions is fairly typical for the nation. Rosstat, Russia's governmental statistics agency, estimated that, nationally, 10,051 newspapers in Russian and other languages were published in 2016.

Together, in 2016, these had a one-time (average one-day) circulation of 217 million copies and a one-year circulation of 6.8 billion copies. In 2016, the average (national) number of newspaper copies per 1,000 people (one-time circulation) was 1,481. The three regions we studied each had about 1,000 copies per 1,000 residents, a 1:1 ratio (Rossiya v tsifrakh, 2018). Newspapers are distributed through subscription and kiosks, and gratis press (typically advertising vehicles) is delivered to mailboxes of residents and distributed in shopping malls.

Just over 98% of urban population and 96% of rural residents in Russia had access to at least one TV channel in 2016, and 90% of urban population and 78% of rural residents had access to at least one radio station. The three regions mirror these national statistics, and TV is the most popular medium in these regions. In 2016, the average rate of broadband access to the internet was 80 per 100 people nationally, with the lowest rate in Dagestan (54 per 100) and the highest in Yamal-Nenets, which had full access. In the three regions we studied, the rate was roughly equivalent or slightly below the national rate, not exceeding 80 per 100 people (Rossiya v tsifrakh, 2018).

Total ad revenue for all segments (TV, radio, print, and outdoor) declined from 2018 to 2019 in Russia, with print affected the most (-19%) (Ob'yem krupneyshikh regional'nykh reklamnykh rynkov, 2019). In regions A and C, the 2018–19 decrease in total ad revenue exceeded the national average. However, in Region B, the 2018–19 decrease in all sectors (TV, radio, print, and outdoor) did not exceed five percent, much less than the national rate of decline—likely because the types of advertisers in Region B were not as affected by economic troubles. According to the Association of Communicative Agencies of Russia, online advertising revenue grew 21% from 2018 to 2019, but experts are unsure about the accuracy of the assessment, with disagreement over what constitutes digital advertising (Ob'yem reklamy v sredstvakh yeye rasprostraneniya, 2019). No data for the three regions' online advertising markets are available, but online ad revenue growth for these regions is not likely to be above the national rate.

Economic Hardships, Political Constraints and Regional Media

Harsh economic times have plagued Russian regions since the collapse of the Soviet Union, and regional media have shared in the misery. The financial crisis of the 1990s resulted in household incomes decreasing by more than twofold across the decade (Zubarevich & Safronov, 2019). According to recent official statistics, 13 to 14 percent of Russians are poor, but academic surveys indicate that around two-thirds of the population live near the poverty line, counting those who cannot afford durable goods (Sätre, 2019). We note that these are pre-pandemic numbers. (At places in the text, we supplement government data with data from independent organizations. Government statisticians often underestimate economic problems: In the case of inflation, for example, academics' surveys reveal levels to be substantially higher than official data [Salikhov, 2019].[4])

The worldwide recession in 2008 also took a harsh economic toll on Russian regions. In 2016, 46% of all national income was received by the top 10% of earners, while the bottom half received 17% of national income (World Inequality Report, 2018). Income disparity grew as government-backed business oligarchs tightened their grip on economic holdings at national and regional levels. Recent regional data show that the stronger the standing of oligarchs' businesses in a region, the higher the income inequality (Fidrmuc & Gundacker, 2017).

Though variable, all regions have experienced economic hardships, and hardships have taken a toll on local media in all regions, growing the media's dependence on government resources, and their vulnerability to political pressure. As mentioned, ad revenue for regional media has declined in recent years across Russia, especially for print media. Both the economic recession (Kiriya, 2019) and international sanctions, imposed for Russia's actions in Ukraine and other issues, deepened the regions' economic miseries, hurting regional businesses and depleting ad revenue (Radikov, 2019), and public weariness over oligarch media owners' conflict also weakened advertising support (Kiriya, 2019). In the 2000s, oil revenue and oil prices rose, and a rise in support for state media followed (Yezhegodnaya informatsiya, 2020). There is some evidence of an inverse correlation over time between oil prices and media freedom (Egorov, Guriev & Sonin, 2009).

Economic challenges for media also have roots in national political decisions. Putin's undermining of regional governors' elections weakened commercial groups' motivation to finance news media for use in local election races, making it harder for news companies to find local non-government revenue, and reducing the number of local news outlets. Also, regional broadcast media subsidiaries were placed under the control of central national headquarters, coinciding with reduced local ad revenue and reduced local content (Kiriya & Kachkaeva, 2011).

Several laws that provided federal money for regional media during the Yeltsin presidency have been repealed in the Putin era. These included laws that protected media from customs duties and a value-added tax; laws that reduced rental rates, postal fees, and phone fees; and laws that provided federal financial help for the poorest media. In 2004, a law was enacted that contributed to a neo-liberal mix of a "constitutional state with a socially oriented market economy," leaving media outlets at the mercy of a weak market economy (Richter [2006] in Dovbysh,

2019, p. 77). As we write this, media industries had not made the list of industries most affected by the pandemic, and so had received no tax relief, according to the Region B newspaper editor.

During the years of our study, the media's financial dependence on the state deepened. In 2019, the founders/owners of most regional newspapers and municipal newspapers were state and municipal authorities. These publications' editorial policies reflect this ownership. Local authorities have sought to turn media into their "assistants," to "carry out their own errands" (Dzyaloshinsky, et al., 2015, p. 39), and coverage of routine and ceremonial government activities has made up much of the reporting (Svitich, Smirnova, Shiriyaeva, & Shkondin, 2016).

Not surprisingly, hard times for the industry have led local journalists to become more financially pragmatic since the perestroika era (Lowrey & Erzikova, 2013; Svitich & Shiriaeva, 2010), and it can be a short step from pragmatism to ethical negligence. Poor living conditions contribute to journalists' low personal and professional self-esteem, and these take a toll on professional standards. Studies have found that most local journalists have perceived taking money for stories and paying sources for confidential information—without transparency—to be acceptable (Anikina, Frost & Hanitzsch, 2017; Klyueva & Tsetsura, 2015). One study found that journalists in the most economically vulnerable areas of the country have been more likely to engage in unethical, financially transactional behavior, making it easier for the state to influence news content (Klyueva & Tstesura, 2011). For journalists in dire financial shape, extortion has not been uncommon. Pasti (2015) studied the case of one commercial regional online newspaper editor who engaged in "racketeering," describing this as a typical "situation of extortion, when journalists come and say to you, 'For [X] money, we will write positively about you or we will not write negatively about you'" (p. 127). Early in our study, one regional newspaper took retribution on a cell-phone company that refused to buy ads or pay for stories by publishing a supposedly science-based story about cell phones causing cancer.

Media, Economy and State: Some Pluralism and Complexities

The existence of business oligarchs and a commercial market—if only a weak market—has allowed, in the past, for some pluralism in financial and political support for Russian media (Dunn, 2009; Koltsova, 2006). Diversity of content and variation in autonomy across regions, though limited and diminished over the last decade, indicate that local press freedom and journalists' autonomy have not been driven entirely by national-level political constraints and economic hardships (Zakharov, 2019; Schulze, Sjahrir & Zakharov, 2016). Local media have played a part in shaping "the regional agenda, regional values and regional identity" in ways that are at least equivalent to the national media (Vyrkovsky & Makeyenko, 2014, p. 5).

Pluralism of media ownership via government and oligarchs has been compared to the Italian "polarized pluralist model" (Gladkova et al., 2019, p. 55) or a "division of the spoils" (Dunn, 2009, p. 46) rather than to the North European model of public service media, with its requirements for political and ideological balance. The comparison to the Italian model is an awkward fit at best, however, given the invasive intervention of the central Russian state (Gladkova et al., 2019). Also, most political views in Russia have not been represented—notably the Communists—and if media pluralism has been aided by the existence of Russian oligarchs, the oligarchs have never had pluralism as an aim (Dunn, 2009).

There are also some alternative media—media that defend "the interests of society from power and capital." However, scholars have described these media as fragmented, ghettoized and marginalized (Kiriya, 2019) and their effects as "negligible" (Dzyaloshinsky et al., 2015). In an in-depth analysis, Slavtcheva-Petkova (2018) found that alternative media are much needed and have been staffed by committed professionals, but they also have been "handcuffed" (p. 193). They have struggled financially and have had a very limited effect on a Russian society that is largely unreceptive to their messages. One of our region's newspapers, born during perestroika, became popular for writing anti-government stories. The regional government first tried to discipline the paper's reporters by sending the Federal Tax Police Service to check, and fine, the paper. Several attempts to close the paper were unsuccessful, and eventually, the government bought it through a loyal business owner, signifying the death of what research participants called the region's last truly free newspaper.

The Intricate Dance of Local Media and State

News media, economics and politics have been intricately intertwined in the recent history of Russia's regions, sometimes leading to unexpected dynamics and relationships. During the Soviet era, regional newspapers were "planned unprofitable" (планово-убыточные) organizations that required state subsidies, and newspaper issues were sold below cost. After perestroika, independent newspapers had to raise prices to stay in operation, and sales lagged. A weak advertising market further undermined sustainability. In response, news outlets began to produce more engaging and/or sensational content to appeal to readers' interests—gardening tips, crime stories, stories about celebrities. They began avoiding "serious" stories about government activities, which sold few copies. This was a rude awakening for local bureaucrats, used to having journalists' attention. Officials realized they would have to pay if they wanted to reach readers, and in the 1990s in Region A, city districts (*raiony*) and government structures (e.g., the Health Ministry) started reaching agreements with various newspapers to cover officials' activities on designated pages. It was a marriage of convenience.

Typically, the relationship between regional media and government is not an entirely coercive situation in which government forces raw power on a resistant but helpless media. In practice, government power can be nuanced and veiled, and both media and state have had some interest in the media's public legitimacy. State pressure often works indirectly—for example, through contractual agreements that provide revenue for coverage: The agreements are ostensibly mutual, but media depend on them. The media follow the state, begrudgingly in some ways, willingly in others, and both parties have some interest in the "dance" being outwardly seen as uncoerced. When media follow voluntarily, they also do so because of an age-old, naturalized logic of obedience to government. Instinctively, "without particular directives, [journalists] understand borders and interests of actors and try not to cross them" (Kiriya, 2019, p. 12).

Decoupling Form from Function

Publicly, government and journalism can become too closely identified with one another. Control of the media through an overt "clientelist" system—where media produce content in service to an elite clientele who compensate them—can undermine media legitimacy and credibility (Hallin, 1996; Hallin & Mancini, 2004), "which poses a problem for both the media and community elites, who need publicly legitimate media messages" (Lowrey & Erzikova, 2010, p. 285). According to Hallin (1994), the media "have to attend to their own legitimacy," and must "maintain the integrity of their relationship with their audience and also the integrity of their own self-image" (p. 7). Regional governments attend to legitimacy as well. As Koltsova (2006) pointed out, maintaining boundaries around journalistic community as being "the only *legitimate* agent of media production" ... "plays to the positive image of both sides [media and state], and that is why it is carefully preserved" (p. 12). Journalists who are seen as having some autonomy are viewed as more legitimate, and such journalists can help sanction and legitimize government messages in the eyes of the region's people and leaders, and in the eyes of national leaders. Therefore, some buffering or decoupling between government mandates and the work journalists produce in response can benefit both sides.

Regional newspapers have decoupled form from function in a variety of ways:

> They promote investigative projects, but no actual investigating takes place; editors seek topics for criticizing officials, but only inconsequential topics; editors hold Q&A sessions with officials, but sessions serve as promotional platforms [for officials]; and story quantity is emphasized over story content to fuel the impression that papers are active and busy and brimming with news (Lowrey & Erzikova, 2010, p. 285).

The Neo-Liberal Turn as Loosely Coupled Control

The neo-liberal turn for Russian media, whereby the media lose regular state support and are thrown to the mercies of an inadequate market, is one example of loose orchestration of state power. Moscow no longer prioritizes the use of regular budget lines to support regional media directly, and so media are supported through an array of less formal, less systematic arrangements. These include a weak commercial market, but also a "parallel market" (Kiriya & Kachkaeva, 2011, p. 10) based on temporary government contracts and grants. These loosely orchestrated means of control include commercial markets where much of the advertising revenue comes from business oligarchs loyal to the government; uneven competition among media for temporary contracts with local governments (for permission to operate and for revenue and information); and media competition for short-term grants that fund narrow government-sponsored projects.

Commercial markets. Media markets are allowed to function, but they may be marginally important, depending on the type of region (donor vs. recipient) and type of area (Russia One, Two, etc.). Ad revenue is meager and concentrated, dominated by business oligarchs loyal to the Kremlin. Local ad money is sucked up by central media sales in Moscow (Dovbysh, 2019). Ultimately, media typically choose subservience to oligarchs: "[D]irect subordination of any media business to oligarchic groups is better than independence and serves as a guarantee from any pressure" (Kiriya, 2019, p. 13). As discussed in later chapters, the *Traditional* in Region A has struggled mightily in its relative independence, and staff have dreamed of attracting a wealthy owner.

Advertising-based markets tend to encourage apolitical, non-ideological and entertainment-oriented media, with a narrow domestic focus (Dzyaloshinsky et al., 2015; Dovbysh, 2019; Dunn, 2009; Beumers, Hutchings & Rulyova, 2009). According to Dzyaloshinsky et al. (2015), commercialization of local media weakens their informational value, but with little outcry from local audiences. In a prior study, we found that Region A journalists who tried to avoid socio-political reporting said their readers had tired of politics and "wished to read practically useful or spiritually helpful stories devoid of political affairs" (Erzikova & Lowrey, 2010, p. 354).

State contracts and grants. Regional media's loyalty to the state is commodified through contractual and grant relationships (Kiriya, 2019; Kiriya & Kachkaeva 2011), which help maintain control over journalists' work, though in indirect ways. Contracts and grants are provided in a sort of market, giving them a veneer of rationality. Ostensibly, they are offered in an open, equitable way that involves voluntariness and negotiation on the part of the media. This system of contracts is a decoupled system, allowing both the government and the media to avoid appearances of direct state coercion, which could erode legitimacy.

Contracts, first offered in the 1990s, may be seen as a "commodification of loyalty." Regional officials pay for good coverage through agreements that spell out the "volume, number, character and themes of information coverage," such as "coverage of governor's policy," and articles about local government initiatives (Kiriya, 2019, p. 13). Dovbysh (2017) lists common types of contracts: "(1) Information contracts for the creation and/or distribution of a media product; (2) contracts for subscription or provision of the state customer with print media; and (3) contracts for the publication of official information (laws, regulations, etc.)" (p. 88).

Grant-seeking and distribution is a more open process for the media, and grants have become a popular way for the state to promote narrow social initiatives. Some common examples: grants from the police to create television programs about road security, grants from the interior ministry to prepare material about police activities, and grants given to popularize "local products, regional tourism and so on" (Kiriya, 2019, p. 14). Ethnic media have also pursued grants: for example, to support "public values" of "patriotic upbringing of the young generation" (Gladkova et al., 2019, p. 58).

Media self-censor in anticipation of landing future contracts, as the more subservient the media, the more the government favors them. In many regions, contracts are concentrated among a few news outlets (Kiriya, 2019). For journalists, landing a contract or grant is seen as an honor, and this is one way that professional motivation is put in the service of state aims (Zeveleva, 2019). Further, for most media owners, regardless of the health of the local ad market, taking contract and grant funding is easier (Kiriya, 2019). Dovbysh (2019) cites Ershov (2012): "it is easier to deal with one 'administrator of credits' in the backrooms of power than to learn sales techniques, create a network of advertising agents and compete for advertisers every day" (p. 81).

There are public service benefits to contracts and grants. They offer both the state and professionally driven journalists a way to provide socially important information for local citizens that commercial markets often fail to provide (Dovbysh,

2019; Lowrey & Erzikova, 2018). "[E]xternal financing [via state contracts] is needed to implement the public-service functions of media (e.g., diversity of information, representation of various social groups and communities, and unprofitable yet socially significant topics)" (Dovbysh, 2019, p. 80).

The Journalist-Citizen Relationship at the Local Level

Local journalists and local citizens have managed to maintain meaningful relationships for centuries, across changing regimes. Roudakova (2017) described the complex links between Soviet-era journalists, citizens and officials—journalists brought citizens' problems to the attention of officials while also monitoring officials' competence in their service to the Russian people and state: "Soviet authorities could not afford to be *seen* as ignoring signals from below without jeopardizing socialism's legitimacy" (p. 31). The pre-Soviet and Soviet-era journalist also served as moral educator for the Russian people (Lowrey & Erzikova, 2018), relying on an internal "finely cultivated moral 'tuning fork'" (Roudakova, 2008, p. 50).

Local journalists can serve similar roles today, though the roles have been less formally sanctioned. During our research, some local journalists sought footholds in both the everyday world of readers and the official world of bureaucratic sources. They tried to connect these worlds, mediate them, and solve daily problems for citizens. Greene (2009) quotes a newspaper editor who sought these connections: "Our reader is used to seeing this newspaper as his last line of defence [and] ... we want to play this role" (p. 69).

But this role, which typically involves helping with small, daily problems rather than systemic problems, is a modest one. Greene (2009) argues that journalists' service to local citizens for their mundane problems is unlikely to develop into shared, meaningful ideas in a "true media space" that fosters social change: "The fact that a newspaper might take pride in serving such a [mundane] role only underscores the profound silence that follows the dropping of these messages into the broader Russian media space" (p. 69).

Kiriya and Kachkaeva (2011) argue that a grassroots public sphere in the grand Habermasian sense has never really existed in Russia's regions. The Soviets "artificially" formed a media audience, and so, outside of a narrow intelligentsia, the people have come to think of media production and consumption from within the framework of state mandates and state activity (Kiriya & Kachkaeva, 2011). Even media diversity and independence during perestroika never led to a "broad sector of the media that championed the public interest," according to Smyth & Oates (2015, p. 289). In 2007, Matveeva wrote of "incoherent goals, unclear roles, and broken communication between journalists and audiences" (Lowrey & Erzikova,

2013, p. 643). Too often, neither owners nor reporters strive to reflect the audience's interests, and while social stability has increased since the early post-perestroika era, it's not at all clear that local audience's interests have been served.

Journalists and Citizens: Beyond the Public Sphere

If we accept the premise that local Russian journalism has never been substantially separate or autonomous from the powers that be, can we see ways forward for journalists who strive to maintain relevance within communities, and do good for citizens? Reporting a faulty elevator to officials (Greene, 2009) may do little to enrich "public discussion," but it seems likely to strengthen social good will and trust between journalist and citizen. We note Hanitzsch and Vos' (2018) suggestion that journalistic service may connect with "community life" and citizens' "everyday life," social domains that are "neither fully political nor private" (p. 151).

One benefit of social trust is found in the ground it prepares for future cooperation and collective action even if there is no apparent immediate value (Putnam, 2002). Roudakova (2017) noted the importance of mutual "trust" as a dimension in the pursuit of truth by journalists, community citizens and community leaders, and she laments the loss of trust and weakening of social tissue connecting journalists, citizens and government. Loss of trust in public news and information systems is not unique to Russia (Schmidt, 2018), but this does not lessen the problem.

Scholars have identified personal social networks in local Russian society—networks that can be latent, informal, private or even underground—as important for enhancing social trust and for sharing social and political information. These were evident during Soviet times and also during "the confusing and overwhelming media environment" of the post-Soviet era (Smyth & Oates, 2015, p. 293). Smyth and Oates (2015) cited online social networks as important in the organization of protests in Russia's capital cities, and while there was some optimism about digital online media encouraging grassroots social mobilization, Smyth and Oates (2015) saw little evidence that these media enhanced the development of public discussion within a shared public sphere.

> [A]uthoritarian states can limit the internet through repressive regulations on internet-service providers, strangling the speed of information delivery by failing to develop technology infrastructure, monitoring citizens online "via" automation or even human oversight, as well as making examples of cyber-protesters in order [to] inculcate online self-censorship and fear (p. 291).

In the offline realm, Smyth and Oates (2015) noted the "tradition of talk around the kitchen table" as important for communal sense-making, as locals balanced media information with lived experiences (p. 293). Also relevant is Yurchak's

(2006) discussion of *svoi*, a kind of latent local community within which Soviet-era citizens participated together in state-sanctioned ritual, which signaled their interpersonal bonds and mutual trust more than their allegiance to state ideology. Svitich et al. (2016) described local journalists' role in reflecting communities' shared needs and values:

> In provincial towns local newspapers carry out the vital mission of preserving journalism, keeping it close to communities, respecting their needs and desires, and ensuring journalistic content is oriented on basic Russian values (p. 17).

Local journalists are proximate to their communities, and they "maintain closer ties with representatives of different social strata and groups of town residents, involving them and moving them towards cooperation" (Svitich et al., 2016, p. 41). These roles aid social cohesion as well as social control.

The flipside of social cohesion is social exclusion. Borders represent and help define a community's commonality, but they also keep others out. Russian regions have seen growing animosity toward the West by both citizens and media (Beumers, Hutchings & Rulyova, 2009), as well as animosity toward the affluent "capitals" and their Western orientations. Many in the regions assume that resources from the West, such as grants to journalists, are provided as a quid pro quo, with expectation of service to Western institutions (Zeveleva, 2019). International sanctions on Russia have bolstered anti-Western feelings (Radikov, 2019), and though varying in economic development, all four of Zubarevich's Russian areas share anti-Western sentiments and a favorable view of restoring a Russian empire (Zubarevich, 2016). In one recent study of "urban, internet-connected, bilingual" students at international universities in Russia, researchers found that "both users and non-users of state-aligned media were inclined to agree more often than disagree that Western media are 'propaganda instruments' of Western governments and that the West has tried to weaken and constrain Russia for centuries" (Szostek, 2017, p. 299).

Discussion

Russia's regions are diverse, but common economic, political and cultural problems have deepened across Russia's regions in the post-perestroika and Putin eras. These trends are evident in the three regions we study. Local media are vulnerable to the effects of these trends, and financial precarity and growing dependence on government seem to have contributed to erosion of journalists' professional standards and aims. Yet, complexities in the relationships between media and state, and between media and citizens, open possible paths—if narrow paths—for journalists' agency in both political and local community spaces. It is unclear if agency can adapt and journalists can continue to nurture social connections and maintain promise for helping local communities in meaningful ways.

This discussion of journalists' social and community contexts takes a more conceptual turn in the next chapter. We explore social "meso-level" theories that can help us explain local Russian journalists' adaptive agency within their complex contexts. Contexts include the nuanced and sometimes puzzling constraints and allowances of political and economic power, as well as the pull of both the occupational community and local community that regional journalists have historically served.

Notes

1. Oblasts are the regions or provinces—the three regions we study are oblasts. Oblasts have their origins in pre-Soviet imperial Russia, but they were fully formalized as administrative units in the Soviet era. Today, they are considered the first-level administrative units in the current federation. Okrugs were administrative units created in the 1920s to provide autonomy to indigenous people in the North. They were later renamed "autonomous okrugs" to signal that they had some autonomous rights and are not merely another type of administrative territory. Republics were designed as districts for specific ethnic minorities; each has its own constitution and legislature and a right to its own language. The autonomous oblast is the Jewish Autonomous Oblast, created during the Soviet era to demonstrate tolerance of religious diversity, but also to resettle Jewish citizens and populate a far eastern frontier area in order to discourage Chinese encroachment. We note that the autonomy of republics, autonomous okrugs and the autonomous oblast is, today, a nominal autonomy. "Territories" or "krais" were originally large frontier areas of Russia. The three cities of federal significance are Moscow, St. Petersburg and Sevastopol in the annexed Crimea (The Constitution, 2020; Petrov, 2002).
2. We provide only general outlines of the regions' characteristics, in order to preserve our participants' anonymity.
3. Officially, for a Russian settlement to become a city, it must have at least 12,000 population; however, this is only a rough criterion in actuality. Some villages are larger than 12,000 and some cities are smaller.
4. Experts (e.g., Salikhov, 2019) say statistics can be manipulated as a consequence of ongoing review/reconsideration of macroeconomic indicators. For example, in April 2019, Rosstat (the Federal State Statistics Service) revised the value of GDP dynamics so that numbers jumped from −0.2% to +0.3%. We therefore supplement official data with data from academic organizations [e.g., Levada-center] and experts [e.g., Natalia Zubarevich].) According to Natalia Zubarevich, director of the Regional Program of the Independent Institute for Social Policy, "This country is not about [economic] development, but about отчетность [reporting]." Statistical reporting becomes a sort of Potemkin village—a façade to conceal mounting serious problems, without success.

References

Alexeev, M., Avxentyev, N., Mamedov, A., & Sinelnikov-Murylev, S. G. (2018). Fiscal decentralization, budget discipline, and local finance reform in Russia's regions. *Public Finance Review, 47*(4), 679–717.

Anikina, M., Frost, L., & Hanitzsch, T. (2017). *Journalists in Russia*. Worlds of Journalism Study. https://epub.ub.uni-muenchen.de/35063/1/Country_report_Russia.pdf

Berg-Nordlie, M., Holm-Hansen, J., & Kropp, S. (2018). The Russian state as network manager: A theoretical framework. In S. Kropp, A. Aasland, M. Berg-Nordlie, J. Holm-Hansen & J. Schuhmann (Eds.), *Governance in Russian regions: A policy comparison* (pp. 7–42). London: Palgrave Macmillan.

Beumers, B., Hutchings, S., & Rulyova, N. (Eds.). (2009). *The post-Soviet Russian media: Conflicting signals*. London: Routledge.

Beumers, B., Rulyova, N., & Hutchings, S. (2009). Introduction. In B. Beumers, S. Hutchings & N. Rulyova (Eds.), *The post-Soviet Russian media: Conflicting signals* (pp. 1–26). London: Routledge.

The Constitution of the Russian Federation. Chapter 3, Article 65. Retrieved April 21, 2020, from http://www.constitution.ru/en/10003000-04.htm

Coronavirus in Russia: The latest news. (2020, April 6). *The Moscow Times*. Retrieved April 21, 2020, from https://www.themoscowtimes.com/2020/04/06/coronavirus-in-russia-the-latest-news-april-6-a69117

Dovbysh, O. S. (2017). *Transformation of structural relations between media companies and the state at the regional media market in Russia* [Unpublished doctoral dissertation]. National Research University—Higher School of Economics, Moscow, Russia.

Dovbysh, O. S. (2019). Commercial or public service actors? Controversies in the nature of Russia's regional mass media. *Russian Journal of Communication, 11*(1), 71–87.

Dunn, J. A. (2009). Where did it all go wrong? Russian television in the Putin era. In B. Beumers, S. Hutchings & N. Rulyova (Eds.), *The post-Soviet Russian media: Conflicting signals* (pp. 42–55). London: Routledge.

Dzyaloshinsky, I. M., Pilgun, M. A., Davydov, S. G., & Logunova, O. S. (2015). *Ecology of media environment: Problems of security and rational use of communicative resources*. APK and PPRO.

Egorov, G., Guriev, S., & Sonin, K. (2009). Why resource-poor dictators allow freer media: A theory and evidence from panel data. *The American Political Science Review, 103*(4), 645–668.

Erzikova, E., & Lowrey, W. (2010). Seeking safe ground: Russian regional journalists' withdrawal from civic service journalism. *Journalism Studies, 11*(3), 343–358.

Fidrmuc, J., & Gundacker, L. (2017). Income inequality and oligarchs in Russian regions: A note. *European Journal of Political Economy, 50*, 196–207.

Gladkova, A., Aslanov, I., Danilov, A., Danilov, A., Garifullin, V., & Magadeeva, R. (2019). Ethnic media in Russia: Between state model and alternative voices. *Russian Journal of Communication, 11*(1), 53–70.

Goode, J. P. (2011). *The decline of regionalism in Putin's Russia: Boundary issues*. London: Routledge.

Goode, J. P. (2013). The revival of Russia's gubernatorial elections: Liberalization or Potemkin reform? *Russian Analytical Digest, 139*, 9–11.

Gorshkov, M. K., & Tikhonova, N. Ye. (Eds.). (2018). *Stolitsy i regiony v sovremennoy Rossii: Mify i real'nost' pyatnadtsat' let spustya* [Capitals and regions in modern Russia: Myths and reality fifteen years later]. Izdatel'stvo Ves' Mir.

Greene, S. A. (2009). Shifting media and the failure of political communication in Russia. In B. Beumers, S. Hutchings & N. Rulyova (Eds.), *The post-Soviet Russian media: Conflicting signals* (pp. 56–70). London: Routledge.

Hallin, D. (1994). *We keep America on top of the world: Television journalism and the public sphere*. London: Routledge.

Hallin, D. (1996). Commercialism and professionalism in the American news media. In J. Curran & M. Gurevitch (Eds.), *Mass media and society* (pp. 243–264). London: Arnold.

Hallin, D., & Mancini, P. (2004). *Comparing media systems: Three models of media and politics*. Cambridge: Cambridge University Press.

Hanitzsch, T., & Vos, T. P. (2018). Journalism beyond democracy: A new look into journalistic roles in political and everyday life. *Journalism, 192*(2), 146–164.

Khachaturov, A., & Kozlova, D. (2019). *Strana nepuganykh median. Chto Rosstat rasskazal o zarplatnom neravenstve v Rossii* [The country of frightened medians. What the Federal State Statistics Service said about salary inequality in Russia]. Novaya Gazeta. https://novayagazeta.ru/articles/2019/07/20/81316-strana-nepuganyh-median-chto-rosstat-rasskazal-o-zarplatnom-neravenstve-v-rossii?print=true

Kiriya, I. (2019). New and old institutions within the Russian media system. *Russian Journal of Communication, 11*(1), 6–21.

Kiriya, I., & Kachkaeva, A. (2011). Economical forms of state pressure in Russian regional media. *Romanian Journal of Journalism and Communication, 6*(2), 5–11.

Klyueva, A., & Tsetsura, K. (2011). News from the Urals with love and payment: The first look at nontransparent media practices in the Urals Federal District of Russia. *Russian Journal of Communication, 4*(1/2), 72–93.

Klyueva, A., & Tsetsura, K. (2015). Economic foundations of morality: Questions of transparency and ethics in Russian journalism. *Central European Journal of Communication, 1*, 21–36.

Kobak, D., Shpilkin, S., & Pshenichnikov, M. S. (2016). Integer percentages as electoral falsification fingerprints. *The Annals of Applied Statistics, 10*(1), 54–73.

Kolenikov, S., & Shorrocks, A. (2005). A decomposition analysis of regional poverty in Russia. *Review of Development Economics, 9*(1), 25–46.

Koltsova, O. (2006). *News media and power in Russia*. London: Routledge.

Kordonsky, S. G., & Molyarenko, O. A. (2018). Umom Rossiyu ne ponyat' [The mind cannot understand Russia]. *EKO, 1*, 5–22.

Kynev, A. (2014). *Vybory regional'nykh parlamentov v Rossii 2009–2013: Ot partizatsii k personalizatsii* [Elections of regional parliaments in Russia in 2009–2013: From partitioning to personalization]. Center "Panorama."

Lipka, M., & Sahgal, N. (2017, May 10). *9 key findings about religion and politics in Central and Eastern Europe*. Pew Research Center. https://www.pewresearch.org/fact-tank/2017/05/10/9-key-findings-about-religion-and-politics-in-central-and-eastern-europe/

Lounsbery, A. (2018). Provinces, regions, circles, grids: How literature has shaped Russian geographical identity. In E. W. Clowes, G. Erbslöh & A. Kokobobo (Eds.), *Russia's regional identities: The power of the provinces* (pp. 44–69). London: Routledge.

Lowrey, W., & Erzikova, E. (2010). Institutional legitimacy and Russian news: Case studies of four regional newspapers. *Political Communication, 27*(3), 275–288.

Lowrey, W., & Erzikova, E. (2013). One profession—multiple identities: Russian regional reporters' perceptions of the professional community. *Mass Communication and Society, 16*(5), 639–660.

Lowrey, W., & Erzikova, E. (2018). Regional Russian journalism: Paths to independence and financial survival. In E. Freedman, R. Goodman & E. Steyn (Eds.), *Critical perspectives on journalistic beliefs and actions: Global experiences* (pp. 94–104). New York: Routledge.

Matveeva, L. V. (2007). Kultura i SMI: razmushleniya o fenomene "razorvannoi kommunikacii" [Culture and mass media: Thoughts about the phenomenon of a "broken communication"]. *Vestnik Moskovskogo Universiteta, seriya 14, Psikhologiya* [Bulletin of the Moscow State University, series 14, Psychology], *1*, 119–132.

Ob'yem krupneyshikh regional'nykh reklamnykh rynkov Rossii v I polugodii 2019 godu sostavil 13 mlrd rubley [The largest regional advertising markets of Russia in first six months of 2019 amounted to 13 billion rubles]. (2019). Retrieved from https://www.outdoor.ru/news/obem_krupneyshikh_regionalnykh_reklamnykh_rynkov_rossii_v_i_polugodii_2019_g_sostavil_13_mlrd_rubley/

Ob'yem reklamy v sredstvakh yeye rasprostraneniya v yanvare-sentyabre 2019 goda [Amounts of advertising in means of its distribution in January-September of 2019]. (2019). Retrieved from http://www.akarussia.ru/press_centre/news/id9024

Panov, P., & Ross, C. (2019). Volatility in electoral support for United Russia: Cross-regional variations in Putin's electoral authoritarian regime. *Europe-Asia Studies, 71*(2), 268–289.

Pasti, S. (2015). A passion for Robin Hood: A case study of journalistic (in)dependence in Russia. In B. Dobek-Ostrowska & M. Glowacki (Eds.), *Democracy and media in Central and Eastern Europe 25 years on* (pp. 117–136). Frankfurt: Peter Lang.

Perevyshin, Yu., Sinelnikov-Murylev, S., & Trunin, P. (2019). Determinants of price level differences in Russian regions. *Post-Communist Economies, 31*(6), 772–789.

Petrov, N. (2002). Seven faces of Putin's Russia: Federal districts as the new level of state—territorial composition. *Security Dialogue, 33*(1), 73–91.

Putnam, R. D. (Ed.). (2002). *Democracies in flux: The evolution of social capital in contemporary society*. New York: Oxford University Press.

Radikov, I. V. (2019). Impact of sanctions on the level of citizens' political confidence in the power of Russia: The incentive role of the media. *Media Watch, 10*(3), 575–585.

Reuter, O. J. (2017). *How Kremlin efforts to control the regions may be backfiring.* PONARS Eurasia. http://www.ponarseurasia.org/sites/default/files/policy-memos-pdf/Pepm467_Reuter_March2017.pdf

Rossiya v tsifrakh [Russia in numbers]. (2018). Moscow: Rosstat. Rosstat. (2019). Retrieved from https://www.gks.ru/regional_statistics

Rosstat. (2010). Retrieved from https://www.gks.ru/free_doc/new_site/perepis2010/croc/perepis_itogi1612.htm

Roudakova, N. (2008). Media-political clientelism: Lessons from anthropology. *Media, Culture & Society, 30*(1), 41–59. https://doi.org/10.1177%2F0163443707084349

Roudakova, N. (2017). *Losing Pravda: Ethics and the press in post-truth Russia.* Cambridge: Cambridge University Press.

Russians return to religion, but not to church. (2014, February 10). Pew research center. https://www.pewforum.org/2014/02/10/russians-return-to-religion-but-not-to-church/

Salikhov, M. (2019). Otkryvaya Rosstat: Mozhno li verit' ofitsial'noy rossiyskoy statistike? [Opening Rosstat: Is it possible to believe official Russian statistics?] *Novaya Gazeta.* Retrieved from https://novayagazeta.ru/articles/2019/04/15/80231-otkryvaya-rosstat.

Sätre, A.-M. (2019). *The politics of poverty in contemporary Russia.* New York: Routledge.

Schmidt, C. (2018, 5 April). *So what is that, er, Trusted News Integrity Trust Project all about? A guide to the (many, similarly named) new efforts fighting for journalism.* Nieman Lab. Retrieved February 18, 2020, from https://tinyurl.com/u399cfx

Schulze, G. G., Sjahrir, B. S., & Zakharov, N. (2016). Corruption in Russia. *Journal of Law and Economics, 59*(1), 135–171.

Shlapentokh, V., Levita, R., & Loiberg, M. (1997). *From submission to rebellion: The provinces versus the centre in Russia.* Boulder, CO: Westview Press.

Sidorkin, O., & Vorobyev, D. (2018). Political cycles and corruption in Russian regions. *European Journal of Political Economy, 52,* 55–74.

Slavtcheva-Petkova, V. (2018). *Russia's liberal media: Handcuffed but free.* New York: Routledge.

Smith, M. (2003). Putin: An end to centrifugalism? In G. Herd & A. Aldis (Eds.), *Russian regions and regionalism: Strength through weakness* (pp. 19–37). London: Routledge Curzon.

Smyth, R., & Oates, S. (2015). Mind the gaps: Media use and mass action in Russia. *Europe-Asia Studies, 67*(2), 285–305.

Svitich, L. G., & Shiriaeva, A. A. (2010). *Teoriya and sotsiologiya SMI. Part 2* [Theory and sociology of mass media]. MGU.

Svitich, L., Smirnova, O., Shiriaeva, A., & Shkondin, M. (2016). Characteristics of the content of Russian local newspapers (a sociological study). *Journal of Russian Media and Journalism Studies, 13,* 13–60.

Szostek, J. (2017). News consumption and anti-Western narratives in Russia: A case study of university students. *Europe-Asia Studies, 69*(2), 284–302.

Trudolyubov, M. (2020, January 16). *Putin's top-down revolution.* The Russia file: A blog of the Kennan Institute. https://www.wilsoncenter.org/blog-post/putins-top-down-revolution

Utsyna, Ye. (2019). Opublikovan perechen' dotatsionnykh sub"yektov RF na 2020 god [List of subsidized constituent entities of the Russian Federation for 2020 was published]. Retrieved from http://www.garant.ru/news/1304783/#ixzz6K1FcyXPu

Vyrkovsky, A. V., & Makeyenko, M. I. (2014). *Russia's regional television: Russia on the threshold of the digital age.* Media Mir.

World Bank Group. (2019). *Russian economic report: Modest growth; focus on informality.* http://documents.worldbank.org/curated/en/332081560895493011/pdf/Russia-Economic-Report-Modest-Growth-Focus-on-Informality.pdf

World Inequality Lab. (2017). *World inequality report 2018.* https://wir2018.wid.world/.

Yurchak, A. (2006). *Everything was forever until it was no more: The last Soviet generation.* Princeton, NJ: Princeton University Press.

Zakharov, N. (2019). Does corruption hinder investment? Evidence from Russian regions. *European Journal of Political Economy, 56*, 39–61. https://doi-org.libdata.lib.ua.edu/10.1016/j.ejpoleco.2018.06.005

Zeveleva, O. (2019). How states tighten control: A field theory perspective on journalism in contemporary Crimea. *The British Journal of Sociology, 70*(4), 1225–1244.

Zubarevich, N. V. (2019a). Poverty in Russian regions in 2000–2017: Factors and dynamics. *Population and Economics, 3*(1), 63–74.

Zubarevich, N. (2019b). Osoboe mnenie. [Special opinion]. Retrieved from https://echo.msk.ru/programs/personalno/2498995-echo/.

Zubarevich, N.V. (2016, January 1). Chetyre Rossii i novaya politicheskaya real'nost' [Four Russias and the new political reality]. Retrieved August 15, 2020 from https://m.polit.ru/article/2016/01/17/four_russians/

Zubarevich, N. V., & Safronov, S. G. (2019). People and money: Incomes, consumption, and financial behavior of the population of Russian regions in 2000–2017. *Regional Research of Russia, 9*(4), 359–369. https://doi.org/10.1134/S2079970519040129

CHAPTER THREE

Local Russian Journalism as a Social Space: Field and Ecology Perspectives

Political elite control money and information, and they hold a grip on the regional Russian journalists who seek these resources. Though the leash can be long, the grip has held. Our study's research questions ask how the structures and logics of the local Russian journalism space constrain and guide journalists: How do they affect journalists' agency (and freedom and autonomy), and how do they affect journalists' ability to bridge the gap between local citizens and local elite?

Given the elite's grip, how meaningfully can we even talk of journalists' agency? This question hangs partly on expectations for journalists' agency and journalism's autonomy. Is the expectation an independent journalism profession that supports a robust and inclusive public sphere, and that can stand up to the powerful and report on them meaningfully and accurately? These are the expectations seen through a liberal democratic lens, with a focus on boundaries between journalists and the powerful. Through this lens, we see only faint boundaries around the local Russian journalism space. This lens is important, but we also consider other perspectives. We agree with scholars who have observed that, while journalism is critical to democracy, there can be journalistic roles beyond democracy (Hanitzsch & Vos, 2018; Josephi, 2013). The journalists we study pursue some roles that may be overlooked when the spotlight is aimed only on manifest power struggles and journalists' efforts to win autonomy.

Meso-Level Spatial Approaches

Local Russian journalism is complex, with manifest and latent purposes and processes, and we argue it can best be understood from within a broad *meso-level spatial approach* (Abbott, 2005b; Benson, 2014; Fligstein & McAdam, 2012; Liu & Emirbayer, 2016; Lowrey & Sherrill, 2019; Mohr, 2005; Scott, 2014). There are different meso-level approaches, most notably field and ecology approaches, and we adopt aspects of each of these in our study. In this chapter, we first discuss some basic shared assumptions of meso-level spaces, including the useful concept of spatial "logics," and their influence. We then explore the differences between fields and ecologies, and we examine how some of these differences have played out in the wider scholarship on local journalism.

Meso-Level Spaces and Their Guiding Logics

From a meso-level spatial approach, journalists, or any social actors (individuals, organizations), may respond to influences in both straightforward and unexpected ways. Journalists think about and practice their work collectively in complex, bounded social spaces that buffer or translate influences from outside, such as powerful political and economic influences. Journalists respond to these influences, but, depending on how autonomous their space is, they may not respond in direct, expected ways. Rather, their responses are shaped by collective interaction and agreement among themselves and other social actors. These shared agreements are channeled by the space's guiding *logic* or logics, which are shared and often taken-for-granted ways of thinking about how things are done in the space. In sum, it follows that the level of the space's autonomy, the nature of social interaction within the space, and the nature of the guiding logics are key in explaining how journalists make decisions and take action.

A little more about logics: Logics are deep-seated "cultural-cognitive" models that organize, channel and enable social action, and that typically have institutional support (Scott, 2014, p. 228). Not all spatial approaches use the term "logics," though we use that term. But, all embrace the idea that that there are shared "interpretive frames" about "what is going on" and what is "legitimate and meaningful" (Fligstein & McAdam, 2012, p. 11) and that these can become "taken-for-granted modes of thinking, perceiving, feeling, and acting" that shape the way people act collectively (Liu & Emirbayer, 2016, p. 67). When people embrace the logic of a social domain, they are more likely to gain legitimacy in this domain; this encourages reproduction of the domain. Social actors of all sorts need public legitimacy as well as money, and the two are related (Collins & Makowsky, 1998; Swedberg, 2006).

Logics are not rigid rules. While they provide people with accepted ways of doing things, there can be more than one logic—a kind of "repertoire" (Silber, 2003, p. 431) or "toolkit" of logics (Thornton, Ocasio & Lounsbury, 2012, p. 9) that is "available to organizations and individuals to elaborate" (Friedland & Alford, 1991, p. 248). Institutional scholars tell us that people do not always rely on the most accessible logics; they may instead "invoke and activate other available logics drawn from other situational contexts" (Thornton, Ocasio & Lounsbury, 2012, p. 101).

When there are multiple social domains and a repertoire of multiple logics, there is more opportunity for human agency. In our study, this means more room for journalists to pursue multiple lines of action, even in oppressive contexts. Without multiple logics providing people with multiple meanings, deviance or to "even think in conflict-oriented terms" would be unimaginable (Thornton, Ocasio & Lounsbury, 2012, p. 44). Journalists may seek legitimacy from more than one domain —for example, government, their profession, or their more immediate community of newspaper colleagues—which makes multiple logics and alternative ways of thinking more likely. Later, we discuss a number of logics relevant to the journalists we study: for example, a *perestroika-era* logic, which encourages journalists' scrutiny of officials, and a *moral education* logic, which encourages or affords journalists in the work of inspiring regions' residents.

Local journalists may also seek legitimacy by thinking and acting in ways that are consistent with their local area, its communities and its citizens. Weber (1978 [1922], p. 902) discussed the importance of geographic "territory" value systems, which order people's behavior in ways that have little to do with satisfying economic or political needs. Local communities are "organized for a shared purpose that may initiate outside of ... formal market or state channels" (O'Mahony & Lakhani, 2011, p. 5), and when people work in local contexts, they are more likely to act in ways that do not reproduce dominant institutions (Marquis & Battilana, 2009). In previous chapters we noted the historical importance of trust between local Russian journalists and citizens (Roudakova, 2017) and the importance of keeping local journalism "close to communities, respecting [community members'] needs and desires, and ensuring [that] journalistic content is oriented on basic Russian values" (Svitich et al., 2016, p. 17). Literature on local-level communication and journalism suggests a range of purposes and practices that are not obviously related to reproducing powerful political-economic institutions: for example, nurturing community members' sense of belonging to their local place, reaffirming the values and normative boundaries of the local place, sustaining local memory, enhancing social trust, and providing inspiration (Costera Meijer, 2010;

Friedland et al., 2012; Kim & Ball-Rokeach, 2006; Lowrey, Brozana & Mackay, 2008; Nielsen, 2015).

The context of fellow journalists, or journalists' "occupational community," is also relevant. Historically, a variety of logics—for example, the moral education and literary logics—have helped bring shared occupational meaning and togetherness to local Russian journalists. Across our findings, these logics have fluctuated in importance, but they have continued to matter, despite evidence that the occupational community is weakening (Lowrey & Erzikova, 2013).

So, while local Russian journalists are highly constrained by political and economic forces and contexts, they are not puppets without agency. And, we suggest, there is more than one measuring stick by which to judge their agency.

Fields and Ecologies

Given this complexity, it's no surprise that there is more than one meso-level theory about social spaces. As mentioned, approaches include ecology theory and field theory (Abbott, 2005a; Liu & Emirbayer, 2016; Mohr, 2005), and we adopt some concepts from each of these in our study. These share the assumptions of the meso-level spatial approach as detailed above, but there are also differences that are worth fleshing out. One key difference is how relatively important political and economic power is in the daily lives of journalists. How strongly do powerful elite influence their decision-making? To what degree are logics of the social space shaped from the top down, by political-economic power, institutions and resources? Conversely, to what degree do logics emerge from the ground up, as shared understandings of the people around you, which develop from the "interactional basis of sociality" in the space (Fine, 2012, p. 4)? Which is more evident: journalists taking an oppositional, normative stance to try to "win" in the face of political-economic pressure, or journalists adapting through a process of ongoing interaction, and getting by, day-to-day? Different spatial theories offer different answers.

Field theories tend to emphasize power and opposition to power, while ecology approaches emphasize adaptation and survival. Given the importance of political-economic power and the concept of autonomy in our study, it makes sense to apply concepts from field theory. However, the tendencies for adaptation and informal, latent practices in Russian society (Gudkov, Dubin & Levinson, 2009; Ledeneva, 2006), as well as the emphasis on enduring hardship suggest the ecological approach will also be helpful. To see and understand local Russian journalism more clearly, we use a broad meso-level spatial approach as a prism, turning between the facets of field and ecology to seek explanation. Below, we provide brief overviews of fields and ecologies.

Field Approaches

Since the mid-2000s, Bourdieu's field theory (1993, 1996) has been used with growing frequency to explain journalism's complex dynamics and contexts (e.g., Benson, 2013; Benson & Neveu, 2005; Powers & Vera-Zambrano, 2016; Robinson, 2017; Ryfe, 2017; Stevenson, 2016). The theory tends toward a critical approach that emphasizes power, dominance and opposition. Other field theories that are similar to Bourdieu's and that are strongly influenced by his approach have emerged as well (Fligstein & McAdam, 2012; Scott, 2014; Wooten & Hoffman, 2008). Field theories have many moving parts. The following are those that are most relevant to our study, and as the reader will see, these are consistent with the description of meso-level approaches discussed above. We draw on aspects of field theory that are found in Bourdieu's approach but that are also found in other field approaches.

Actors (individuals, organizations) operate in relation to one another within a bounded social space—a *field*, which is variably autonomous in the face of pressures from the environment. A field may include multiple guiding logics that are accessible to actors, but there is often a dominant logic for any given field. The relative domination and subordination of actors are important in Bourdieu's theory especially, and these are shaped by availability of different types of capital across the field—or "resources" as they are called in other field theories. The ways capital or resources are distributed across the field are shaped by political and economic power. Field theory studies of journalism have tended to focus on effects of economic capital (money) and cultural capital, i.e., "cultural competence" (Johnson, 1993, p. 7) or the benefits that come from knowing how to do things appropriately within the field—and how one may be converted into the other. People compete for capital as they take oppositional positions in the areas available to them, and there is always something "at stake" in a field, as "[w]ho gets what and why are the core questions at the heart of the analysis" (Fligstein & McAdam, 2012, p. 217). People's actions are channeled, constrained and enabled by the field's structures and logics. People's actions, in turn, tend to reproduce the field. In Bourdieu's approach, this takes place through *habitus*, a kind of muscle memory or a "feel for the game" in the field (Johnson, 1993, p. 5). However, there can be change too, especially when people can access multiple domains and logics (Bourdieu, 1993; Johnson, 1993; Wooten & Hoffman, 2008).

We take a moment to highlight the roles of institutions in social fields and the behaviors they encourage, especially the pursuit of legitimacy (Scott, 2014; Wooten & Hoffman, 2008). Social actors like journalists and officials seek to show legitimacy in their actions. To have legitimacy is to fit with, or be in accord with, recognized social domains, institutions and taken-for-granted ways of doing things in one's field (i.e., the field's logics) (Thornton, Ocasio & Lounsbury, 2012).

Studies of institutional influence in fields explore the steps people take to maintain legitimacy, especially when they seek to be consistent with conflicting social domains or logics: Journalists may seek legitimacy in the contexts of government, their local community, and their fellow journalists, and these efforts may be at odds. For us, the most relevant steps involve the ways they "decouple" their behaviors in these situations. For example, throughout our study, we saw journalists and officials saying one thing but doing another, or taking superficial half-steps so they could be seen as legitimate, even when they were pulled in contradictory directions (Scott, 2014).

Ecology Approaches

Ecology approaches and assumptions are common in the study of local and community journalism and journalistic change (Anderson, Coleman & Thumim, 2015; Boyles, 2017; Coleman et al., 2016; Nielsen, 2015; Wahl-Jorgensen, 2016). They have roots in natural sciences, with the social system often described as a body, or an ecosystem with interconnected spaces and actors (Lowrey & Sherrill, 2019). Ecology studies explore how social actors adapt and survive over time within changing ecosystems. Later ecological scholars adopted interactionist processes, which allow for fluid, unpredictable and informal change in social situations and ways of thinking (e.g., Abbott, 2016). People's shared assumptions (similar to "logics") and their "lines of action," are shaped by considering the perspectives of others. People "modify what they are doing so as to fit in more or less easily with what others have in mind to do" (Becker, 2008, p. 201). This kind of approach fits well with studies of community-level interaction.

According to Abbott (2016), who is often cited in literature on journalism change (Carlson, 2015; Lowrey, 2006; Usher, 2016), ecological social space is relatively unpredictable, continually being remade from moment to moment (Abbott, 2016; Jouvenet, 2016). This stands in contrast to Bourdieu's field, which "emphasizes the concept of domination" (Abbott, 2005a) and which is "firmly ordered by mechanisms ... of domination and reproduction" (Swartz, 2013, p. 21), as actors take oppositional positions structured by power. Generally, ecological approaches are less critical, less normative, less formal, and less likely to foreground political-economic power (Lowrey & Sherrill, 2019). In unpredictable ecologies, when people accumulate resources and reach relatively dominant positions, they gain mostly "short-run power" (Abbott, 1988, p. 141). Those who appear at any moment to be the dominant or the dominated could find the structures and logics change out from under them. So, for the dominated, like the journalists we studied, the ability to endure can matter in the long run.

Comparing Field and Ecology Approaches

In field theory analyses of journalism, the stakes are typically grounded in democratic governance, and journalists struggle with political and economic forces that challenge their autonomy and their ability to support this governance (Benson, 2013; Hess & Waller, 2017; Powers & Zambrano, 2016). Analyzing local Russian journalism as a definable field seems problematic: There are many interlopers in the field (officials, business owners, bloggers), and boundaries and autonomy are faint. However, boundaries are still evident. Local journalists still claim normative roles, challenge officials, and seek resources in order to play these roles.

Ecological assumptions about people's behavior are generally less normative, which is a weakness and a strength. People do not just take oppositional positions and seek to win within a field shaped by "external, trans-situational forces" (Fine, 2012, p. 5). People also adapt and continue on, day to day, in varied, unpredictable ways, with their behaviors shaped by ongoing social interaction. Continuing to survive is ultimately more consequential than securing clear boundaries in the face of dominant force, and there are many ways social actors may adapt, gain footholds and carry on.

The Wider Scholarship on Local and Community News

Before we explore our research findings on Russian regional journalism, we situate our research within the broad, burgeoning literature on community and local journalism. We focus specifically here on problems in Russia's regional journalism that are consistent with the mounting problems found in the local media space, worldwide. So, the following exploration of this literature accomplishes two main goals: (1) It reveals commonalities between the local Russian journalism space and other local news systems, and (2) it sheds light on the relative helpfulness of field approaches and ecological approaches in understanding the local journalism space. Along those lines, we explore studies on local journalists' autonomy and their democratic purposes, and other studies on journalists' interaction with their communities and the emerging possibilities for change.

There has been a small flood of research literature on local journalism around the world over the last five to 10 years, including high-profile reports (Friedland et al., 2012; Knight Commission, 2009; Pew Research Center, 2015; Radcliffe & Ali, 2017), books (Ali, 2017; Anderson, 2013; Hess & Waller, 2017; Nielsen, 2015; Reader & Hatcher, 2012; Robinson, 2017) and special journal issues (Guimerà,

Domingo & Williams, 2018; Robinson, 2014; Wall, 2017). This research cuts across nations, but much of it focuses on liberal democratic and social democratic media systems, assuming that local and community journalism naturally serve "the societal role of providing a means for common dialogue in a democracy" (Hatcher, 2012, p. 130).

Ties between journalists and local community is also a recurrent research topic. The "notion of 'a nearness to people' provides a common theoretical anchor" for local journalism scholars (Reader, 2012, p. 5). Conversely, some scholars think journalists who prioritize connections with local community risk ignoring universal truths "in favor of community loyalty and conformity" (Barney, 1996, p. 140). This argument suggests that journalists should serve "a general 'public interest'" that transcends "particular interest" and local tradition (Hallin & Mancini, 2004, p. 56).

However, the dispassionate journalistic system proposed in liberal democratic theory can fall flat at the local level. Some scholars cite local power constraints as the reason, and some point to lower levels of expertise and resources in local news outlets (Berkowitz, 2007; Nielsen, 2015). But others see problems in dispassion itself, arguing that local journalists are more successful when citizens see them as "in their corner" rather than as members of a high-minded, distant profession (Heider, McCombs & Poindexter, 2005; Rosen, 2001). They urge local journalists to view community members as neighbors with needs, as many of our journalist respondents did, rather than as an abstract public that exists to animate democracy. This goal is as relevant to quasi- and non-democratic systems as to democratic systems. According to one survey study of local citizens (Costera-Meijer, 2010), local media should help people "navigate their local community," "provide inspiration," "ensure representation of different groups," "increase ... understanding between different groups," "maintain a form of local memory or chronicle" and foster a "sense of belonging" (Nielsen, 2015, p. 11). Of course, a fine line separates neighborliness from advocacy, and studies suggest that local journalists, especially in smaller local areas, can step over this line too willingly (Gutsche, 2015; Tichenor, Donohue & Olien, 1980). Both the critical emphasis on journalistic autonomy (the "field" facet) and the interactionist emphasis on nurturing communal meaning (the "ecology" facet) can shed light on the meanings and implications of journalist-community relationships.

Local News: Political-Economic Power, Control and Opposition

Much recent scholarship on local journalism has looked at the contexts of political and economic control and local journalism's vulnerabilities to these contexts. Most of these studies do not appropriate field theory, but they share its critical focus on power and autonomy.

In Russian regions, government subsidies coupled with the local media's dire need for resources have encouraged submissiveness to government by local media. However, government support for money-strapped news operations is increasingly common around the world, in liberal, pluralistic and corporatist media systems, causing controversy in Western nations especially (Zahariadis, 2013). Governments have provided subsidies to grow diversity in local media markets in Scandinavian countries, Austria, Belgium and France, and have supported innovation in financially struggling local media in Denmark (Hess & Waller, 2017). The UK's National Union of Journalists called on the government for help in navigating the industry's uncertain future (Cawley, 2017). Political parties and political figures commonly fund media in Italy, providing media-state arrangements that have been seen as similar to Russia's, though government support for Russian local media does not encourage meaningful political pluralism (Dunn, 2009; Gladkova et al., 2019). Some worry that government involvement may discourage media pluralism in Western democratic states. The publisher of the Winnipeg (Canada) Free Press complained that publications cannot compete with the online content from government-backed public broadcasting: Citizens view it as free despite paying taxes for it (Cox, 2016).

Research shows that local political-economic power encourages local journalists to avoid conflict. Media seek to "get along" with local elite, who influence availability of revenue and information, especially in tightly knit small communities (Harry, 2001; Nah & Armstrong, 2011; Tichenor, Donohue & Olien, 1980). We see this in media systems around the world. For example, local journalists in Spain avoided confrontation with elites by framing a local industry's chemical spill as an economic problem rather than an environmental problem (Castelló, 2010). This research is consistent with studies of campaign, advocacy and boosterist journalism, which supports "dominant cultural positions of collective identities" (Hess & Waller, 2017, p. 132) through the production of media messages of "approved behaviors" (Gutsche, 2015, p. 498). One prominent research program focuses on the tendency for media in less "structurally pluralistic" communities—small towns with few centers of power (businesses, government agencies)—to avoid conflict and promote harmony. In smaller, less pluralistic communities, local media are more likely to avoid investigation of conflict and to soft-pedal local problems, and this supports the local power structure and the status quo (Tichenor, Donohue & Olien, 1980). Similarly, media system research in Norway found that smaller media in smaller communities focused relatively less on political and public-issue news (Sjøvaag, Pedersen & Lægreid, 2019).

Conceptualizations and discourses of the local are generally framed by market boundaries, such as "designated market areas" in the U.S. According to Ali (2017), these have facilitated control by the political-economic elite, as government regulators aid powerful media corporations. Scholars have noted a neo-liberal turn in Russian regions and in government discourse about media (Richter, 2006); cuts in regular government subsidies have left media vulnerable to businesses, which are themselves dependent on government, and have also left media more dependent on paid government contracts (Kiriya, 2019). In both cases, the stakes of struggle for local journalists, from a field theory perspective, relate to the ability of journalists to make authentic local meaning in the face of political-economic power.

Much recent research on local journalism around the world focuses on financial hardships facing local media organizations and journalists (Barnett & Townend, 2015; Franklin, 2014; Hess & Waller, 2017; Napoli, Weber, McCollough & Wang, 2018; Nygren, 2019). These situations are not uniform. Local TV tends to be financially healthier than newspapers (Nielsen, 2015), and we find somewhat healthier local outlets in corporatist systems, such as those in Scandanavia, where competition has been weaker (Sjøvaag, Pedersen & Lægreid, 2019). But, generally, local media have been challenged by digital fragmentation, shifts in audience use patterns, waning revenues, and concentrated ownership, and we see some similar challenges for journalism in our three Russian regions. Staff cutbacks at the local level have been dramatic (again, we see this in Russian regions), and news organizations now increasingly share their already thin reporting, editing and production resources (Cawley, 2017; Collaborative Journalism Database, 2020; Stonbely, 2017). According to Galletero-Campos (2019), 29 provincial newspapers closed in Spain between 2001 and 2016, and print sales have been cut in half, or more, in Finland and Sweden. In the U.S., around 20% of newspapers disappeared over the last 15 years (Abernathy, 2018), and news staffs were slashed 25%, on average, from 2008 to 2018 (Grieco, 2019).

Depleted local news outlets have struggled to provide "quality public interest journalism," and have focused increasingly on entertainment and public relations content at the expense of "investigation depth, accuracy and public accountability" (Nettlefold, 2019, p. 75). There is a growing worldwide problem of local news outlets disseminating information that is not local (Hess & Waller, 2017; Napoli, Weber, McCollough & Wang, 2018), and producing stories that matter little to locals (Hess & Waller, 2017). Cash-strapped outlets, from China to Africa, India and Oceania, too often feel obligated to provide state-subsidized information, which local residents see as irrelevant (Hess & Waller, 2017). All of these challenges were evident, to varying degrees, in the regional newspapers we studied.

Local News, Survival, Adaptation and the Long Game

Ecological perspectives in local journalism scholarship are common (Anderson, 2016; Boyles, 2017; Coleman et al., 2016; Lowrey, 2012; Nielsen, 2015; Wahl-Jorgensen, 2016; Weber et al, 2016) though often, ecological concepts such as boundaries (Carlson, 2015; Winch, 1997) and ecosystems (Anderson, 2010, 2016; Nygren, Leckner & Tenor, 2017) are used informally or piecemeal (Lowrey & Sherrill, 2019). As do critical studies, ecological studies examine economic hardship and its consequences, but the focus is less on revealing effects of political-economic constraints on journalists' freedom, and more on finding sustainability and opportunities within a changing news media "ecosystem." Processes of survival and sustainability often receive more direct attention than the nature and quality of news content (Abernathy, 2018; Wadbring & Bergström, 2017).

The tone and goals of ecological research are relatively optimistic, or at least prescriptive. They are more "can-do" than critical. Research stresses the authenticity of journalists' identification with local place and local people, and vice versa (Hatcher & Haavik, 2014; Thomson, Bennett, Johnston & Mason, 2015). "Concrete face-to-face interaction" (p. 287) between media and community residents can foster shared meaning-making about the local area (Lowrey, Brozana & Mackay, 2008), and journalists and citizens may engage in "neighborhood storytelling" (Kim & Ball-Rokeach, 2006, p. 413).

In Chapter 2, we discussed the importance of trust in relationships between Russian journalists and community members, and this importance is recognized across diverse media systems (Hess & Waller, 2017). Local initiatives aimed at building social trust between journalists and the communities they serve have emerged around the world (Fischer, 2018; Schmidt, 2018a; Schmidt, 2018b). In the editor's introduction to a special *Journalism Practice* edition on community journalism, Robinson (2014) observed:

> From our review of the community journalism literature, we know that one of the fundamental tenets is that the reporters become one with the community, attending local events as citizens first and then as reporters and serving as an adviser and advocate (p. 118).

This tenet seems to encourage "communicatively integrated" community (Friedland, 2001, p. 360) more than political autonomy. Ecological studies do not always draw overt cause-effect connections between community integration and democratic goals, though they are often assumed.

From the ecological perspective, hope springs eternal, and studies assume journalists can adapt to changing media systems in functional ways, especially in diverse systems (Friedland et al., 2012). There has been extensive research on emerging non-legacy media forms—for example, hyperlocal or "citizen journalism" online news outlets, which have sprouted in the margins of local news ecosystems, especially in urban areas. These sites have been studied worldwide—in France (Bousquet, Smyrnaios & Bertelli, 2014; Smyrnaios et al., 2015), Belgium (Paulussen & D'heer, 2013), the UK (White et al., 2017), Australia (Hess & Waller, 2017) and the U.S. (Bobkowski, Jiang, Peterlin & Rodriguez, 2019). The hope has been that user-generated news outlets will renew dying media spaces and offer alternative voices. However, sustainability of these citizen-based media has been a problem (Williams, Harte & Turner, 2015), and the content has often disappointed (Carey, 2014; Karlsson & Holt, 2014; Usher, 2017). Emerging media were a mixed bag at best for journalists in our study, as we discuss in later chapters. They have offered some opportunity for independent voices, but resources for such ventures have been meager in these controlled economic systems, and according to many of the experienced journalists, they have undermined quality in content.

The Local Russian Journalism Space: Ecology or Field?

In an ecological study, Nygren (2019) discussed other problems with the advent of "user-generated media." For example, "strong actors like local authorities" are developing their own online/social media platforms for communicating directly with regional residents (p. 65). For years, Russian governors have been promoting their agendas through blogs and social media. While the ecological approach helps us see a wide range of possibilities in media ecosystems, it does not always emphasize critical thinking or problems of institutionalized power. The ecological framework helps reveal the unexpected ways journalists and news outlets seek to adapt to changes and pressures, as they pursue alternative logics and try new practices to maintain their social space and their relationships with audiences. But, what is often missing in a pure ecological perspective is a clear-eyed view of political-economic power, and critical assessment of how power may undermine both citizens' ventures and journalists' efforts to connect local citizens with the resources and mechanisms that can help them.

Yet critical approaches such as field theory studies, with their attention to power and responses to power, may frame the social world narrowly, overlooking the creative, diverse and nuanced ways that journalists adapt to constraints and hardship. In ecological approaches, social change can play the long game, taking a circuitous path: Nurturing of trust between journalists and citizens helps make the social space fertile for opportunities that may arise, eventually, as the social system shifts. How much this happens is an empirical question. But, the possibility exists, offering rationale for adopting both approaches.

In the opening chapter, we asked about local journalists' ability to connect the people and their needs to the powerful and their resources, and vice versa. The literature on local Russian journalism, and on local journalism generally, offers some evidence for this linkage, but also reveals formidable barriers. It is highly difficult to act based on relationships of trust when mired in relationships of dependency. The following chapters explore the political, economic, organizational and community contexts of the three regions under study, and the complex social interaction within them, offering rich material for exploring these questions from both field and ecology perspectives.

References

Abbott, A. (1988). *The system of professions: An essay on the division of expert labor.* Chicago: University of Chicago Press.
Abbott, A. (2005a). Ecologies and fields. Retrieved December 6, 2018 from http://home.uchicago.edu/aabbott/Papers/BOURD.pdf
Abbott, A. (2005b). Linked ecologies: States and universities as environments for professions. *Sociological Theory, 23*(3), 245–274. https://doi.org/10.1111/j.0735-2751.2005.00253.x
Abbott, A. (2016). *Processual sociology.* Chicago: University of Chicago Press.
Abernathy, P. M. (2018). *The expanding news desert.* UNC School of Media and Journalism. Retrieved August 19, 2020 from https://www.usnewsdeserts.com/
Ali, C. (2017). *Media localism: The policies of place.* Urbana, IL: University of Illinois Press.
Anderson, C. W. (2010). Journalistic networks and the diffusion of local news: The brief, happy news life of the "Francisville Four." *Political Communication, 27*(3), 289–309. https://doi.org/10.1080/10584609.2010.496710
Anderson, C. W. (2013). *Rebuilding the news: Metropolitan journalism in the digital age.* Philadelphia: Temple University Press.
Anderson, C. W. (2016). News ecosystems. In T. Witschge, C. W. Anderson, D. Domingo, & A. Hermida (Eds.), *The SAGE handbook of digital journalism* (pp. 410–423). London: Sage.
Anderson, C. W., Coleman, S., & Thumim, N. (2015). How news travels: A comparative study of local media ecosystems in Leeds (UK) and Philadelphia (US). In R. K. Nielsen (Ed.), *Local journalism: The decline of newspapers and the rise of digital media* (pp. 73–93). London: I.B. Tauris & Co.
Barnett, S., & Townend, J. (2015). Plurality, policy and the local. *Journalism Practice, 9*(3), 332–349. https://doi.org/10.1080/17512786.2014.943930
Barney, R. D. (1996). Community journalism: Good intentions, questionable practice. *Journal of Mass Media Ethics, 11*(3), 140–151. https://doi.org/10.1207/s15327728jmme1103_2

Becker, H. (2008). *Art worlds*. Berkeley: University of California Press.

Benson, R. (2013). *Shaping immigration news: A French-American comparison*. Cambridge: Cambridge University Press.

Benson, R. (2014). Strategy follows structure: A media sociology manifesto. In S. Waisbord (Ed.), *Media sociology: A reappraisal* (pp. 25–45). Cambridge: Polity Press.

Benson, R., & Neveu, E. (2005). *Bourdieu and the journalistic field*. Cambridge: Polity Press.

Berkowitz, D. (2007). Professional views, community news: Investigative reporting in small US dailies. *Journalism, 8*(5), 551–558.

Bobkowski, P. S., Jiang, L., Peterlin, L. J., & Rodriguez, N. J. (2019). Who gets vocal about hyperlocal? *Journalism Practice, 13*(2), 159–177.

Bourdieu, P. (1993). The field of cultural production, or: The economic world reversed. In P. Bourdieu (Ed.), *The field of cultural production: Essays on art and literature* (pp. 29–73). New York: Columbia University Press.

Bourdieu, P. (1996.) *The rules of art: Genesis and structure of the literary field*. Cambridge: Polity Press.

Bousquet, F., Smyrnaios, N., & Bertelli, D. (2014). What is the impact of the web on local journalism?: Two case studies in Toulouse, France. *Brazilian Journalism Research, 10*(1), 144–161. https://doi.org/10.25200/BJR.v10n1.2014.630

Boyles, J. L. (2017). Building an audience, bonding a city: Digital news production as a field of care. *Media, Culture & Society, 39*(7), 945–959. https://doi.org/10.1177/0163443716682073

Brock, G. (2013). *Out of Print: Newspapers, Journalism and the Business of News in the Digital Age*. London: Kogan Page.

Carey, M. C. (2014). Facebook interactivity rare on community news sites. *Newspaper Research Journal, 35*(2), 119–133. https://doi.org/10.1177/073953291403500209

Carlson, M. (2015). Introduction: The many boundaries of journalism. In M. Carlson, & S. C. Lewis (Eds.), *Boundaries of journalism: Professionalism, practices and participation* (pp. 1–16). New York: Routledge.

Castelló, E. (2010). Framing news on risk industries: Local journalism and conditioning factors. *Journalism, 11*(4), 463–480. https://doi.org/10.1177/1464884910367592

Cawley, A. (2017). Johnston Press and the crisis in Ireland's local newspaper industry, 2005–2014. *Journalism, 18*(9), 1163–1183. https://doi.org/10.1177%2F1464884916648092

Coleman, S., Thumim, N., Birchall, C., Firmstone, J., Moss, G., Parry, K., Stamper, J., & Blumler, J. G. (2016). *The mediated city: The news in a post-industrial context*. London: Zed.

Collaborative Journalism Database (2020). Retrieved April 17, 2020 from https://collaborativejournalism.org/database-search-sort-learn-collaborative-projects-around-world/

Collins, R., & Makowsky, M. (1998). *The discovery of society* (6th ed.). Boston: McGraw-Hill.

Costera Meijer, I. (2010). Democratizing Journalism? Realizing the citizen's agenda for local news media. *Journalism Studies, 11*(3), 327–342. https://doi.org/10.1080/14616700903500256

Cox, B. (2016, August 19). Local journalism in Canada needs a boost. Retrieved August 15, 2020 from https://nmc-mic.ca/blog/2016/08/19/local-journalism-needs-boost-full-text/

Dunn, J. A. (2009). Where did it all go wrong? Russian television in the Putin era. In B. Beumers, N. Rulyova, & S. Hutchings (Eds.), *The post-Soviet Russian media: Conflicting signals* (pp. 42–55). London: Routledge.

Erzikova, E. & Lowrey, W. (2012). Managed mediocrity? Experienced journalists' perspectives on "pampers generation" of Russian reporters. *Journalism Practice, 6*(2), 264–279.

Fine, G. A. (2012). *Tiny publics: A theory of group action and culture.* New York: Russell Sage Foundation.

Fischer, S. (2018). How pro-trust initiatives are taking over the internet. *Axios.* Retrieved August 15, 2020 from https://www.axios.com/fake-news-initiatives-fact-checking-dfa6ab56-3295-4f1a-9b38-e61ca47e849f.html

Fligstein, N., & McAdam, D. (2012). *A theory of fields.* Oxford: Oxford University Press.

Franklin, B. (2014). The future of journalism. *Journalism Studies, 15*(5), 481–499. https://doi.org/10.1080/1461670X.2014.93025

Friedland, L. (2001). Communication, community, and democracy: Toward a theory of the communicatively integrated community. *Communication Research, 28*(4), 358–391.

Friedland, L., Napoli, P., Ognyanova, K., Weil, C., & Wilson, E. J., III. (2012). *Review of the literature regarding critical information needs of the American public.* Communication Policy Research Network. Retrieved August 15, 2020 from http://transition.fcc.gov/bureaus/ocbo/Final_Literature_Review.pdf

Friedland, R., & Alford, R. R. (1991). Bringing society back in: Symbols, practices and institutional contradictions. In P. J. DiMaggio, & W. W. Powell (Eds.), *The new institutionalism in organizational analysis* (pp. 232–263). Chicago: University of Chicago Press.

Galletero-Campos, B. (2019). The disappearance of provincial printed press: analysis of the causes and consequences based on the case study of Castile-La Mancha. *Communication & Society, 32*(2), 139–155.

Gladkova, A., Aslanov, I., Danilov, A., Danilov, A., Garifullin, V., & Magadeeva, R. (2019). Ethnic media in Russia: Between state model and alternative voices. *Russian Journal of Communication, 11*(1), 53–70. https://doi.org/10.1080/19409419.2018.1564355

Grieco, E. (2019, July 9). *U.S. newsroom employment has dropped by a quarter since 2008, with greatest decline at newspapers.* FactTank: News in the Numbers. Pew Research Center. Retrieved August 15, 2020 from https://www.pewresearch.org/fact-tank/2019/07/09/u-s-newsroom-employment-has-dropped-by-a-quarter-since-2008/

Gudkov, L. D., Dubin, B. V., & Levinson, A G. (2009). Fotorobot rossiiskogo obuvatelya [A sketch of the Russian everyman]. *Mir Rossii, 2,* 22–33.

Guimerà, J. À., Domingo, D., & Williams, A. (2018). Local journalism in Europe: Reuniting with its audiences. *Sur le Journalisme, About Journalism, Sobre Jornalismo, 7*(2), 4–34.

Gutsche, R. E., Jr. (2015). Boosterism as banishment: Identifying the power function of local, business news and coverage of city spaces. *Journalism Studies, 16*(4), 497–512. https://doi.org/10.1080/1461670X.2014.924730

Hallin, D. C., & Mancini, P. (2004). *Comparing media systems: Three models of media and politics.* Cambridge: Cambridge University Press.

Halpern, M., & Humphreys, L. (2016). Iphoneography as an emergent art world. *New Media & Society, 18*(1), 62–81. https://doi.org/10.1177/1461444814538632

Hanitzsch, T. & Vos, T.P. (2018). Journalism beyond democracy: A new look into journalistic roles in political and everyday life. *Journalism 192*(2), 146–164. https://doi.org/10.1177/1464884916673386

Harry, J.C. (2001). Covering conflict: A structural-pluralist analysis of how a small-town and a big-city newspaper reported an environmental controversy. *Journalism & Mass Communication Quarterly, 78*(3), 419–436.

Hatcher, J. A. (2012). A view from outside: What other social science disciplines can teach us about community journalism. In B. Reader, & J. A. Hatcher (Eds.), *Foundations of community journalism* (pp. 129–150). Los Angeles: Sage.

Hatcher, J., & Haavik, E. (2014). We write with our hearts. *Journalism Practice, 8*(2), 149–163. https://doi.org/10.1080/17512786.2013.859828

Heider, D., McCombs, M., & Poindexter, P. M. (2005). What the public expects of local news: Views on public and traditional journalism. *Journalism & Mass Communication Quarterly, 82*(4), 952–967. https://doi.org/10.1177%2F107769900508200412

Hess, K., & Waller, L. (2017). *Local journalism in a digital world*. London: Palgrave.

Johnson, R. (1993). Editor's introduction: Pierre Bourdieu on art, literature and culture. In R. Johnson (Ed.), *The field of cultural production* (pp. 1–25). New York: Columbia University Press.

Josephi, B. (2013). How much democracy does journalism need? *Journalism 14*, 474–489.

Jouvenet, M. (2016). Contextes et temporalités dans la sociologie processuelle d'Andrew Abbott [Contexts and temporalities in Andrew Abbott's processual sociology]. *Annales: Histoires, Sciences Sociales, 71*(3), 597–630. https://doi.org/10.1353/ahs.2016.0116

Karlsson, M., & Holt, K. (2014). Is anyone out there? Assessing Swedish citizen-generated community journalism. *Journalism Practice, 8*(2), 164–180. https://doi.org/10.1080/17512786.2013.859830

Kim, Y.-C., & Ball-Rokeach, S. J. (2006). Community storytelling network, neighborhood context, and civic engagement: A multilevel approach. *Human Communication Research, 32*(4), 411–439. https://doi.org/10.1111/j.1468-2958.2006.00282.x

Kiriya, I. (2019). New and old institutions within the Russian media system. *Russian Journal of Communication, 11*(1), 6–21.

Knight Commission on the Information Needs of Communities in a Democracy. (2009). *Informing communities: Sustaining democracy in the digital age*. The Aspen Institute. Retrieved August 15, 2020 from https://knightfoundation.org/wp-content/uploads/2019/06/Knight_Commission_Report_-_Informing_Communities.pdf

Ledeneva, A. V. (2006). *How Russia really works: The informal practices that shaped post-Soviet politics and business*. Ithaca, NY: Cornell University Press.

Liu, S., & Emirbayer., M. (2016). Field and ecology. *Sociological Theory, 34*(1), 62–79. https://doi.org/10.1177/0735275116632556

Lowrey, W. (2006). Mapping the journalism-blogging relationship. *Journalism*, 7(4), 477–500. https://doi.org/10.1177/1464884906068363

Lowrey, W. (2012). Journalism innovation and the ecology of news production. *Journalism and Communication Monographs*, 14(4), 248–287. https://doi.org/10.1177/1522637912463207

Lowrey, W., Brozana, A., & Mackay, J. (2008). Toward a measure of community journalism. *Mass Communication and Society*, 11(3), 275–299. https://doi.org/10.1080/15205430701668105

Lowrey, W., & Erzikova, E. (2013). One profession, multiple identities: Russian regional reporters' perceptions of the professional community. *Mass Communication and Society*, 16(5), 639–660. https://doi.org/10.1080/15205436.2013.770031

Lowrey, W. & Sherrill, L. (2019). Fields and ecologies: Meso-level spatial approaches and the study of journalistic change. *Communication Theory*. https://doi.org/10.1093/ct/qtz003

Marquis, C., & Battilana, J. (2009). Acting globally but thinking locally? The enduring influence of local communities on organizations. *Research in Organizational Behavior*, 29, 283–302. https://doi.org/10.1016/j.riob.2009.06.001

Mohr, J. W. (2005). Implicit terrains: Meaning, measurement and spatial metaphors in organizational theory. In J. Porac, & M. Ventresca (Eds.), *Constructing industries and markets* (pp. 1–38). Amsterdam: Elsevier.

Nah, S., & Armstrong, C. L. (2011). Structural pluralism in journalism and media studies: A concept explication and theory construction. *Mass Communication and Society*, 14(6), 857–878. doi:10.1080/15205436.2011.615446

Napoli, P. M., Weber, M., McCollouth, K., & Wang, Q. (2018). *Assessing local journalism: News deserts, journalism divides, and the determinants of the robustness of local news*. Duke University Sanford School of Public Policy. Retrieved August 15, 2020 from https://dewitt.sanford.duke.edu/wp-content/uploads/2018/08/Assessing-Local-Journalism_100-Communities.pdf

Nettlefold, J. E. (2019). Listening at the local level: the role of radio in building community and trust. *Media International Australia*, 172(1), 74–88. https://doi.org/10.1177/1329878X19858662

Nielsen, R. K. (2015). Introduction: The uncertain future of local journalism. In R. K. Nielsen (Ed.), *Local journalism: The decline of newspapers and the rise of digital media* (pp. 1–25). London: I.B. Tauris & Co.

Nygren, G., Leckner, S., & Tenor, C. (2017). Hyperlocals and legacy media: Media ecologies in transition. *Nordicom Review*, 39(1), 33–49. https://doi.org/10.1515/nor-2017-0419

Nygren, G. (2019). Local media ecologies: Social media taking the lead. *Nordicom Review*, 40(2), 51–68. https://doi.org/10.2478/nor-2019-0026

O'Mahony, S. O., & Lakhani, K. R. (2011). Organizations in the shadow of communities. *Research in the Sociology of Organizations*, 33, 3–36. https://doi.org/10.1108/S0733-558X(2011)0000033004

Paulussen, S., & D'heer, E. (2013). Using citizens for community journalism. *Journalism Practice*, 7(5), 588–603. https://doi.org/10.1080/17512786.2012.756667

Pew Research Center. (2015). *Local news in a digital age.* Retrieved August 15, 2020 from https://www.pewresearch.org/wp-content/uploads/sites/8/2015/03/PJ_MediaEcology_completereport.pdf

Powers, M., & Vera-Zambrano, S. (2016). Explaining the formation of online news startups in France and the United States: A field analysis. *Journal of Communication, 66*(5), 857–877. https://doi.org/10.1111/jcom.12253

Radcliffe, D., & Ali, C. (2017). *Local news in a digital world: Small-market newspapers in the digital age.* Tow Center for Digital Journalism.

Reader, B. (2012). Community journalism: A concept of connectedness. In B. Reader, & J. A. Hatcher (Eds.), *Foundations of community journalism* (pp. 3–23). Los Angeles: Sage.

Reader, B., & Hatcher, J. A. (2012). *Foundations of community journalism.* Thousand Oaks, CA: Sage.

Richter, A. (2006). Ekonomicheskaya pomosch SMI i zhurnalistam so storony gosudarstva na postsovetskom prostranstve [Economic support of mass media and journalists from the state in the post-Soviet space]. *Izvestiya of Ural State University, 45,* 176–190.

Robinson, S. (2014). Introduction: Community journalism midst media revolution. *Journalism Practice, 8*(2), 113–120. https://doi.org/10.1080/17512786.2013.859822

Robinson, S. (2017). *Networked news, racial divides: How power and privilege shape public discourse in progressive communities.* Cambridge: Cambridge University Press.

Rosen, J. (2001). *What are journalists for?* New Haven: Yale University Press.

Roudakova, N. (2017). *Losing Pravda: Ethics and the press in post-truth Russia.* Cambridge: Cambridge University Press.

Ryfe, D. M. (2017). *Journalism and the public.* Cambridge: Polity Press.

Schmidt, C. (2018a, April 5). So what is that, er, Trusted News Integrity Trust Project all about? A guide to the (many, similarly named) new efforts fighting for journalism. Nieman Lab. Retrieved August 15, 2020 from https://tinyurl.com/u399cfx

Schmidt, C. (2018b, April 25). Who's who in local news: A guide to the biggest brains and bank accounts in the fight for local journalism. Nieman Lab. Retrieved August 15, 2020 from https://www.niemanlab.org/2018/04/whos-who-in-local-news-a-guide-to-the-biggest-brains-and-bank-accounts-in-the-fight-for-local-journalism/

Scott, W. R. (2014). *Institutions and organizations: Ideas, interests and identities.* Los Angeles: Sage.

Silber, I. F. (2003). Pragmatic sociology as cultural sociology: Beyond repertoire theory? *European Journal of Social Theory, 6*(4), 427–449. https://doi.org/10.1177/13684310030064004

Sjøvaag, H., Pedersen, T. A., & Lægreid, O. M. (2019). Journalism and the political structure: The local media system in Norway. *Nordicom Review, 40*(2), 63–89. https://doi.org/10.2478/nor-2019-0034.

Smyrnaios, N., Marty, E., & Bousquet, F. (2015). Between journalistic diversity and economic constraints: Local pure players in Southern France. In R. K. Nielsen (Ed.), *Local journalism: The decline of newspapers and the rise of digital media* (pp. 165–184). London: I.B. Tauris & Co.

Stevenson, M. (2016). The cybercultural moment and the new media field. *New Media & Society, 18*(7), 1088–1102. https://doi.org/10.1177/1461444816643789

Stonbely, S. (2017, September). Comparing models of collaborative journalism. The Center for Cooperative Media.

Svitich, L., Smirnova, O., Shiriaeva, A., & Shkondin, M. (2016). Characteristics of the content of Russian local newspapers (sociological study). *Journal of Russian Media and Journalism Studies, 13*, 13–60.

Swartz, D. (2013). Metaprinciples for sociological research in a Bourdieusian perspective. In P. S. Gorski (Ed.), *Bourdieu and historical analysis* (pp. 19–35). Durham, NC: Duke University Press.

Swedberg, R. (2006). The cultural entrepreneur and the creative industries: Beginning in Vienna. *Journal of Cultural Economics, 30*(4), 243–261. https://www.jstor.org/stable/41810929

Thomson, C., Bennett, D., Johnston, M., & Mason, B. (2015). Why the where matters: A sense of place imperative for teaching better indigenous affairs reporting. *Pacific Journalism Review, 21*(2), 141–161. https://doi.org/10.24135/pjr.v21i2.125

Thornton, P. H., Ocasio, W., & Lounsbury, M. (2012). *The institutional logics perspective: A new approach to culture, structure and process.* Oxford: Oxford University Press.

Tichenor, P. J., Donohue, G. A., & Olien, C. N. (1980). *Community conflict & the press.* Beverly Hills: Sage.

Usher, N. (2016). *Interactive journalism: Hackers, data and code.* Urbana, IL: University of Illinois Press.

Usher, N. (2017). The appropriation/amplification model of citizen journalism: An account of structural limitations and the political economy of participatory content creation. *Journalism Practice, 11*(2–3), 247–265. https://doi.org/10.1080/17512786.2016.1223552

Wadbring, I., & Bergström, A. (2017). A print crisis or a local crisis? Local news use over three decades. *Journalism Studies, 18*(2), 175–190. http://dx.doi.org/10.1080/1461670X.2015.1042988

Wahl-Jorgensen, K. (2016). The Chicago school and ecology: A reappraisal for the digital era. *American Behavioral Scientist, 60*(1), 8–23. https://doi.org/10.1177/0002764215601709

Wall, M. (2017). Introduction: Mapping citizen and participatory journalism: In newsrooms, classrooms and beyond. *Journalism Practice, 11*(2–3), 134–141. https://doi.org/10.1080/17512786.2016.1245890

Weber, M. ([1922] 1978). *Economy and society: An outline of interpretive sociology* (G. Roth & C. Wittich, Eds.; E. Fischoff et al., Trans.). Berkeley: University of California Press. (Original work published 1921–22)

Weber, M. S., Fulk, J., & Monge, P. (2016). The emergence and evolution of social networking sites as an organizational form. *Management Communication Quarterly, 30*(3), 305–332. https://doi.org/10.1177/0893318916629547

White, D., Pennycook, L., Perrin, W., & Hartley, S. (2017). The future's bright but the future's local: The rise of hyperlocal journalism in the United Kingdom. *Journal of Applied Journalism & Media Studies, 6*(1), 71–82. https://doi.org/10.1386/ajms.6.1.71_1

Williams, A., David H., & Turner, J. (2015). The value of UK hyperlocal community news. *Digital Journalism*, 3(5): 680–703.

Winch, S. P. (1997). *Mapping the cultural space of journalism: How journalists distinguish news from entertainment.* Westport, CT: Praeger Publishers.

Wooten, M. & Hoffman, A.J. (2008). Organizational fields: Past, present and future. In R. Greenwood, C. Oliver, K. Sahlin & R. Suddaby (Eds.), *The SAGE Handbook of Organizational Institutionalism* (pp. 130–147). Los Angeles: Sage Publications.

Zahariadis, N. (2013). Industrial subsidies: Surveying macroeconomic policy approaches. In P. Murschetz (Ed.), *State aid for newspapers: Theories, cases, actions* (pp. 59–72). New York: Springer.

SECTION II

FINDINGS: THE THREE REGIONS, THEIR JOURNALISM, JOURNALISTS AND COMMUNITIES

CHAPTER FOUR

Russian Regional Journalism and Its Environments

In June 2019, an elderly couple walked into the newsroom of the Traditional newspaper. The woman sank heavily into a chair, and shared her story. The previous year, the woman had surgery at a local hospital, and since, she has been in constant pain, unable to rotate her legs. She needed the surgery after jumping from a fourth-floor window to escape her drunken son-in-law's attempts to stab her. She did not press charges, though she cannot work and receives no disability. Her two daughters are alcoholics, and her grandchildren were placed in an orphanage. She lives in a village with a man who receives a monthly 10,000-ruble pension. He brought her to the city to seek assistance and justice, and the Traditional was first on their list. A reporter asked for the woman's passport and called an insurance agency. The agency found the case and provided a clear plan of action, bringing the woman to tears. After the couple left, reporters said they frequently handle situations like this—if not every day, then at least every week.

When a regional newspaper helps residents who seek justice, the power of the local community's pull on journalists is evident. But other factors and contexts pull on journalists as well. Scarcity of time and resources, government constraints, and the demands of newsroom owners and managers may discourage such decisions. This chapter explores the economic, political, organizational and community contexts of the regional journalism under study, how these contexts have changed over time, and how they work differently across different regions and outlets. Fleshing out these environments will help make sense of the characteristics and behaviors of journalists we explore in the chapters that follow.

The Regional Media Infrastructure

Prior to perestroika, the media ecosystems in our three regions were nearly identical to one another and to other regional media ecosystems across Russia. Each region supported only two socio-political newspapers: the organs of the regional Communist Party and the Komsomol (Communist youth organization) committee, and the papers did not compete. Today, dozens of newspapers across the three regions position themselves as socio-political papers, or serious, "quality" papers that report on public issues. Around 40% of these papers are published in regional capitals, while the rest are published in mid-size and small towns and rural districts. There are also a number of print publications that misleadingly position themselves as traditional socio-political city newspapers but are actually short-lived advertising vehicles providing promotional content with only a few city news stories. As of May 2020, around 10% of the newspapers in Region A that were positioned as socio-political in nature were actually "pretend socio-political" newspapers.

Although socio-political papers have different owners, ranging from state to private, they compete for the same readers in their respective areas and for the same major "advertiser"—the government, whether a regional, city or district administration. In addition to the state-run TV and radio stations, several private stations that launched in the '90s operate in each region, as do several online news portals established in the 2000s. Though these stations and online outlets are independently owned, they depend on government funding.

In each Russian region, a government Mass Communication Department oversees and regulates media operations. These departments perform a number of other specific control functions, including developing and maintaining relationships with media to ensure residents are told about government actions and decisions; developing small town and rural media; and providing educational opportunities for media professionals, such as seminars on changing skills. A typical department may include 10 or 15 managers and staff members. For example, in the Yaroslavl region, 13 employees operate the department: the head, two deputies, three heads of sub-units and seven staffers (Upravleniye massovykh kommunikatsiy, n.d.).

Typically, a regional government signs a decree that allocates budget revenue and regulates financial relations between the government and the media, facilitating control over media. For example, the Tula region, with a 2014–2020 program budget of 1.15 million rubles (about 15,000 US dollars), implemented programs providing both general and specific support for print and electronic media (Avrutina, 2016). Typically, in poorer regions especially, the media are expected to cover government activities ("government assignments") in return for general support. The Tula government also offered money for programs on specific topics, such as "Society and the Power," a series of publications with information about the government. These specific programs are essentially the same as the targeted "grants" offered by specific government divisions, discussed in Chapter 2 (e.g., grants for coverage of tourism, coverage of regional police, etc.). The regional government attempts to control the news agenda by telling media participating in these various programs what topics to cover, what issues to address in round-table discussions between officials and media, and which press conferences to attend. In return, participating media receive unrestricted access to socially important information and an opportunity to negotiate contracts with officials (Avrutina, 2016).

The head of the Region A government's Ideological Department, which oversees the Mass Communication Department, shared his perception of state-media relations in the region. State-supported media "have to be micromanaged to get a result," he said. He blames what he sees as reporters' weak professionalism: "One out of ten thinks before he writes, and nine write just to write something." Frustration ran both ways, with journalists expressing dissatisfaction over officials' poor decisions because of a lack of journalism knowledge.

Nearly all Russian newspapers are poor and need financial assistance from governments and corporations: A 2011 study (Vartanova & Azhgikhina) reported that only 5% of print media were profitable and 10–15% were self-sustaining. These numbers have not improved. However, not all of these desperate outlets receive government support, and among recipients, some get more support than others. Government assistance—through direct subsidies, contract agreements and grants/programs, and "government ads" (paid publication of government announcements)—strongly shape regional news outlets and their daily decisions. As the editor of the *Traditional* newspaper said, government assistance gives "friendly" newspapers priority access to information sources, and also provides them with government-guaranteed subscriptions and/or government encouragements to local businesses to place ads.

During periods of limited advertising and consumers' low purchasing power, the need to survive spurs rivalry among news outlets and among journalist colleagues, and many journalists saw rivalries for government subsidies as professionally destructive rather than as an incentive for quality. The head of Region C's Journalism Union said government subsidies in her province has divided news outlet from news outlet and weakened journalism. Newsrooms without state support often accuse those with support of receiving unfair advantages. The editor of the *Government* said the *Traditional* "with its [very low] circulation took away part of our subsidies," while the *Traditional's* editor called the distribution "fair," and much needed for circulation growth.

The Economic Context: How Regional Papers Find Money

Newspapers in all three regions need economic capital urgently, but they obtain it in different ways. Government subsidies, whether direct or through contracts and grants, are the dominant revenue source, and most content is paid for by the government, either through regular subsidies (in the case of the Government newspaper) or through payment for specific kinds of content, through contracts or grants. Generally, this content is not labeled as paid content, and so readers are not made aware of this arrangement.

The Region A government encourages the newspapers it subsidizes from its budget to pursue ad revenue from private sources to supplement government payment, and the government also encourages companies to advertise with favored papers. Private ads take the form of both "hidden advertising," or promotional content that is not labeled as advertising and "module ads," which are labeled. Though private ad revenue is scarce, the papers that manage to acquire it tend to operate at a higher level, in the view of the government. These papers use government subsidies more efficiently, their news content and production are higher quality, and they have more readers, which means more eyes on government messages. According to the head of the Region A government's Ideological Department, journalists need to seek private revenue more aggressively: "The time they [the media] spend in the government building asking for subsidies should have been spent on targeting businesses with projects that business people would see as beneficial for their companies." Officials worry little that revenue from businesses might increase newspapers' autonomy in relation to the government, and embolden their reporting. There is too little private ad revenue for that to happen, the journalists are short on business savvy, and the government can pressure local businesses.

Region A, our primary focus, is the poorest region among the three, and revenue for Region A's news outlets comes almost exclusively from the government. The *Traditional* newspaper has been the most financially strapped publication in Region A across the 13 years of study, and the gap between it and other newspapers has grown. While a local oligarch supported the *Private* newspaper, and the regional government supported the *Government* paper, the *Traditional* has had no champion since the city's mayor lost control over the paper prior to our period of study. Management and staff have struggled to keep their heads above water. In 2017, the local government began to provide some subsidies for the *Traditional*, but these have been meager. A *Traditional* reporter drew a vivid analogy:

> The government is like a homeowner who graciously allows a stray dog to stay in the yard and eat leftovers but refuses to provide any care. And yes, the dog is obligated to bark at strangers.

A pastime of *Traditional* staffers and managers was to dream up possible solutions to their financial misery. The editor said he wished for a selfless, affluent and absent sponsor who demanded no accountability and rained money on the paper: "'Work, folks!,'" this sponsor would yell, "and after that he would be gone to the woods."

The *Government* newspaper in Region A sits closest to the region's political and economic power. The paper received the most government support during the study period, a situation that competing regional papers see as unfair. In the early years of our study, the regional government encouraged local businesses to advertise in the *Government* and in other favored newspapers. In 2007, a *Traditional* manager complained that, after offering a client a page of advertising for 5,000 rubles, "the *Government* comes and offers the client *two* pages for 5,000 rubles." As ad revenue diminished over the years, favoritism toward the *Government* newspaper took other forms, such as requiring state employees to subscribe to the publication.

Government staff view their subsidies as enabling the practice of "normal" journalism, as opposed to "sensational" or "yellow" journalism. But this "normal" journalism tends to be timid and subservient, and according to interview participants, the *Government* possesses limited social trust with its readers. Readers doubt the paper will back them should they complain to officials. Observations showed that when readers visited the *Government* newsroom to seek help for problems such as illegal layoffs, the staff were unlikely to offer direct help and instead used their connections with other groups in the region to try to maintain trust with readers.

> It makes sense to start a war if you have backups, resources. One woman appealed to us and we ... advised her to go to the Left Front, who would use her case as a means to fight the regime. She owned land downtown. She thought [government] compensation for the land was not big enough. Often times, instead of investigating, we suggest seeking help from oppositional forces like communists.

In 2018, the regional government cut subsidies and salaries at the *Government*, ending a period of stability for the newspaper's staff and leading to hardship. Across the study period, the *Government* paper, with the easiest access to government revenue, has been the most financially secure publication in the province, and despite the recent cuts, the paper remains in much better financial shape than the *Traditional*. In terms of type of revenue source, the *Private* newspaper lies at the other end of the spectrum. The *Private* seeks ad revenue and focuses on tracking readership, though it too receives government support. The publisher said in 2015 that content must be "sellable," even if some perceive their content as "yellow":

> We want to write about psychics—and [we] do it! We found out that every district has 10 to 15 psychics, who help people at least psychologically. The phenomenon exists in our life—why not write about it?

Private reporters said they thought their relative financial independence has resulted in more independent decision-making, helping them produce content readers want, and providing a type of cultural capital that helps them with citizens. According to the editor, the paper worked for years to gain a measure of financial independence so it might position itself as the ordinary people's advocate and defender. However, the staff define this "defending" as helping readers with everyday problems rather than advocating for systemic change at a public level.

The Region B newspaper also desires financial independence, and though the Region B government supports its media, officials expect papers to supplement the subsidies. While the paper receives government revenue through short-term contracts, much of their revenue comes from advertising. There is more advertising available in Region B than in Region A, though it is scarce across all regions. According to the editor, his paper should be rewarded for their active search of advertisers. He says that while other papers in the region wait for the next government money transfer, his paper "floats on its own"—though he admits that having guaranteed government support too would be ideal.

In Region C, which has the most affluent administration and the most commercial wealth among the three regions, the local government routinely and quietly distributes subsidies to various publications. A vice-editor of a Region C private paper is highly skeptical that ad revenue can support media in the way that government subsidies can:

> Take any regional media, look at "direct" advertising (ad modules), correlate the number [of printed ads] with the rates - and after 15 minutes of simple calculations you will understand that it is not advertising that "feeds" the media.

There was relatively less discussion of (and no rancor over) government subsidies among journalists and news managers in Region C, as compared to the more economically desperate newsrooms in Region A—likely a consequence of Region C's greater wealth. Region C newspaper managers and staff said they were moderately satisfied with the money they received from the government, though editors still thought they deserved more. Apparently, government support, with its reliable and long-term commitment, has somewhat decreased the incentive to seek private advertising, despite greater commercial wealth in the region.

The Local Political Context: Administration and Officials

Most typically, journalism in these regions is produced either in service to the government or in avoidance of government disapproval, and financial dependence on government is a major reason. For a variety of reasons, relationships between journalists and officials can be contentious, but they are hardly volatile. In 2015, a reporter from the *Government*, the most directly controlled publication, spoke of the power of the government "boss":

> Ideally, the government supports its newspaper, but it doesn't intervene with its operation. A problem in Russia is that the power is sacral here. Everything that a boss says is the truth. ... In Russia, the [government] boss can do whatever ... In the US, it [would] be a scandal [and] it can be a social reaction ... But to change something in Russia ... It is impossible—never ... Or maybe in 300 years.

In the early years of our data collection (2007–2009), respondents were more likely to mention cases in which journalists acted in defiance of officials. A healthier economy and reduced dependence on government loosened restrictions somewhat, though the situation was restrictive even then. There was more animosity by journalists toward media owners who "bend the back like waitresses do," as a *Traditional* journalist put it (Lowrey & Erzikova, 2010, p. 281).

There was some evidence of mild defiance. In 2007, *Regional Branch* newspaper reporters pointed to a section in their paper that reported verbatim "bloopers" from public officials—one example: "Public transportation doesn't exist for people; people exist for public transportation." A small local paper (not one we studied) reported on officials who gullibly spent government funds to host hundreds of uncredentialed "foreign businessmen," with no apparent benefits for the region. There are other incidents, explored in more depth in Chapter 8. Such actions diminished over the years as the reins tightened. The region's worsening economic situation resulted in fewer advertisers and declining subscriptions, and economic capital came increasingly under government control. Typically, private newspapers now depend on well-paid contracts to cover government activities, and state-owned newspapers depend on government subsidies, and this lack of journalistic autonomy provokes feelings of powerlessness and vulnerability. Even in Region C, which has a relatively stronger commercial base, ad revenue is still too scarce and government subsidies too reliable for managers to feel that it is worth chasing after private advertising.

Censorship is common, and excessive editing by the government usually means a story will be softened or given another angle. During a focus group in 2015, a *Government* reporter recounted problems with a story that put the governor in a bad light:

> I had a story about a hospital being constructed. All TV stations showed the governor yelling at the workers, but his cursing was eliminated. I wrote a story, which circulated in the government for 3 days. I got back an altered story and was told that I needed to be loyal. I couldn't understand why my story had to contradict what was shown on TV.

This anecdote reveals a disconnect with regional residents, who can be well aware of an issue from other media. Yet, *Government* reporters are not allowed to report it – the words are unmentionable. Reporters derisively referred to such a situation as "Жопа есть, а слова нет" or "'ass' is there but there is not a word for it."

Yet, officials from the Mass Media Department do give lip service to the need for socially important journalism. A *Government* reporter in 2010 complained:

> We are told at newspaper meetings, 'Let's make a bomb! But ... it should be a bomb that will not touch anyone.' Government officials say what they are supposed to say: 'The newspaper must address social concerns.' But bureaucrats know they would censor such stories.

In this "decoupling" of rhetoric from actual practice, reporters pretend the request is real but do not act on it—as readers of novels suspend disbelief, so do regional reporters who want to keep their jobs. We discuss "decoupling" and "facades" in more detail in Chapter 8's exploration of autonomy.

In more recent years, most journalists have come to view government oversight of the region's journalism as business as usual. Older journalists have been more likely to chafe and even engage in mild disobedience, perceiving government authority over media as unfortunate, but a painful necessity. Younger journalists have been more likely to shrug. But neither view government power as an inherently illegitimate affront, and there is little question that the government will oversee the media's work. Generally, both have accepted this government-service logic as the "rules of the game" in the field. As a *Government* focus group participant said, matter of factly, "The regional government subsidizes us, and we inform residents about what government does." A *Traditional* vice-editor echoed this:

We found a niche—we serve those [bureaucrats] who need to prove that they do a good job, and we write about their great deeds and how good they are. We create a nice picture of the reality.

However, we do see some outrage from these regional journalists over the nature and quality of the government's oversight. In fact, an indication of journalists' fundamental acceptance of government control is found in journalists' narrow focus on the incompetence and indifference that officials display in controlling them. In all three of the regions, journalists had low opinions of the Mass Communication Department officials who were in charge of the provincial media.

Journalists' frustration mainly derives from officials' lack of a journalism background. A *Traditional* editor said officials were too poorly educated and journalistically inexperienced to "provide an overall strategy for the coverage of bureaucrats' activities." According to seasoned reporters, regional officials practice an incompetent "check-mark" oversight, merely counting the number of stories about the region's governor, and dismissing the need for longer "thought pieces," or the need for journalistic quality. Officials create "state assignments," or monthly lists of events and topics that must be covered routinely—a seminar for managers of sugar refineries, or the installation of GPS on state school buses—regardless of changing circumstances or reader interest. An editor from Region B bemoaned the poor state of the media in his province: "It would be a different story if we had adequate … people in the regional government that manage mass media … The head of the mass media department is not professional."

In contrast, several older journalists spoke of late Soviet-era authorities as competent administrators who viewed reporters more as partners and less as subordinates. These reporters, who experienced censorship in the USSR, said Soviet authorities were less arrogant toward reporters than are today's officials, and more knowledgeable about journalistic practices, principles and quality. Participants also said they approved of the pre-perestroika practice of appointing a local newspaper manager as the head of the region's ideological department. According to a manager for the *Government* in 2016:

Who worked in the government apparatus before? Well-prepared officials who understood the place and role of the media in society. In the last 10 years, the apparatus has started changing—random people have come [there]. The purpose of the newspaper is oblique to them.

Post-perestroika bureaucrats regularly breach previously observed boundaries, behavior that was common across the entire period of study. A *Private* reporter complained about treatment of the press at government meetings:

> The government wants to be open and invites us to attend their meetings. But we are asked to leave the room [after] 10 minutes; the government wants us to inform people about a meeting without details ... It's a very strange "open government."

As discussed in a later chapter, seasoned reporters have developed small ways to push back, despite journalists' general accommodation of government processes. In 2016, one senior *Traditional* reporter says he merely disregards many government-mandated assignments—*obyazalovka* (обязаловка)—as they are pointless and uninteresting to readers. A senior *Government* reporter said she refuses to cover political topics during election campaigns: "I don't respect [political candidates]. I can't write 'he is good and brave' while he is bad and a coward." Despite the risk, insubordination by seasoned reporters can actually benefit editors if it affords more room in the paper for content that attracts readers.

One explanation for problems in regional media administration is the frequent turnover among regional heads of mass media departments. None has lasted for more than three years. A manager for the *Government* paper said ongoing administrative turnover leads to unclear and inconsistent goals: "A new boss starts with disregarding what the previous one has done, and all his ideas will be also dismissed after he is fired." Some heads from outside the region returned to their native regions after failing to establish good relationships with local elites, and others were fired for misconduct, such as money laundering. In the studied regions, several appointees have used their state positions as a springboard to launch their own (non-media related) businesses, leaving the position when the businesses became profitable.

A bitter consensus was that bureaucrats will neglect the provincial press until they figure out how to make serious money from newspaper production, both officially and personally. The varieties of "shadow" opportunities that officials consider reveal a rich, if shady, ecology—one with both manifest and latent resources. Yet the newspaper business, especially a struggling one, is difficult to exploit. As one journalist said in 2018:

> The newspaper production is not a construction business. You can steal millions by stealing asphalt and making a road narrower by 10 centimeters. You can't steal millions by cheating on circulation—claiming you printed 100,000 copies while in reality, printing 10,000 copies.

The vice-editor of the *Government* noted that it is difficult to launder money by creating new publications because "imitation of news production" takes real effort. However, officials did gain funds by launching their own internal media ventures, according to reporters and editors in all three regions. Regional budgets provide generous support for these efforts, and, according to respondents, some officials have hired relatives to run the organizations. In Region A, the city administration launched a newspaper that resembled a newsletter, and the city official's wife, who had no journalism background, was given the editor's position and a lucrative salary.

Despite their animosity toward officials, nearly all participants stressed the importance of good relationships with the government. The *Traditional's* editor valued government connections because of the "positive moments" that came from state-assigned stories of local citizens. The editor of the *Private* had a more practical reason. His paper relies on periodic contracts rather than ongoing state subsidies, and so, developing personal, informal relationships with government officials keeps information timely for residents, as officials are often late in providing information. The *Private* editor says personal relationships with officials keep residents happy:

> You have to be friends with the government. And, for example, if an official will call me and ask to publish information about the resettlement of residents from dilapidated housing, I will say "yes." First, I know this kind of info will be interesting for our readers. Second, I know when I will have a question, she will help me out ... Thank God, the officials didn't give this info to another newspaper. Well, they knew that people [in the province] read the *Private* and would follow the instructions about the resettlement published there.

Bureaucrats often share information with only one newspaper, a selectivity that helps control newspapers' actions. The *Private* has benefited from this tendency. The *Private's* competent management and ability to gain marginally more ad revenue than competitors have increased staff motivation and professionalism, leading to a more reputable and popular product. Because of its higher quality, greater reach, and more assertive and accomplished staff, the *Private* has had success establishing priority relationships with government agencies (Health, Agriculture, etc.). Officials are supposed to communicate information through the governor's press service, but instead, they often take their information directly to the *Private*. Consequently, the *Private* has become the top source of timely information for the regional government about itself. It serves the latent function of an internal newsletter, and according to a seasoned reporter, the *Private* is the first thing the Region A governor reads in the morning. The regional government tracks the *Private's* success and directs its own paper, the *Government*, to learn from it—interesting, as the *Government* would normally serve as the leading "newsletter." So, the *Private's* greater legitimacy in the eyes of the public and the government—its greater cultural capital—translates to economic capital in the form of better government contracts.

The *Private*'s success has even allowed it to distinguish between useful information for readers and boasting by officials about organizational activities, and to charge the government accordingly. "If it's a report about [government] achievements," the editor said, "it's considered advertising and it's paid." The *Private* charges for such articles more than other publications. To do otherwise, the editor said, would be "a damage to the paper."

At the Region B paper, reporters work to develop relations with business elites by reaching out for expert opinions. This approach can serve as a defense against government backlash. As a journalist put it, "We reporters just communicate what the expert, a respected business person, said." This strategy is also adopted by one of the reporters at the *Private* in Region A, but it is not an organization-wide strategy.

Publications in the wealthier, larger Region C looked superior in terms of developing relationships with business elites, compared to both Region A and B newspapers. One Region C publication with an extensive digital presence positions itself as an expert by regularly writing analytical stories on the state of economy in the region. Editors and staff at another Region C publication expressed pride in the fact that readers grab its free weekend supplement from delivery workers as they walk to the newspaper stands. A close look at both main (paid) and weekend (free) editions showed that around 4/5 of their content is actually hidden advertising or unmarked promotional stories, mostly from the government. Nevertheless, the weekend supplement was better in quality than most of the gratis (distributed for free) press, as it actually contained original content (much of it so-called branded advertising.).

The Organizational Context: Newsroom Management

A more immediate context for the question of reporters' control is news organization management. The boundaries are fuzzier here, as managers and journalists share the same social space. Managers are journalists themselves and are often on familiar terms with the staff, but managers also answer to higher-ups and have the authority to affect the daily work and daily financial situation of the staff.

News organizations included in this study have similar managerial structure. The editor-in-chief and vice-editor represent top management; below these top editors are department (section) editors (начальники отделов); and below department editors are senior and rank-in-file reporters (writers, social media managers and photographers). Proofreaders (корректоры) are generally at the lowest level: They perform the "technical" duties of correcting grammar, punctuation and spelling. Proofreaders do not re-write text or produce headlines; however, a team of proofreaders who worked for the *Traditional* early in our data gathering (2007–2010) were regional legends because of their encyclopedic knowledge, acute sense of style, dedication to the newspaper and supportive attitude toward newcomers. One reporter said she learned how to write "by going over proofreaders' edits." Only one of these four proofreaders still works at the *Traditional*. She is paid less, though her workload has doubled.

The position of managing editor was eliminated across all newspapers in the three regions during the 2008 recession, due to tight budgets. The editor-in-chief or vice-editor now performs the editing duties. When we started our research in 2007, all Region A newspapers had content departments (e.g., information, medicine and public health, culture, and sports) with at least two staffers, one of whom was the head of the department. Over the years, the number of reporters has decreased and now single reporters at the *Private* and *Traditional* represent entire departments—a so-called человек-отдел (one-man-department). In contrast, in 2007 the *Government* paper increased the number of staff writers and even created a separate department for digital media.

Region B and Region C newsroom staff sizes fell over time as well, but it appears they have managed better by optimizing news production rather than simply overloading the remaining reporters. One Region C newspaper targeted reporters' efforts more efficiently by analyzing online audience preferences to identify stories that drew fewer readers. Reporters were then prohibited from working on these stories.

Across the papers, relationships between news managers and reporters generally appeared warm and respectful. Descriptions of subordinates from interviewed managers include: "hardworking," "responsible" and "reliable," while reporters' descriptions of managers include: "protective," "caring" and "reasonable." A variation to this is the Region B newspaper, with a substantial age gap between management and reporters that seemed to encourage purely professional relationships.

All news managers in this study started their professional careers before or during perestroika, and the perestroika-era identity helped them earn respect among other journalists, as perestroika is considered a golden time for Russian journalism. Even young reporters divided the journalistic community into "from perestroika" and "not from perestroika" (Lowrey & Erzikova, 2013).

Government newspaper reporters said their editor acts as a shield when the regional government expresses disfavor with reporters. In 2018, the editor stood up for a reporter who criticized bureaucrats on her social media account for failing to remodel a road on time. The government must pay the price, the editor told officials, if they want a talented reporter on the staff. A senior *Government* reporter, who came to journalism inspired by perestroika, linked professional assertiveness with talent: "Everything depends on a reporter's ability to fight and resist [and] the reporter can't fight if he does not have talent."

However, numerous editors from this era complained that too few journalists prioritized their professional work. The vice-editor of the *Government* often criticizes young reporters for apparent admiration of public officials, while the editor of the Region B newspaper complained of reporters' susceptibility to the allure of officials' power: "The reporter likes to accompany the governor in his trips—she said, 'He is my favorite man!' [and] she has a map on the wall in her office where she marks all the towns and villages she has visited with him."

Other managers were more tolerant of journalists' acceptance of authority and weak critical thinking, and in more recent years, some managers have appeared to lower their standards. For the *Private* manager, the bar that job seekers must clear had become "an interest in journalism." "If her eyes are sparking ("глаз горит"), there is promise." The *Government* vice-editor has eased up on the strictness of her editing. She said she realized reporters would one day look back on her as a "negative and mean person," and so she became "softer" with subordinates. Subordinates noticed: "She is not as critical and unaccepting," one reporter noted. The editor of the *Traditional* said he does not have "a moral right to demand dedication and quality from reporters who are paid minimal salaries." The editor fosters a highly informal, even lax newsroom atmosphere that would not have been tolerated in earlier years. A simple example: During an interview with the editor, an accounting staffer walked in and interrupted the editor mid-sentence: "Do you have salt? I am trying to cook fish in the microwave." The editor handed her a saltshaker and a tomato he had grown.

Evidence suggests that leniency in the *Traditional* newsroom may correlate with slipping professionalism. Over the last seven years, three relatives of newspaper managers have been hired, and there is little evidence that they have been qualified or productive—one rarely reports to work. Observations also indicate that staff reporters are often more passive than professional, for example, talking on the phone with friends while passing up story opportunities. The *Private*'s publisher found it necessary to hire an additional reporter because, he said, existing reporters did not produce enough content to fill issues. Newsroom observations supported his worries—for example, at a weekly planning meeting in 2019, no one volunteered to provide stories for three pages in an upcoming issue. Reporters voiced complaints about his decision to hire an additional reporter: "The pie is too small to share."

The Community Context: Readers and Audiences

Journalists often point to their readers and community as their most important context, if not always the most influential. Journalists regularly reach out to community citizens—sometimes for PR, sometimes out of altruism, and sometimes both. During the May 9 celebration in 2015, the editor and a reporter from the *Private* newspaper donned military uniforms, "hired an accordionist, went to the street to sing songs and give carnations to WWII veterans." For the next week, they said, they received thank-you calls from readers. They had engaged with citizens, and they gained grateful readers.

Readership research for these papers is practically non-existent, though some regional polling and social research was conducted in 2007 by the Moscow "parent" company of the *Regional Branch* newspaper. According to these studies, a typical Region A reader could be portrayed as a married woman, over 35, with children. This typical reader was more educated than most in the region, though family income was close to the region's average. As a child, her parents would have subscribed to two national papers, one local paper and a few magazines. She herself subscribes to no publication but buys at least two weekly newspapers from a kiosk. She loves the feature writers, and she talks about their stories with relatives or co-workers. She uses the internet to find gardening tips ("why are leaves on my dacha's apple trees turning dark?"). Her main news source is TV. As with the internet, TV news usage is mainly for awareness (быть в курсе) of local happenings and foreign dealings of the nation's leader. The regional newspaper for her was a glimpse into the lives of fellow residents—people she might know personally. In more recent years, our participants in Region A described their core audience as equally likely to be male or female, as older than the female prototype described here, and likely retired. It appeared readers aged along with the study's journalist participants.

Journalists increasingly viewed audiences in terms of online vs. offline. The *Government* staff perceived their online audiences as more diverse in age and socio-economic status than their print readers, and Region C participants said older generations prefer print issues. According to one Region C reporter, "people [who] read news online … might not even know that a print edition of their favorite news source exists." Region B participants bucked this trend, describing both print and online audiences similarly, as relatively heterogeneous.

Region A journalists have typically taken a paternal and personal orientation toward their readers. On one hand, many of these journalists feel they have not been very successful addressing citizens' needs through their stories. During the first year of our study, a reporter for the *Traditional* called their relationship with readers "broken" because the government-driven "socio-political" news content is too often meaningless for readers, failing to connect with their daily lives—for example, stories on government meetings that do not report what was decided. This problem persisted across the years of the study. On the other hand, journalists have been more successful addressing readers' individual daily needs on a one-by-one, personal basis. A 2016 quote from the *Traditional's* vice-editor details widely varied interactions with readers, who were destitute, frustrated, or just curious:

> They write letters to us and call often. The system of public health has been re-organized, and many villages don't have even a paramedic point [first-aid units in rural areas without hospitals]. Readers call and write, and ask questions like "I am 80 years old, my birthmark is bleeding, what should I do?" We published this letter and advised to see a doctor. Another reader called and said he is a disabled person with no money to go to the city to seek medical advice. I asked our former editor to ask his wife to consult this person on the phone. She agreed. One reader sent a letter saying he was facing an anniversary. He was turning 90. He said he heard a song and wanted to sing it at his celebration, but he didn't remember all the words. I found the song, made 10 copies and mailed to him. Later, we received a thank you letter. He said his girlfriends were singing and he was playing an accordion. It was a great celebration. It's typical that our readers call us and share their stories through the phone. Life is difficult everywhere; life in Russia is a drama. One young lady with cerebral palsy told me she reads every issue of our gardening supplement because she wants to [learn what wives need to know and] get married. She grew up in an orphanage for disabled children, and now she lives in a dormitory. Recently she visited her parents and hopes they would take her back. But she is not sure.

The *Government* outreach to citizens tends to be less personal and more formal. In 2019, its editor explained that today, media can adopt the role of non-profit organizations: "We install streetlights, put out asphalt, organize sporting events, and collect books for libraries." The editor said these activities have nothing to do with journalism, but said they are "one of the [paper's] methods to survive":

> It's work with audiences, it is showing the audience need us. For example, we collected books for a library, and [regional residents] subscribed to us. When we organized this project and got results, we shared them with government [officials]—"look, it's a model, take it, implement it." But the power disregarded our project.

He said projects like this demonstrate how problems can be addressed in ways that bring the powerful and the people closer together, but he said his pitch has fallen on deaf ears: "The powerful don't care about people's problems."

Journalists have also embraced a mission to enlighten readers culturally and morally. The *Government* editor said newspapers serve this purpose, much as an arts-and-culture magazine does:

These days, a newspaper is a magazine for the poor. My [own] art education happened in a barn of our neighbour, uncle Vitya. The walls of his barn were covered with posters cut from famous Soviet magazines, like *Ogonek*, that published reproductions of world-famous paintings. Say a villager comes to the city, he goes to the market and mall; he would never visit an art gallery. Maybe in childhood he visited the gallery while on his class trip to the region's centre. That's it. He would not find reproductions of famous paintings on the internet. Our mission is to raise our reader. We need to lift him slowly to a new level. We don't need to push him down.

While enlightenment for the *Government* is defined by high culture, the *Traditional* promotes the Orthodox faith, especially in its gardening supplement. Nominally farming-related, the supplement is broader in scope. It is a family digest that, in addition to providing useful gardening tips (for example, how to increase your strawberry harvest), publishes a Church calendar and stories about Russian saints. According to a *Traditional* reporter, the supplement urges higher-order thinking: "The supplement helps [people] stop thinking about consuming goods and start thinking about God." Reporters said none of the other regional papers leads a dialog with readers about "eternal values like faith, compassion and forgiveness." These reporters tend to view their readers as individuals, with individual-level needs, rather than as a public with political needs. This is a relatively narrow niche in the media ecology for journalists, but it is an old one, and it remains open.

In 2015, a reporter at the Region B paper said readers need their community newspapers for this kind of small, intimate news, and that all types of papers are needed, "regardless of their quality and circulation":

> A newspaper is a living organism that connects different territories (of people). People read, get information and take actions. For example, we write that a famous poet is buried in a particular village. People read and fundraise money to build a monument for him ... [The paper] is a chronicle of life in the region. It gives a systematic and full understanding of what happens in the region. If the [paper] is gone, a stratum is gone. It will be an impoverishing process.

Most of our participants embraced the idea of serving readers and community. The *Government* newspaper writes "not just for the government but for the people too," as a *Government* reporter said. The paper divides its issues into two parts— "the state order" (*goszakaz*), which includes news about government, and the section "for people," containing uplifting and entertaining stories about interesting people, events and trends. A reading of *Government* issues showed that the stories varied in geography to assure the region was broadly represented. For example, a story about an urban celebrity (a regional theater actor) neighbored a story about a forester from a remote village.

Face-to-face feedback from readers was common. Observations in the *Government* and the *Traditional* showed that readers visited editors, discussing current events and sharing personal stories over tea. Hospitable staff tried their best to work while conversing with guests; however, ongoing reader interaction could wear thin (Erzikova & Lowrey, 2010). There were instances where reporters viewed readers as social dependents (социальные иждивенцы) who suck their time, and this frustration grew over the study period, as citizens' daily challenges mounted and news staffs diminished. When, in 2009, a city telephone help desk became a paid rather than free service, residents began calling newsrooms to ask for phone numbers. Observations at the *Government* revealed different reactions from reporters: While one female reporter tried to help callers, her office mate would grunt, "Don't know!" and hang up.

A bigger challenge surfaced when residents demanded that journalists solve community problems. When a new road was needed in Region A in 2012, a group of "concerned citizens" attacked reporters at the *Private* for "not doing their jobs"— i.e., for not ensuring that the road is built. However, when the road was built, the same group attacked reporters, demanding the road should be closed because traffic caused too much "noise in the neighborhood." One *Private* reporter developed a reputation as a zealous defender of her community's citizens, and *Private* readers often wielded her name as a scare tactic when bringing problems to public officials. Eventually, however, she burned out—not an uncommon phenomenon. "This is why I hate my job," she said. "You would be blamed for everything you've done or haven't done." She left the *Private* for a news agency to "work at a news assembly line" where she no longer had to meet with dependent citizens. While the urge to help citizens is undeniably evident across the regions' papers, low pay, long hours, and ongoing administrative problems take their toll.

Discussion

Economic times have been harsh during our 13-year period of study, leading to ongoing financial, political and work-task pressures for journalists. Competition for scarce government money has tended to divide and weaken the journalistic space in these regions, eroding occupational community and professional motivation as the government plays one news outlet off against another through acts of favoritism. Managers and senior reporters do sometimes profess the need to defy officials; however, defiance has grown rarer across the years. Increasingly, both older and younger journalists have come to accept government control as normal and even natural, reserving their animosity for perceived malpractice of government dominance rather than for the dominance itself. Across the papers, we see how political-economic power has shaped the field, but we also see more evidence of journalists' adaptation—shifting of the frames and premises—than we see acts of opposition.

Ad revenue is generally scarce, though this varies somewhat across the three regions. However, even in the wealthier Region C, managers feel that advertising cannot support their papers. The combination of government support and scarce ad revenue helps ensure newspapers' dependence on the government, but these dynamics play out differently across regions. In the wealthier Region C, government support is the most stable and predictable over the long term, and so Region C newspaper managers do not pursue private ad revenue aggressively—securing ad revenue can be unpredictable in comparison, despite the region's stronger business environment. In the poorer Region A, government support is less stable, and the government tends to reward papers that pursue ad revenue as a supplement to smaller government coffers.

Relationships between management and staff are generally congenial and supportive across the papers, but tight resources have pushed managers to make unpopular decisions about pay, especially in Region A, causing some friction. As discussed in Chapter 5, there has also been significant friction with younger, less experienced reporters, who may demonstrate less traditional professionalism. However, some managers have abandoned the "tough line" in these struggles, seeking to just get along.

In general, news content either serves the government or is apolitical. Too often, the result is bland content focused on official events that bores the papers' aging readers or sensational content that briefly distracts them. Yet, the local community, as a social space, does pull on these journalists, and they have found ways to serve readers by addressing their personal requests and engaging in community projects. The will to connect with citizens is often strong, and these journalists' efforts to help citizens reflect the creativity of ecological dynamics, as journalists take advantage of the opportunities presented them. But underpaid and overworked journalists on shrinking staffs are experiencing burnout as they try to help needy regional residents. These journalists—especially in Region A in the last few years—say they have had little success in interesting officials in the problems they hear from citizens and in their efforts to address them.

References

Avrutina, L.G. (2016). SMI Tul'skoy oblasti: sovremennyye tendentsii vzaimodeystviya s vlast'yu [Media of the Tula region: current trends in interaction with the government]. *Mezhdunarodnyy Zhurnal Gumanitarnykh i Yestestvennykh Nauk, 1,* 50–55.

Erzikova, E. & Lowrey, W. (2010). Seeking safe ground: Russian regional journalists' withdrawal from civic service journalism. *Journalism Studies, 11*(3), 343–358.

Lowrey, W., & Erzikova, E. (2013). One profession—multiple identities: Russian regional reporters' perceptions of the professional community. *Mass Communication and Society, 16(5)*, 639–660.

Upravleniyemassovykh kommunikatsiy. (n.d.). Retrieved from https://www.yarregion.ru/depts/umk/default.aspx.

Vartanova, E., & Azhgikhina, N. (2011). Dialogi o zhurnalistike[Dialogs about journalism]. IREX Russia: MGU.

CHAPTER FIVE

Regional Journalists: Scarcity, Divisiveness and Persistence

In 2018, a reporter at the Traditional newspaper stepped through the newsroom's doorway. "Tomorrow at noon," she announced, and journalists nodded. Reporters from several newspapers planned to picket the Health Ministry to protest poor treatment of the reporter's mother at a local hospital. The woman was dying, and after the reporter used her Moscow connections to obtain a rare, costly medication, it appeared hospital personnel had stolen it. Anticipating dishonesty, the mother asked a nurse who was about to inject her to show her an empty ampule so she could ensure it was the right medicine. The nurse, becoming nervous, left the room. This situation prompted the reporter to call colleagues to support her picket in front of the Health Ministry. A dozen journalists from different papers arrived, holding signs. Officials also arrived and promised to resolve the issue. Within the hour, the reporter's mother was moved to a new room and had started receiving the right treatment.

Wider societal contexts and age-old logics and roles shape the field of Russian regional journalism in real, ongoing ways. But it is in the day-to-day working and living—daily newsroom conflicts, financial worries, inspiring moments, professional camaraderie—that journalists truly feel pressures and motivations. This chapter explores these more intimate contexts and their meanings for local journalists.

Who are these journalists? As we have interviewed most of the working journalists in Region A since 2007—around 100 total—their demographics provide a good picture of the overall journalism workforce of the region. Around 60% of these interview respondents have been female. Most either had more than 20 years or less than 10 years of experience at the time of their interviews, and over the years, senior respondents at the regions' newspapers expressed concern over a shortage of journalists in the "in-between generation" (10–15 years of experience)—those between the newcomers and the "мастодонт" ("mastodons" or seasoned reporters with 20 or more years). Over the last six years, the newcomers of the early years have filled the "in-between" gap, as a number of senior journalist respondents died or retired. Years of experience correlated well with age: Journalists with less than 10 years of experience were almost invariably in their 20s or early 30s. Around a quarter of the respondents were managers at some point during the 13 years. Only two of our respondents came from outside the region, and nearly all were born and received higher education degrees in the region, consistent with the Russian saying that one is Где родился, там и пригодился (needed where born). However, a minority had journalism degrees while other common degrees included language and literature, public relations, history, law, finance, and engineering.

This chapter focuses mostly on Region A, but we note that journalists in regions B and C were similar in terms of gender, though somewhat different in years of experience. In the legacy newspaper studied in Region B, most reporters had at least 15 years of professional experience and their ages ranged from 40 to 65, with the exception of a 22-year-old reporter with one year of experience. At the three newspapers studied in Region C, the majority of reporters were younger and had less than five years of experience. Like Region A, a minority of journalists in the other two regions had journalism degrees, and in these regions, which had healthier economies than Region A, reporters' salaries were higher. Across papers within each of the three regions, respondents generally knew one other, and almost all senior-level reporters had worked together at some point in their careers.

Journalists and Personal Financial Struggles

In 2007, participants from all Region A papers—the *Private*, *Traditional* and *Government*, as well as the *Regional Branch*, included in our study until 2013—said the shortage of qualified cadres was the biggest problem for their papers' operations. Times changed, and in 2018, falling salaries topped the list. Reporters' personal financial hardships became progressively acute over the last decade, following the recession, as economic capital diminished across the field. Reporters in Region A are paid the minimum allowable wage, at around 13,000 rubles, the equivalent of around 200 US dollars or 175 Euros per month. In addition, reporters at the *Government* and the *Private* are paid *honoraria*, or extra payment for helping managers fill out the newspapers' pages. *Traditional* reporters are not paid honoraria, due to a leaner budget. As a *Government* reporter said, the rock-bottom cost of the product cannot support quality journalism and cannot support journalists personally: "The 6-month subscription is 360 rubles (around 6 US dollars); a supply of toilet paper for 6 months is more than 360 rubles." During the last three years of the study, there were several observed cases of reporters asking colleagues to borrow money for emergencies—shoes for children or medication for aging parents.

Reporters said their own need to survive had become all-consuming, sapping the time and incentive to produce reporting that helps the region's poor—difficult anyway because of a government that does not want to see bad news reported. They saw this as devastating to a craft that requires complete immersion. One seasoned reporter drew a comparison with one of Russia's revered arts: "It's hard to imagine a ballerina that dances at Bolshoi Ballet would do folk dancing in her spare time to make ends meet."

Reporters pursued a number of strategies to stay solvent. One was to churn out stories for honoraria. Honoraria amounts have plummeted since 2013 across all papers. Reporters can earn up to 13,000 rubles (around 200 US dollars) a month at the *Private* and the *Government*, but in 2019, *Traditional* managers decided the paper could no longer afford to pay honoraria, and reporters lost at least a third of their monthly earnings. Honoraria amounts have been tied to story length, and not to story quality or significance. This practice has discouraged in-depth, time-consuming investigations as well as the pursuit of journalism awards, drawing journalists away from work that supports local civic life and from the pursuit of symbolic capital. Neither can help reporters pay their bills. A second earning strategy has been to take on supplementary work, such as reporting secretly for rival publications, editing other organizations' publications, running PR efforts for small businesses, or writing books. We note that while some journalists have left their news organizations for other cities or for other lines of work—often, PR—we have not seen a mass exodus, mainly because of the poor job market.

The *Traditional* has been the poorest publication in Region A, battling insolvency during the period of study. The paper started receiving government subsidies in 2017, but too little too late for staff. The subsidies helped pay bills (rent, printing), but have not increased salaries. One *Traditional* staff photographer, a father of two, worked as a taxi driver at night to make ends meet, and the vice-editor said they use archive photos rather than ask him to shoot for no honoraria. "We let him work as a taxi driver and earn money to feed his children."

Relatively speaking, journalists at the *Government* have had reasonable workloads and stable salaries. However, stability ended recently when the regional government slashed its funding for the paper. One *Government* reporter said she never opens her bills before going to work to avoid frustration. An experienced, award-winning *Government* reporter confessed "fear of starvation." In contrast, *Private* reporters appeared fairly secure in their finances in the most recent years of the study, though they balked at new hires, which sliced the paper's budget more finely.

In 2007, newspapers across the province had distinct goals, according to the *Regional Branch* advertising director: "Some aim at surviving, others aim at making profit." By 2018, profit was a distant dream. At all papers, managers and staff—particularly, senior staff—had largely embraced survival mode. "It's not about money," the *Traditional's* vice-editor said. "It's about having a hub to hold out for two to three years until we retire."

Journalists, Their Colleagues, and Newsroom Culture

Personal relationships within newsrooms were an important means of support in trying times, and the importance of коллектив, "the collective," of journalists has become stronger, at least among co-workers within the same news outlets. A seasoned *Private* reporter said these collectives demonstrate clear boundaries and strong internal trust.

> We don't love newcomers, and they don't feel like they fit. We are a good team. We agreed a long time ago that if management says bad things about one of us, we would share it. We would not have secrets from each other.

All three of the Region A newspapers studied across the entire period have a "core" of staffers—a group that has worked together for at least 10 years. Unlike the *Private*, the *Traditional's* core welcomed newcomers unconditionally. The *Government* core seemed to accept newcomers so long as they shared its values and complied with house rules. Digitally savvy reporters who moved to the *Government* from the *Regional Branch* in 2012 said they felt somewhat alienated at first. The obstacle was the digital reporters' sensationalistic view of news; however, the staff's "core" warmed to them.

Participants commonly spoke of fellow reporters as family. At the *Government* newsroom, reporters often congregated in offices to talk and drink tea after work. The *Government* vice-editor's office became a welcoming after-hours hub. A journalism legend, she has an everyday stream of visitors: former colleagues, officials and people she has written about. The vice-editor's office is a mini art gallery displaying her admiration for local artists, who visit her office too. Visitors serve as a sort of ongoing focus group for her. In summer 2019 a retired editor visited, along with seven of his former colleagues, and a potluck dinner lasted until midnight with guests recollecting, reading poetry and singing folk songs, all staples of Russian social gatherings.

Observations revealed camaraderie in the *Private* and the *Traditional* as well, though the atmospheres differed. One informal gathering of journalists at the *Private* demonstrated informal collegiality with reporters sharing funny stories, but companionship ended at the office doors. *Private* reporters made fun of colleagues from other publications, speculating what would happen if they were to join other staffs: "The [*Government*] paper will need to get rid of at least three reporters." The noise quieted when the publisher walked in, but there was little tension. After a short meeting—"where are we at with the current issue?"—reporters hurried to leave the newsroom. No one wanted to work overtime, and no plans were made to socialize after.

Reporters at the *Traditional* drew no line between themselves and management. They were a tight-knit group, all trying to survive. Unhappiness about their dire financial situation (a monthly salary of 13,000 rubles or around 200 US dollars) was offset by comforting relationships within the newsroom. Staffers described colleagues as "family," and the atmosphere as "soulful." Like *Private* reporters, *Traditional* staffers shared secrets and concerns with each other and provided emotional support. Unlike *Private* reporters, *Traditional* reporters said they would trade their newsroom for a workplace that paid a decent salary, though they would prefer to abandon together, arm in arm. The strength of the collective, where what you do is not as important as with whom you do it, was crucial for them in enduring difficult days.

At each paper in Region A, social cohesion emerged among staff for different reasons. At the *Government*, a bonding force was antipathy toward regional officials, though bonds were strengthened by warmth and accommodation from daily interaction. Only *Government* reporters regularly gathered outside of work hours, for picnics or get-togethers at someone's dacha (summer garden home). Bonds at the *Private* were born of the same daily interaction, but also from common professional respect. Shared pride in their work was an important social glue. A shared history of hard times seemed the social glue for journalists at the *Traditional*.

The papers in Region C demonstrated similar collectiveness, evident across staff and newsroom managers. The strength of the editor contributes to cohesion in one of the Region C papers. Both senior and younger reporters referred to this editor as a "life-long mentor" and "greatest supporter" who turned his newsroom into an "educational institution." They say the editor takes care of reporters' professional growth by guiding their topic choice, developing interview questions and editing story lines and attributing story success solely to reporters. Staff referred to the newsroom as "хороший коллектив" (a good team) and "a family."

An exception to the importance of коллектив (the collective) was the newspaper in Region B. A generation gap appeared to be a key factor, and the editor was interpersonally distant. According to a young reporter, a few retirement-age reporters were "stuck in the 1970s" in their news and writing styles and were unwilling to adapt. The young reporter said the different generations have virtually nothing in common, and "an awkward silence typical for strangers is common in our newsroom." However, professional dispassion and indifference were more evident than conflict. Generational division was common across the regions' papers, and it is explored in more detail below.

Journalists' Occupational Community and Fragmentation

While individual newsroom environments have been collegial, or at least conflict-free, the broad "occupational community" of journalists across each region appears fragmented. Interviews showed that journalists, loyal to their own newsroom colleagues, can be disparaging of other regional organizations. The *Government* staff "relaxes and stuffs their paper with nonsense," according to one *Private* reporter in 2015. In 2016, the *Traditional* vice-editor suspected the *Government's* editor of forbidding his staff from socializing with *Traditional* staff: "He said we are crooked and can get all their secrets." Despite disdain toward other news organizations, journalists are friendly enough with other organizations' journalists, and there can even be a moderate sense of solidarity in common struggle, though this is rarely acted on.

Journalists' bonds across local news outlets have been stronger historically, as in the past, journalists looked to one another for support during difficult times. The Journalists' Union, founded in 1959 and especially active in Soviet times, helped the regions' journalists and news outlets maintain their standards, their self-esteem, and their connections with citizens and with one another during trying situations. The Union served Soviet aims, striving to advance Soviet journalism abroad, but it also helped members' grow professionally at home (French, 2014). French (2014) argued that the Union was formed less to control journalists, and more "to expand their responsibilities and improve their qualifications" (p. 424). The Journalists' Union localized its activities through regional branches, which held regular meetings, resolved conflicts among members, encouraged unity, and defended members' rights. However, the Region A local branch has been inactive for years.

The concept of "occupational community" is helpful for understanding the relative cohesiveness and coherence of the region's journalists, both formal and informal (Lowrey & Erzikova, 2013; Van Maanen & Barley, 1984). The concept is consistent with ecology approaches, as it emphasizes negotiated shared meanings as a basis for community, and accommodates a range of interactions—formal, informal, professional and personal. Occupational communities consist of people who believe they do the same sort of work, who share norms and values that apply to daily work and beyond work, (Fine, 1996; Trice, 1993; Van Maanen & Barley, 1984) "and whose social relationships meld work and leisure" (Van Maanen & Barley, 1984, p. 287). While work positions are "organizationally created and sanctioned, the work that comprises such a position often has a history of its own and, therefore, a context that is not organizationally limited" (Van Maanen & Barley, 1984, p. 291). Identities of occupational communities may strengthen, weaken, alter or fragment, depending on a variety of structural factors including government pressure on (or support for) the occupation; centralization of the market (Van Maanen & Barley, 1984); and technological change. But they are also affected by cultural factors such as the task rituals, ceremonies, interactions, routines and standards of daily work, and workers' shared accounts of these, which reproduce cultural factors.

Generally, respondents in our study saw the forces undermining their occupational community as stronger than supportive forces. We see both field and ecology dynamics at play. Reporters from all publications said the regional government has wielded power over newspapers and journalists by controlling economic capital and informational resources, a sort of centralized market that increases dependency on government and weakens occupational identity, autonomy and cohesiveness (Van Maanen & Barley, 1984). The resulting competition over scarce capital has, in some cases, increased oppositional position taking by players in the field toward one another (Bourdieu, 1993); for example, news managers complain about rivals jockeying for additional government revenue. However, there is also evidence that hard times have led, over the years of our study, to a discouraged resignation, and to a slide into a logic of mere daily survival—this is especially evident at the troubled *Traditional*. In either case, occupational harmony and unity are hardly being encouraged.

Journalists across the papers acknowledged the benefits of more meaningful communication among the occupation's members, but most saw this as unlikely given the "hostile environment of competition" over resources, as one journalist put it. In Region A, *Private* and *Regional Branch* reporters resented their colleagues from the *Government* and the *Traditional* for living off the regional budget—particularly the *Government*, which has received annual financial and administrative support from the regional government by default. *Traditional* journalists were discouraged at receiving a fraction of what the *Government* newspaper received, while *Government* journalists generally thought regional government funding for the *Traditional* was a waste of money.

According to one Region A senior journalist, journalists are bound to their organizations, and to their organizations' owners: "Newspapers are not perceived as the medium that belongs to journalists [generally]," he said. "We are journalists hired by the power ... [and are] alienated property." It's not clear how prevalent this view was though it seemed to grow with the worsening economic situation. But findings did show that journalists' understanding of their professional roles was shaped significantly by their particular organization's goals and revenue sources. In 2007, a young reporter for the profit-driven *Regional Branch* newspaper argued that the "quality of the language" should not matter and that "readers are only interested in getting news fast." Similarly, this paper's Moscow-based manager said in 2008 that "classical literature" was the place for "high quality text," and not newspapers. In 2012, the reporter moved to the *Government*, and his view of journalism changed. The *Government* was less focused on profit, and, according to the *Government's* vice-editor, the paper urged writing that informs but also "guides and educates." In 2016, the reporter, reflecting on his old position, said *Regional* management had treated him dismissively, merely as a "news supplier." His job had been to churn, he said, rather than instruct and inspire.

News outlets have made money in different ways, and this has contributed to varying norms and values, challenging the coherence and cohesiveness of the local journalistic community. The *Regional Branch* focused heavily on local business advertising, and its staffers tended to value fiscal soundness—"the most self-reliant publication in the city" according to their general manager, though the paper also willingly accepted local government revenue. *Private* reporters also said that a "real newspaper" must be financially sustainable, and they too accepted government subsidies, but unlike *Regional Branch* reporters, they tended to believe government subsidies undermined good journalism. Some *Traditional* and *Government* reporters, particularly in more recent years, said that having more financial support from the local government helps their papers avoid the sensationalistic content and mercenary processes they perceived at the *Private*. One reporter said papers like the *Private* publish stories that capitalize on citizens' concerns—about pensions, for example—because the anxiety they produce grows paper sales. For his part, the head of the Region A mass media department said state-supported papers serve citizens, and private papers serve themselves:

> Subsidized papers inform readers better. Yellow newspapers would not write about agriculture, unless a combiner is killed by lightning. But my goal is to honor the foremost workers.

Across all Region A papers, reporters said concrete, active efforts to cultivate occupational community amid these divisive influences were weak and sporadic: "Reporters from different newspapers get together only at someone's funeral," said a *Traditional* vice-editor. It appeared the only time the province's journalists collected on a regular basis was at the annual national press day. The Union of Journalists last held a regional branch meeting in the mid 2000s, and many journalists did not even know who headed the local Union branch. Although some respondents thought the Union could help promote dialog among journalists, they doubted it would enhance autonomy in any meaningful way.

Yet, there was some evidence of occupational community, typically emerging in personal and informal contexts rather than professional contexts. Personal difficulties by fellow journalists would prompt gatherings. In 2019, Region B journalists raised funds for a reporter whose parent passed away, and the same year they took care of a child whose mother, a regional reporter, died from a medical error. In 2017, Region C reporters raised money for a reporter who had adopted three children. Over the years, Region A reporters showed support in many ways. They stood in line to give blood to a sick colleague, and they raised funds for a journalist killed in a car accident, for another journalist with cancer, and for a third whose house was destroyed by flooding. "Not everything comes down to business," a Region B editor noted. "There is room for human feelings." There was even an example of connectedness for professional reasons when Region C journalists signed a petition demanding the release of a reporter for covering a mass protest. These kinds of actions were most likely in Region C papers, which had the most resources, stability and professional expertise.

Informal occupational community was encouraged by job-hopping. Journalists regularly work at rival papers, and across the years of data collection, there was little mention of workplace tension because of this nomadic practice. In all three provinces, journalists have stayed in touch with former newsroom colleagues, offering help when asked. Across the 13-year study period, secretly writing stories for rival publications emerged as an informal routine. A *Government* reporter admitted she helped friends from other newspapers with news they missed or events they were unable to cover, and this was common practice across papers. And while newspapers' rules generally forbid reporters from writing for other outlets, managers have groused rather than enforced. A *Private* reporter in 2015 said she could not recall anyone being fired for it: "Management just keeps warning them."

Not all reporters were willing to help colleagues and earn honoraria. Those indoctrinated into the profession at the *Regional Branch* learned fierce professional competition rather than camaraderie. *Regional Branch* managers and staff perceived all comparable newspapers in the region as rivals, viewing exclusive information as a lure for readers and ad revenue, and reporters declined to help colleagues at other papers because they feared retribution from a management that actually enforced these rules. As a *Traditional* reporter said, "When we worked [at the *Regional Branch*], we were afraid that similar information would appear in another paper." The reporter said photographers were often the source of information leaks because they knew that without information, their photos would not be published.

Journalists also occasionally criticized one another's work publicly, and this was most common in Region C. One seasoned reporter at a Region C paper bashed his colleagues on social media for producing stories on topics like "Fishermen start a new fishing season"—stories, he said, that have no depth and meaning.

> Where is journalism? "News? Viewpoints? And—God forbid—the truth? I get it, I get it—99% of journalism is a copy-paste craft, but still ... somebody needs to write stories—for others to steal it."

About a hundred of his colleagues "liked" the post and a few shared this outcry on the social media network. Though potentially divisive, this criticism is also an alternative expression of community—a "tough love," where journalists challenge one another because they long for the community to improve.

Between 2007 and 2010, relationships among reporters in Region A were damaged by confrontations in an online chat room. A young reporter for the *Traditional* said the tone was hostile:

> If someone wants to assess relationships among local reporters, he needs to visit a specific website and see how they attack each other. Every "writer" has a [pseudonym] there, but almost all of them were blown out [revealed] in fiery debates.

Yet, by 2015, the chatroom lost popularity after the key "nasty chatters" left journalism, according to a *Government* reporter. By 2019, there was no mention of the chatroom or chatroom animosity.

This loose and tenuous occupational community generally diminished over the mid-years of our study (Lowrey & Erzikova, 2013), but some unity seemed to be reviving around 2018, as journalists found themselves sharing a growing frustration with the local government, which they viewed as incompetent and unfair in managing regional media. Journalists at all papers agreed that regional officials simply did not understand the level of resources needed to run a daily newspaper: "The news production process, if done properly, is costly," as the *Government* vice-editor said. In the mid 2010s, a handful of government officials launched a series of websites, funded by the regional budget, in order to demonstrate their loyalty to the governor, and journalists' resentment heated up. As a *Traditional* reporter said:

We earn money, but officials don't want to support us. They want to spend all money on their websites. Who visits these sites? A few thousand, while if we had resources, the *Traditional* would become a source of information for a half-million residents.

Despite shared frustration, staffers and managers across the papers have taken no meaningful joint action. There has been no organized effort to confront officials or to assert unity and autonomy.

While journalists acknowledged the fragility and fragmentation of their "community," most journalists held their occupation in esteem. It still provides symbolic capital. As a young reporter for the *Private* said in 2010:

> You don't have a right to belong to the community because you have been hired by a paper yesterday. You earn the right [only through] dedicated work for years.

Fragmentation and the Newsroom Generation Gap

The young reporter's comment touches on another key reason for the occupation's fragility and fragmentation—a generation gap, which widened across the post-perestroika era. According to Bourdieu (2005), individuals' orientations and decisions are shaped by the trajectories they have traveled, and the two paths of perestroika-era journalists and post-2000 generation journalists have continued to diverge, fueling animosity and division within the local journalism workforce. Consistent with past literature on Russian journalism (Pasti, 2005; Coman, 2000), older reporters in this study perceived that younger journalists were tracking "deviant trajectories" (Benson & Neveu, 2005, p. 6), openly valuing commercial sensationalism and political opportunism over press freedom and responsibility to the local community. For their part, younger reporters saw older reporters as unwilling or unable to adjust to changing commercial and technological realities, and as failing to mentor the next generation. In this section, we discuss the various characteristics and outcomes of this generation gap. We note that the gap was more salient in the minds of journalists earlier in our study period, but it remained relevant across the 13 years.

The "imprinting" of one's environment is a stubborn factor, strengthening dependency on the paths people have taken and the investments they have made, and making it less likely people will adapt to changing circumstances (Aldrich & Ruef, 2006; Erzikova & Lowrey, 2012). A question is whether the different socializing "imprinting" of these journalists' generational groups takes an ecological direction, encouraging dynamic and diverse interaction within the social space and encouraging new meaning-making—or if instead, oppositional position-taking divides and fragments the occupation.

Findings suggest that fragmentation was a more obvious outcome than beneficial diversity, at least in the short term. Most of our respondents said that the pursuit of sensationalism weakened professional cohesiveness and principles. Older reporters said Russian journalism should follow the age-old tradition of personal, philosophical, moral and literary writing—writing that "lifts up" the people (Erzikova & Lowrey, 2010)—what we call a *moral education logic*, discussed in Chapter 7. They disapproved of younger reporters' deviation from this traditional path. The older generation's perestroika experiences help explain their entrenched defense of this centuries-old tradition. The late 1980s and 1990s brought waves of reform-minded proponents of Western journalism to Russia, through NGO-supported workshops, conferences and consultants (Miller, 2011). At first, Russian journalists enthused over Westernization and its promise of a long-desired editorial independence, but over time, journalists, especially in "heartland" regions, grew uncomfortable with Western approaches. The subjugation of personal assertions to "fact" was troubling. Regional journalists commonly equated neutral journalism and its commercial origins with cold indifference to a craft that has deep moral and literary roots (Lowrey & Erzikova, 2013), rich in letter writing, personal comments, and clashing viewpoints (Vartanova & Azhgikhina. 2011). For these journalists, the promise of perestroika was less about production of public facts and accountability, or entrepreneurial business success, and more about the liberation of their writing so that it could be personal, reflective, and inspirational. At every stage of our data collection, perestroika and perceptions of its lessons emerged as a meaningful and persistent generational boundary marker for journalists. In Chapter 7 we discuss a *perestroika-era logic* and the ways it interacted with other logics and shaped the local journalism space.

In the earliest years of our research, 2007–2010, senior journalists commonly referred to junior reporters as a "rootless generation," unmoored from motherland and region, and indifferent to the plight of disadvantaged everyday local people. They saw this indifference as eroding connection and commitment to poor local citizens, which senior journalists saw as fundamental to local Russian journalism values, stretching back to pre-Soviet times. The editor of the *Regional Branch* lamented that its parent company's push toward westernization of news production ("the faster, the better") and an emphasis on meeting quotas for story quantity, diminished reporters' interest in engaging with their immediate surroundings.

> Neither brain nor heart are involved when they write. They don't insert themselves into local life, don't socialize with colleagues from other papers, and don't spend time with government officials on Saturdays fishing for story ideas.

Observations at the *Regional Branch* newsroom supported the editor's concern: Reporters, who were typically younger and under quota demands, tended to sit isolated in their newsrooms, searching the web for information, rarely discussing story ideas. These reporters perceived the quota demands as legitimate, and they expressed pride that their Moscow-based, Western-oriented parent company had processes that were more up-to-date than the provincial publications.

These twenty-somethings came of age in the mid-2000s, a post-Soviet Russia absent the fervent anti-Westernism of the Cold War. But some (not all) senior staffers who experienced the Cold War suspected the West of foul play, believing their efforts to democratize Russia were a ruse, and they saw younger Russians as uncritical, and therefore vulnerable. In the words of one seasoned *Traditional* reporter:

> The West is totalitarism, surveillance and brainwashing mass media. Blood is spilling over from a TV set. It's mentally damaging, especially young people are susceptible.

His colleague from the *Government* echoed this, believing the West sought to undermine Russian values: "The goal is decay."

Older journalists typically viewed younger journalists as obsessed with consumerism, a cultural capital they saw as non-native to Russia. Some older reporters said regional media were not up-to-date enough to meet expectations of the younger generation, who seem to follow other sets of rules, who "live in another dimension and speak another language." According to a *Regional Branch* newspaper manager:

> The generation of people who are 18–20 is not interested in journalism in its real sense. They ... evaluate everything through a single prism—glamour or not glamour. The modern newspaper, accordingly, is not glamour. So it is out of their interests ... Russia is a temporary home [to them], whereas their real home is somewhere in Europe. If they don't feel any ties with their native country, how can they have interest in getting a job at a provincial newspaper?

A few senior journalists said they thought the political-economic uncertainty of perestroika and post-perestroika had undermined the socialization of younger reporters. In a 2011 interview, one seasoned manager from the *Government* paper found it "a puzzle and disappointment" that younger reporters should pander to officials, as it was her generation that was "born in captivity" while "youngsters were born free." Another manager for the *Government* said the new generation of journalists merely seeks to "fit in the corridors of power":

> They are transmitters. They are excited about the governor's speech about offshore zones. I am tired from editing their stories to eliminate this excitement. They are not just transmitters; they are idealizers.

In the mid 2000s, a prominent veteran reporter literally found herself on the side opposite her younger colleagues. While she and a group of citizens gathered outside a government building to protest the removal of trees from a children's park,[1] younger colleagues gazed down on them from government office windows. She said she thinks the new generation actively "kisses up" to authorities. Young reporters, she said, "spend more time in government offices than in newsrooms" and are "proud" to receive government awards for their coverage of government activities.

However, what older journalists viewed as the personal and professional challenge of dealing with authority, younger journalists see as weakness by senior journalists in the face of powerful, savvy officials, who are the more alluring role models. Younger reporters often witnessed senior journalists' lack of control over their work: At one newspaper, the government hired and fired editors every three months during a two-year period.

Further, newsroom observations revealed that management routinely assigned younger reporters to stories that required minimal ability and were unlikely to aid skill development. Younger reporters were regularly sent to cover "which-bureaucrat-said-what" stories, such as routine news conferences. Most senior journalists thought young journalists incapable of tough assignments, and so the senior journalists took on the in-depth stories that resonate with readers and evoke emotion. However, from the perspective of younger reporters, seasoned reporters avoided routine pro-government stories because they bring "neither money nor glory," as one young staffer put it. More than one observation revealed young reporters cutting off conversations about story ideas when older reporters entered the room, for fear their ideas would be stolen.

Relative distribution of capital across the field also plays a part in this generational clash. Centralization of capital by the regional government has led newer journalists to seek money and status though interactions with powerful officials. Older perestroika-era journalists perceived service to the government as necessary but coerced; however, for many younger reporters, the harsh environment has further normalized service to the powerful and wealthy, eroding critical distance. Service to community and profession seems, to these reporters, quaint notions of a previous generation.

The same may be said of following the logics of literary quality and moral uplift. During a focus-group discussion in 2007, four young *Regional Branch* reporters said their main purpose was to inform and entertain using "simple language," and avoiding "smart words," a practice for which older "stiff" journalists could not be retrained. In the eyes of many younger journalists, the harsh times demanded less idealism and more realism—more on-the-ground hustling and more online clicks. A *Government* newcomer said she was surprised by the slow pace and lack of competitive attitude among older colleagues, while a *Government* vice-editor commented on young reporters' "insane" productivity: "Newcomers gather more information and much quicker—but the quality suffers." However, observations showed that this editor visited younger journalists' offices to discuss story ideas more frequently than he visited senior journalists.

Interview respondents' critical talk of a "rootless" younger generation began to fade around 2011, and virtually disappeared in 2015, as the country's financial situation worsened. To survive, newsrooms shrank and stopped hiring new staffers. However, some tension between the two generations persists.

Journalists and Local Education and Training

In the eyes of the older generation, journalism's future in Region A is jeopardized by an inadequate local educational system that fails to train individual journalists. Interviewed senior staff perceived Region A's journalism school, launched during perestroika, as a diploma mill that failed to produce well-prepared, committed and energetic journalists. A recent national survey of Russian journalists revealed a widely shared perception that local journalism schools, generally, provide a broad education but, in the words of one survey respondent, "no longer teach the profession" (Glowacki, 2015, p. 74).

This stands in contrast to the Soviet system in which newspapers published by regional committees of the Communist Party and Komsomol hired college graduates as reporters, and graduates were obligated to work three years at the papers (Приказ от 18 марта 1968 г.). As a rule, individuals with non-journalism degrees—e.g., pedagogy, engineering—could also become staff writers, after years of freelancing.

A *Government* reporter's scathing assessment of the Region A school was typical: "Losers go to the journalism department to buy a diploma" and "other losers—university teachers—hand out the diplomas to them without educating them." The editor of the *Regional Branch* said the school attracts individuals with no drive to study but who still accept the cultural stereotype that "a person must have a university diploma." The editor of the *Private* said she had no idea where the school's journalism graduates obtain jobs. She recalled a competition launched by her paper to fill two positions, which ended in the hiring of individuals with no journalism training:

> About 50 people responded to the ad, and none of the candidates was affiliated with the local journalism department. After a few candidates worked for us for about a month, we hired a nurse and a teacher.

A government official said he recognized the need to improve education at the school, but he admitted the "region does not have the resources to invite good teachers and supply them with good salaries." Monthly incomes for Ph.D. faculty in the province are low, and overload teaching was often required. The official said it is no wonder that "professionals with a high potential" seek a better life in large cities outside the province.

If the local "supply side" of education is weak, so is local demand. The traditional cultural capital of the community-oriented, literary journalist is worth much less in a cash-starved, politically constrained environment, and there is little demand for university degrees and professional training, especially as these require owners/managers to pay higher salaries. To save money, publication owners have literally hired staffers off the street. A new generation of "reporters" found that "journalism is not that hard," given the reduced expectations. For these untrained staff, newspaper readers are not local citizens with needs but content consumers, and journalism is an office job requiring mostly online search skills and a vivid imagination. A senior manager for the *Traditional* recalled a time when he thought a new reporter had finally learned the basics of professional writing:

> I was so excited. But a quick internet search showed that her story was an article published in a [another region's] newspaper. She simply copied and pasted the text and changed the city's name.

The reporter herself told the editor she had no qualms because "everyone does it."

During the mid-1990s through the early 2000s, news work became an assembly-line production that invited ethical violations. Staff were observed "borrowing" sensational stories from national or other regions' online publications—e.g., a story about a crocodile found in a backyard—and changing the geography so that it appeared to happen to a local resident. Staffers also invented stories out of whole cloth. A senior reporter for the *Private* said that after she read a story in a local paper about a deadly explosion in a private bathroom, she checked police records and found no mention. This practice, which abated in the late 2000s, had two main causes. First, younger, less educated staffers were more likely to thieve others' stories, in a desperate effort to appease managers who were critical of their work. Second, mainstream yellow newspapers that spread from Moscow to the provinces regularly "borrowed" online stories from regional papers and adapted them, a practice they called "optimization," according to a former editor of a regional yellow newspaper. Free domestic publications also emerged and spread, adopting similar unethical practices.

Many professional journalists from failing legacy publications—some interviewed for this study—preferred to leave the profession than to join new commercial publications staffed by less educated and under-socialized younger workers. For them, a growing commercialism "kills the paper and the kids [young employees]," as one editor put it. A journalist interviewed in 2018 was typical. Now in another line of work, he said he enjoyed "journalism of the perestroika time," but "when times changed, I didn't feel 'the new journalism' fitted to who I am." His desire to quit journalism was reinforced after an extortion scandal in which one local commercial newspaper's publisher threatened to "throw mud" at a high-level official if the official refused to pay. The publisher was arrested, but other publishers still instructed their reporters to blackmail potential advertisers.

There is little evidence of the Soviet-era tradition of informal mentoring between seasoned and young reporters in the typical post-perestroika newsroom in Region A. However, senior journalists from Regions B and C appeared to be more helpful to beginners and less critical of their lack of preparedness. Located in bigger cities, Region B and Region C newsrooms attracted relatively more graduates with reputable journalism degrees. Also, it appeared management sought to retain talent and worked to educate the newcomers. A reporter who moved to Region C after graduating from a prestigious journalism program said she hadn't realized her education at the newspaper itself "would be more in-depth and more encompassing than her schooling."

Findings suggest senior reporters in Region A do not think investing in young reporters is worth the trouble, though their help is needed. The *Traditional* editor said those without Soviet-era journalism degrees are professionally helpless, and yet, he said, it seems the less education and experience they have, the higher their self-esteem: "They don't see themes for stories and don't look for them, but they think they are great writers—as a minimum, Remarque and as a maximum, Tolstoy." In 2007, a reporter with one year's experience complained that the *Traditional* editor had refused to change her status from a freelancer to a columnist, a full-time high-level position:

> He told me I haven't written a real feature article. This is unfair. His friend and colleague—the head of the news department—doesn't write news but he remains the news head.

She left the profession in 2009, an occurrence, according to Region A seasoned journalists, that is not uncommon. They said reporters without journalism degrees who were socialized to the profession at commercial newspapers were likely to leave the field. Senior journalists were not unhappy to see them go, but still, they longed for a better way to introduce new journalists to the field. "A bitter taste" from dealing with "copy-paste" reporters lingers in traditional newsrooms, particularly for those who remember better days.

Discussion

Personal poverty and the pressures to cater to officials hinder journalists' professionally. In this environment, it is difficult to find the time and the motivation to produce coverage that makes a difference in the lives of regional citizens. Journalists feel the pull of the community's needs and are sympathetic, but enterprise reporting to help people in the community is challenging, to say the least. The system that ties honoraria to story-churn does not encourage thoughtful investigative work.

Journalists draw strength from the social bonds of their organization-level relationships, but competition over scarce resources and a lack of meaningful professional structures—no meaningful journalists' union and poor educational programs—hinder "occupational community" among the regions' journalists across news organizations. Journalists show connectedness in personal, informal ways—when a colleague is ill or in trouble, for example. There are also interesting latent forces in the news ecosystem that have encouraged informal, loose community across papers: (1) Journalists know journalists from other organizations, as they rotate from paper to paper, and they maintain these connections; and (2) difficult economic times and small staffs encourage journalists to seek help in covering news from colleagues at other papers, and journalists earn extra money this way. There is also some recent stirring of occupational cohesiveness, born of current frustration with the government's media administration. These informal bases of interaction encourage collectivity across the journalism space even as top-down political-economic forces generally divide journalists—a complex situation that can be examined by turning the prism between the facets of social ecology and critical field theory.

A generation gap in newsrooms has also hindered occupational community. Differing sets of values between seasoned reporters who came of age during perestroika and the younger generation, more enamored of government service and chasing online audiences and honoraria, have led to divisive positions in the field. Older journalists have been disappointed in younger journalists' apathy toward the journalistic craft and its mission to serve the local community, and they have been frustrated by younger journalists' admiration of officials. For their part, younger journalists viewed older journalists as weak, stuck in the past and as resistant to mentoring. Older journalists and managers lay part of the blame on journalism education, which they viewed as increasingly inadequate for preparing younger journalists for traditional and emerging challenges; however, newsroom environments diminished by political and economic pressures are also an important part of this story.

Note

1. During perestroika, some journalists joined and/or actively supported emerging non-profit organizations and activist groups. This particular reporter became known for her involvement with citizen advocacy groups, for example, organizing protests against government officials for activities generally considered unlawful.

References

Aldrich, H. E., & Ruef, M. (2006). *Organizations evolving*. Thousand Oaks, CA: Sage.
Benson, R., & Neveu, E. (2005). *Bourdieu and the journalistic field*. Cambridge: Polity Press.
Bourdieu, P. (1993). The market of symbolic goods. In P. Bourdieu (Ed.), *The field of cultural production: Essays on art and literature* (pp. 112–141). New York: Columbia University Press.
Coman, M. (2000). Developments in journalism theory about media 'transition' in Central and Eastern Europe 1990–99, *Journalism Studies 1*(1), 35–56.
Erzikova, E., & Lowrey, W. (2010). Seeking safe ground: Russian regional journalists' civic service journalism. *Journalism Studies 11*(3), 343–358.
Erzikova, E. & Lowrey, W. (2012). Managed mediocrity? Experienced journalists' perspectives on "pampers generation" of Russian reporters. *Journalism Practice, 6*(2), 264–279.
Fine, G.A. (1996). Justifying work: Occupational rhetorics as resources in restaurant kitchens. *Administrative Science Quarterly, 41(1)*, 90–115.
French, M. C. (2014). *Reporting Socialism: Soviet Journalism and the Journalists' Union, 1955–1966*. Publicly Accessible Penn Dissertations. 1277.
Glowacki, M. (2015). "Who is a journalist today? Mapping selected dimensions for comparative study on journalism. In G. Nygren & B. Dobek-Ostrowska (Eds.), *Journalism in Change: Journalistic Culture in Poland, Russia and Sweden* (pp. 63–95). Frankfurt am Main: Peter Lang.
Lowrey, W. & Erzikova, E. (2010). Institutional legitimacy and Russian news: Case studies of four regional newspapers. *Political Communication, 27*(3), 275–288.
Lowrey, W., & Erzikova, E. (2013). One profession—multiple identities: Russian regional reporters' perceptions of the professional community. *Mass Communication and Society, 16*(5), 639–660.
Miller, J. (Spring 2011). Questioning the Western approach to training. *Nieman Reports*. Retrieved August 20, 2020 from https://niemanreports.org/articles/questioning-the-western-approach-to-training/
Pasti, S. (2005). Two generations of contemporary Russian journalists, *European Journal of Communication 20*(1), 89–115.
Prikaz (1968). ПРИКАЗ Минвуза СССР от 18.03.1968 n 220 ОБ УТВЕРЖДЕНИИ ПОЛОЖЕНИЯ О ПЕРСОНАЛЬНОМ РАСПРЕДЕЛЕНИИ МОЛОДЫХ

СПЕЦИАЛИСТОВ, ОКАНЧИВАЮЩИХ ВЫСШИЕ И СРЕДНИЕ СПЕЦИАЛЬНЫЕ УЧЕБНЫЕ ЗАВЕДЕНИЯ. Retrieved October 3, 2018 from https://www.lawmix.ru/docs_cccp/6149

Rating of socio-economic situation of subjects of the Russian Federation. [Рейтинг социально-экономического положения субъектов РФ по итогам 2017 года]. (2018). Retrieved January 22, 2019 from http://www.riarating.ru/infografika/20180523/630091878.html

Trice, H. M. (1993). *Occupational subcultures in the workplace.* Ithaca: ILR Press.

Van Maanen, J., & Barley, S. R. (1984). Occupational communities: Culture and control in organizations. *Research in Organizational Behavior, 6,* 287–365.

Vartanova, E., & Azhgikhina, N. (2011). *Dialogi o zhurnalistike* [Dialogs about journalism]. IREX Russia: MGU.

CHAPTER SIX

Russian Regional Journalists in a Digital Era

For years, Private reporters have considered their newspaper a model for other local publications in finding topics that resonate with readers. "We take care of our readers," the Private editor said in 2015. "We help them. We listen to them." "Thinking outside the box," said a young reporter, is the "norm" in the Private newsroom. The Private's reporters also took pride in their ability to "hunt down" bureaucrats, a senior reporter said in 2019, and get first-hand information. Yet, one day, shortly before an issue went to print, the editor-in-chief told the staff he lacked three news stories to fill a hole. Reporters rushed to their computers to search other news organizations' websites, predominantly online news agencies. After finding a few stories, reporters decided which would appeal most to Private readers, and they re-wrote them. Surfing other news organizations' websites was a quick way to fill pages with recent information, and this practice appeared to be routine.

Consistent with worldwide trends (Hess & Waller, 2017), in Russia, digital online technologies are shaping the work of local journalists in varied and often unexpected ways, and with functional and dysfunctional consequences for journalists and communities. None of the newsrooms in our study was a digital native (founded online) and relative to audiences generally, the papers' readers are not highly active online. While some of the newspapers' management and staff have heard the call to digitalization and embraced the challenge, more have ignored it or wavered and hedged, amid uncertainty. Based on interviews, observation and close reading of online content, journalists' digital practices generally increased in volume and quality over the period of study, though this varied across regions and papers. We have seen a stronger emphasis on digital online news practices in regions B and C than in Region A, with Region C publications being the most aggressive and sophisticated in their practices. Regional governments have also been direct players in the online space over the years. Notably, the Region A governor started a blog in 2011 (as did other governors around the country), and the Region A government launched its own news portal in 2018, allowing it to bypass newspaper journalists.

In Region A, only the *Government* newspaper's website, started in 2006, was actively managed across the entire study period, and today the paper's online production is managed at least 18 hours per day. The *Government's* online managers originally worked for the *Regional Branch* paper, which had the most advanced online presence early in the study period. Managers learned the craft of online journalism from the *Regional Branch's* Moscow-based parent, and they were hired by the *Government* in 2012, tasked with ramping up the paper's online presence. The *Private* had no website during the period of study, and the *Traditional*, which started its website in 2014, used the site only as a digital archive for print stories, uploading stories after print publication. The *Private* started social media accounts for the paper in 2018, but only the *Government* has had active newspaper accounts, starting them in 2012. The *Traditional* has no newspaper social media accounts. Reporters at all three papers are active on their own personal accounts, using them to find story ideas and information.

The Region B newspaper launched a website in 2001, the first newspaper site in the region according to the editor. By 2014, the website had 100,000 visitors per month, which the editor saw as "a huge victory." The Region B editor said in 2015 that only about 15% of the print audience overlaps with their online audience, and he has little faith in the site's long-term financial sustainability. However, he has continued to commit time and resources to the site and to social media. He holds out hope they will prove to be a useful "promotional tool," to lead online users to the print product, particularly younger readers who seem unaware that a print product exists.

Region C papers started their websites in the early 2000s. In 2016, Region C reporters said their print and online audiences overlap somewhat, with the print audience being "more educated and demanding" about the quality and depth of publications. The most devoted online readers, according to a social media editor, were Facebook group users, consisting of both online and print readers. The importance of digital practices in Region C, relative to the other two regions, is evidenced by one Region C editor's recent use of social media to find digitally savvy reporters, who have been rare: "Only 10% of journalism graduates end up working for a medium, and [of these] only one graduate is multimedia capable."

Online Audience Access and Usage

Internet access grew by 5 to 10% in the studied regions from 2014 to 2018, according to the Federal Service for State Statistics. Recent levels of internet access and usage by residents were largely consistent across the three regions and were just under the national levels of 77% for access and 87% for usage among those with access. According to a national report by a private firm, 78% of Russian adults in 2019 said they primarily obtained their news and information from online sources, compared to 40% in 2015. Percent obtaining news primarily from social media specifically increased from 14% in 2015 to 37% in 2019 (Tendentsii monetizatsii kontenta v Internete, 2019).

The three regions have substantial rural populations, particularly A and B, with C being more urban and closer to the national rural vs. urban ratio. The rural vs. urban make-up of the regions affects rates of internet access and use. Nationally, fewer rural than urban households had internet access in 2013 (50% rural vs. 73% urban) and in 2018 (67% rural vs. 80% urban). In 2013, 63% of rural adults and 73% of urban adults across the nation reported having no interest or need for the internet at home, but within five years these percentages declined dramatically, with only 15% of urban residents reporting no need for home access in 2018, compared to 21% of rural residents (Rosstat, 2018). Rural and urban users differ in their online content choices, according to national government statistics, though news usage online makes up a small portion for both groups: 11% of rural Russian residents reported reading news and books online in 2018, compared to 21% of urban residents (Rosstat, 2018).

Though growth in online use in the three regions is similar to national trends, Region A managers said they still do not view their newspaper readers as heavy online users, as many are older and live in more rural areas. In 2010 the *Traditional* editor described readers as living a "real, not a virtual, life," and for the most part, this perception persisted across the study period. The editor of a *Traditional* supplement said her readers mail her letters requesting that the paper print information they had heard was published online. Still, "they say they actually don't need the internet." The *Government* newspaper's online managers lamented that the region's younger, better educated and digitally active residents tend to follow national online media.

Social media dominated the internet use of Russians who are regularly online, consistent with trends around the world (Kemp, 2020). In 2018, 78% of urban and

77% rural Russian adult internet users said they used social media platforms—typically, either VK (formerly vKontakte), Odnoklassniki.ru or Facebook—a four-percent increase from 2013 for both groups. According to Pfanshtil (2019), use of VK, the most popular platform, averages in the mid 80% range nationally, consistent with use in the three regions.

In 2014, one Region C editor described the behavior of his paper's various social media audiences: The VK fan group reacts within an hour with hundreds of likes to a humorous photo, while the Facebook group is "the quality group [that is] most loyal." The Facebook-using audience is more likely to read, "like," comment on, and share public-issue and analytical stories. When his paper published a story naming companies that bought buildings that formerly held kindergartens, which are scarce in his city, "the biggest [negative] reaction came from the Facebook group that shared the story a hundred times."

In 2019, the Region B newspaper website had about 700,000 unique visitors, while newspapers in Region C, the wealthiest and most highly educated region, had roughly three times this number. Consistent with online use around the world (Kemp, 2020), online users skewed young. For both Region B and C newspaper websites in 2019, the 35–44 age group was the largest user group (26% and 30%, accordingly), followed by 25–34 year olds. Mobile and social media links were more common as sources of traffic for Region C newspapers than for Region B papers, making Region C more similar to worldwide usage. Region C papers appeared most proficient at tracking online audiences, and in 2016, one Region C paper designated a reporter to analyze online traffic. In 2016, this reporter said the heaviest traffic came from personal computers in the morning when people arrived at work, and site traffic was seasonal, increasing on spring and fall Friday afternoons when readers "go to dacha" (summer/year-round second houses). She also said data show niche news areas are most popular, which suggests the strategy of "more news is good news" is ineffective.

Region A newspapers do not track audiences as carefully as papers in regions B and C, and what statistics they have, they keep to themselves, according to *Traditional* and *Government* managers. A *Government* digital media manager explained that they make these data available to potential advertisers only, and if it were widely spread, competitors could take advantage. However, given these papers' sparse resources for online production, audience traffic is likely lower than the other two regions.

Reaching Out to Readers Online

Increasing focus on online analytics suggests an economic orientation has been on the rise at these papers, especially at Region C papers and the *Government* in

Region A. The trends at these papers are consistent with recent research on analytics and news in the U.S. and Europe (e.g., Zamith, 2018).

However, an orientation toward the local community was also evident. Senior reporters, especially, were less interested in commoditizing online readers and more interested in using the internet to connect with them personally. Some interacted with readers individually, and most combed through social media and websites for incidents that would spur story ideas. Usually, these were local stories, and interaction was local. A *Traditional* reporter who is active on social media said in 2019 she regularly engages online with readers and combs through forums for stories:

> Recently, one lady from a different city sent me a message that I had a spoilage [curse] on me. She told me she needs 1,200 rubles to buy candles to pray for me. I engaged in a dialogue with her and published a story about this con artist. Wandering on public forums, I also found a person who collects and restores old cars. He works as a free taxi driver for older people.

Though the *Private* has no digital issue, *Private* reporters said they routinely use social media to aid their reporting and "keep up with residents' interests," as a reporter said. The social media manager said she searches hashtags, which enabled her to find a local family that rescues wild animals.

Journalists and managers also increasingly felt the pull to look beyond their own regions and communities for stories, particularly to gain more online traffic. As their regional readers are not avid users of online local news, Region A managers have seen little reason to motivate journalists to produce online content. The result has been low-quality local stories written by staffers who are underpaid and sometimes under-trained. Indicative of a vicious cycle, younger, better educated and wealthier readers have drifted away to national media platforms with a more sophisticated understanding of news consumption patterns. During a 2014 interview, the *Traditional* online editor demonstrated this reader exodus by opening a fan page of lenta.ru, a Moscow-based online newspaper:

> More than 2,000 people from our region belong to [lenta.ru's] fan page on odnoklassniki.ru [a social networking service]. Let's look at stats … here we go—75% of them are people under 30. I believe lenta.ru has powerful resources. A good number of talented reporters who travel and report from all over the world. Lenta.ru does analytics and knows precisely which content is popular.

Journalists also worried about a deeper, existential problem with readers—that, in a fragmented, perplexing media environment, readers no longer know what news is. New, emerging forms of digital online media are increasingly confused with professionally produced content, and this, journalists say, undermines the informational roles of journalism in the community and weakens social links between journalists and the people. A focus group session at the *Traditional* demonstrated the anxiety over this problem among journalists who were already anxious from financial struggles. One seasoned reporter voiced frustration with growing confusion among the paper's readers:

> The task of a reporter is to uncover informational value for people in the facts he reports. To explain why it's important. But people think that posts in Instagram are journalism. I tell them it's informational slag.

Reporters around the room nodded agreement, and one reporter echoed this point:

> Even educated people might say, "It is written on a website," and when you ask for details, you will find out that it wasn't a news story, it was a comment on social media.

A second seasoned reporter entered late, grumbling about a grocery bill and about having to choose between butter and milk. A focus group participant offered the reporter a tongue-in-cheek suggestion: "Go find a company that pays for social media posts, and you would have enough money to buy both." The "grocery shopper" declined the "offer." Journalism and social media "do not overlap," she said, and besides, she already had a job on the side.

Sensationalism in online content was viewed as a related and growing problem. As increasingly, journalists thought readers were failing to distinguish professionally produced content from "informational slag," journalists across all regions spoke of the need to maintain standards of "socio-political" quality—news of social importance, though typically government-subsidized. The Region B editor noted that his website's fast start ("100,000 monthly visitors by 2014") was accomplished without "scandalous or sensational news." During a focus group in 2016, Region C reporters said that while they report news of accidents online, they try to avoid scandal or stories that would lead readers to "be disgusted with a topic." "Such a story might bring 10,000 visitors," said one reporter, "but reputational loss would be huge."

The Regional Government and Emerging Media

Online production in the regions is complicated by the dual and sometimes duplicate roles of newspapers and government offices. Region A offers a good example. In addition to the *Government* newspaper's website, the regional government launched a news portal in 2018, though without clarifying to readers that government officials supervise the site. The regional government also hosts several social media platforms, including the governor's social media accounts, which started as a blog. Journalists at the *Government* newspaper are upset about the diversion of resources to the regional government's online products that bypass journalists, especially the recently launched news portal, which they see as a redundancy.

Nevertheless, newspapers' online efforts in the region depend on government resources and bend to government demands—often, resources are withheld, and newspapers' online efforts wither. One area that received growing attention and funding over the last few years of the study is social media, but social media efforts are centrally controlled. The head of Region A's Mass Media Department said in 2019 that residents' social-media activities are monitored by both regional and national officials. In the department head's opinion, not many newspapers "engage with readers online" and staff's social-media activities "are not satisfactory." A Region C editor shared recently that his region's government spends "almost all money [budgeted for regional media] on management of social media." The editor said he still managed to negotiate some funding for the newspaper itself, but only because "we are the oldest in the region and most respected."

Despite their growing attention to social media, regional governments and media have done little to attract young readers. The *Traditional* editor lamented this problem in 2016, and the problem has continued:

> Young people and intelligent people don't read newspapers and don't watch TV. The youth doesn't go to vote. It is clear regions have failed when it comes to the media. Look at rural or regional newspapers across Russia—they all look like Siamese twins. Nothing is there.

A social-media manager at the *Government* said officials haven't yet "figured out" how to produce state news for online platforms: "One day they will, but for right now, they publish their news releases on our websites." This means journalists at the *Government* paper are tasked with both disseminating government news in its traditional form and trying to attract readers, which seems futile to these journalists. Typical "official" news turns off online readers, they say, and older, more traditional readers prefer print.

The cultural capital required for journalists to engage both audiences is of two very different kinds, and the economic capital needed to produce this cultural capital has not been forthcoming. In 2019, a digital reporter at the *Government* called traditional state news "laughable and uninteresting," while the regional government's own online portal, created in 2018, is allowed to publish more engaging content and has more financial and human resources than the online platforms operated by the newspapers:

> Money is being poured on them. And their editor can publish sensational stories to attract readers. We can't. We are told we need to form a positive image of government.

Look ... (She opens website). This is how we are forced to work: government cuts a ribbon here, an agricultural event there. And here, this is them [the new portal]: an official was arrested, a man's body was found in a well. God forbid if we publish something like that. We are prohibited.

Social media and blogs produced by the Region A government have not been responsive to readers. In 2014, a freelance reporter was quite critical of the governor's blog, which appeared to be 'interactive' in name only:

> Anyone could go to the governor's blog and say that he is a bastard. He didn't delete comments ... He said he was building roads. People came to his blog and called him a liar because he didn't build roads [but he did not respond]. This is a paradox: A blog demonstrates openness and at the same time, there is no openness in his blog.

Five years later in 2019, the newly elected governor launched accounts on VK, Odnoklassniki.ru, Facebook, Twitter and Instagram. According to interviews and observation of the site, the new governor is no more responsive, but critical comments are now deleted.

Online Production at the Government Newspaper

A closer look at the recent structures, processes and staff roles for online production in the *Government* news organization since 2012 can help demonstrate the influence of the regional government on online news production. Online practices in the *Government* paper also shed light on the ways different kinds of journalists think about their readers and interact with them online.

In 2007, when websites were just vague notions for the *Traditional*, and the *Government's* online activities were rudimentary, the *Regional Branch* newspaper had a well-maintained online presence. The paper required its reporters to write for both print and online editions and to supply photo, audio and video files along with their stories. As mentioned, the online news managers for the *Regional Branch* were later hired by the *Government*, aiding the *Government's* online efforts, which were relatively sophisticated for Region A papers.

Since 2013, reporters have been divided into three groups: "digital only" reporters who write short news for the web; "digital and print" reporters who produce different stories for the web and print edition; and "seasoned reporters" who see little or no capital to be gained from digital journalism. The "digital only" reporters are young—all under 30, around the same age as the "digital and print" reporters, and younger than the "seasoned reporters." Two are male, while all print reporters are female, and their educational background is similar to the print reporters (typically, they studied Russian language and literature).

Digital only Reporters

The three digital-only reporters worked in an office on a floor separate from the main newsroom, and the operation looked like a separate news organization. These reporters focused narrowly on audience engagement and on competition with regional online news outlets. Conversations focused frequently on the portal's online ranking and number of views, and the financial implications.

One digital-only reporter said that from 2014 to 2019, "regional online news portals grew like mushrooms after rain, and almost all of them [have used] dishonest approaches to attract readers." For example, the reporter said, one outlet temporarily became the online traffic leader after publishing a story about twins found in a dumpster. "But it was a clickbait headline—a photo showed the twins were not inside the dumpster, but outside of it, trying to get a football out." He added that as a government organ, the *Government* newspaper site does not use clickbait adjectives like "horrible, atrocious" when describing harmful incidents or accidents. This is one reason, he thought, that the paper trailed more aggressive competitors in pageviews.

Aside from designing online ads, re-writing government press-releases and writing their own stories, digital reporters at the *Government* monitored social media sites to find incidents worth covering (or re-writing), and to be first on a story. "If the story 'shoots,' [gains attention], we would work on an update," the reporter explained in 2018. He said the ultimate goal was "to be picked up by Yandex," the national news aggregator, which is like winning a professional competition—though, one that can undermine professional standards. His colleague added:

> As for online journalism, nobody corrects style, language. All thoughts are about how to get into the top, how to get into Yandex. We are not doing well in terms of Yandex because we don't have time to create news. I don't have time to work on news that has a good chance to get into Yandex because I work on stories about the regional government that Yandex doesn't need. Plus, we need to work in social media to promote our stories. How much time do you think it takes—to write a story without errors, find a photo, publish, and share on social media. It is up to 30 minutes. Ten news [stories] a day is госзаказ ("goszakaz—the government order for stories) ... Plus [time spent on] advertising, phone calls, technical problems ...

These "digital only" reporters also managed their newspaper's social media accounts—VK, odnoklassniki.ru, Facebook, and Twitter—and they found this work more rewarding than filling the website with government news. Relative to the main news edition, the newspaper's social networking sites were off the regional government's radar, and digital reporters did not share official news there. In 2019, the paper's VK attracted the most online traffic (about 900 visits per day), followed by Facebook (89) and odnoklassniki.ru (39).

Digital reporters said they see more and more people getting their news through social media. The paper's social media posts are unburdened by "boring political information like government meetings," said one reporter in 2019. "If I didn't work at a newspaper, I would never look at official media websites, only social media." Different social media attracted different types of audience, according to digital reporters. They labeled Facebook group members as "intelligent and ironic" and the odnoklassniki.ru group as "mainly housewives, who like cats and prayers." Theatrical performances, art exhibitions and movie releases were covered on Facebook and crime and religious news on odnoklassniki.ru. A digital reporter said that official religion-related stories "не заходят" ("do not go in")—in other words, they do not resonate with readers:

> News about the church is not popular, except news about relics. We get many views if we write that relics of such and such saint would be delivered to the city. People want to know what illnesses these relics cure, where the relics would be displayed and when. And people go to receive treatment. News about myrrh-streaming [myrrh emanating from religious icons] is popular, too. Half of the comments would be [angry and sarcastic]. But still ... it's important that people read news.

Any attempt to include the government in an important issue in social media posts—for example, a Health Ministry official talking about a growing number of cancer patients—has been met with "radio silence." The newspaper's social media accounts have attracted relatively little reader comment and interaction, though more than the *Government* paper's website has attracted. Even hostile comments aimed at the paper have been welcomed by reporters: "Thank God they react somehow to our stories."

While news managers have discouraged reporters from posting official government news and mentions of officials on social media, viewing it as unappealing to readers, news aimed at humanizing the governor's image was allowed. One post showcased the governor resting at a river over a weekend, and reporters clearly enjoyed reading angry comments by readers who were no fans of the local government or who were simply bored by these posts: "Stop writing about the governor! Don't you have other topics to cover?"

A reporter said the *Government* newspaper's social media users don't typically confront officials. The publication's readers are relatively docile, in a political sense. He said it is mainly the regional government's social media sites—primarily, the governor's social media site—that are attacked by politically active critics of the Russian government.

> The social media group of the governor deletes a lot of comments. Governor doesn't debate with opposition, he pretends he doesn't notice them. He is not supposed to start a fight with the opposition.

Asked in 2019 if they planned to add Instagram to their social media, they almost panicked—"Please don't plant this idea in the head of our editor!" Their workload was already double the rest of the staff, and the difference was striking when observing the leisurely pace of the print journalists. Other reporters joked that "digitals" were "glued" to the chairs, and in fact, they had a six-day work week. At least one "digital" worked on Saturday and Sunday, monitoring online content from home, though weekend work was officially unpaid, rewarded only with honoraria (about 700 rubles, or 10 U.S. dollars).

Digital and Print Journalists

Reporters who were both "digital and print" prioritized the print edition over the online edition but were required to produce for both. These journalists tended to be socialized to print work, and the use of social media as a reporting tool did not come naturally. One reporter said in 2019 that he looked at social media posts, but it was more of a gesture than a real effort: "I am visiting regional паблики ['publiki'—social media forums], and I find topics there, but I don't do it with intent. With intent, it is our сайтовики ['saitoviki'—digital reporters]." A second reporter said he understood the need for online platforms, "but not with my heart."

In weekly staff meetings, these journalists hear statistics about site visits and story popularity, and, as one reporter put it, these numbers are "sad and disturbing" because stories of crime and tragedy are typically most popular. One reporter summarized a focus group conversation with print reporters: "Reporters do not feel motivated to write for the web because the online audience does not appreciate real journalism." These *Government* reporters do communicate with their readers, though less frequently than journalists at the *Traditional* and the *Private*, but they prefer to imagine positive feedback from the print audience than to deal with "offensive" feedback from the online audience. A more prosaic reason for reluctance to do online work is the significantly lower honoraria for digital stories. *Government* newspaper management explained that a web-based story is only a slightly altered print copy in their view, and the minimal honoraria they offer these journalists for online stories reflects the minimal work required.

Seasoned Reporters

Seasoned reporters expressed even more reluctance to engage with online media, and because of their status, they were not required to write for the web. Though they said they recognized the importance of the internet for disseminating information, they felt the online space was inadequate for the craft as they believed it should be practiced, and it was no place for heartfelt conversations with readers.

In 2013, in a typical comment, one award-wining *Government* reporter equated internet work with blogging, which he thought offered no insight or substance:

> The internet is not able to replace traditional journalism. Bloggers are nonsense. A journalist is doing work that other people can't do. He finds and delivers stories. Bloggers are like aqsaqals (male elder, community leaders)—[they only] sing about what they see around them. It's boring to read them. I read journalists who tell me what I don't know.

Still, legacy reporters recognized that the internet could be a legitimate source for story ideas. It offered a route to community news that bypassed official sources. In 2013, a senior reporter found a story on a private newspaper's website about a group of teenagers suspected of stabbing a classmate. The private paper had learned of the case from a reader. The editor agreed the reporter should dig into the story. Asked why the reader did not call the *Government* newspaper, the reporter smiled sardonically: "My paper? Well … A minister or another kind of an official usually calls my paper …"

Online Community and Ethics: Sharing and Stealing

The Regional Branch was the first news organization in Region A with an online presence, and it was also the first to address the issue of online plagiarism, with policies that required reporters to "call and meet with sources to obtain first-hand information," as the paper's editor said in 2007. Reporters were prohibited from searching information online, and only one reporter was allowed to access social media during work hours, to monitor accounts of high-profile news sources. *Regional Branch* reporters said they noticed unusual usage patterns among a handful of website visitors who popped in and out every two to three hours. Also, content they produced started appearing on other sites, particularly on TV news sites. It was upsetting, a reporter said. "Our reporters work hard finding high quality information, while TV reporters copy and paste our news, without acknowledging the source." The problem continued. In 2018, a Region C editor said he had the same concern, "It's common that TV reporters don't look, don't dig for stories. They graze at our website."

"Stealing" stories from competing news outlets and from reporters' personal accounts emerged as a major concern among our study's respondents around halfway into our period of study, and it began to shape reporting practices. In 2013, a *Traditional* reporter stormed through the editor's office door and said that her friend's neighbor, a little girl, had drowned at a foreign resort, and people had collected money to bring the casket back to Russia. "Should I tweet about the case?" the reporter asked. "They will steal our information immediately!"

> If we wait until the next print issue [in 6 days], another paper might find out about the case. If we post it on our website or tweet about it, a TV or radio [station] will report about the case within hours. And they will not give us credit!

None of the reporters believed the issue of plagiarism could be successfully addressed with broadcast outlet staffers. The *Government's* vice-editor said that in more recent years, "bloggers have joined the army of TV thieves" who monitor their website. "If we have exclusive information, they steal it in a heartbeat."

However, the *Government* vice-editor admitted this practice is not a one-way street. "We monitor others and borrow stories too," he said. "Ethics don't exist. If it's a large story, [our social media managers] give credit. If it is a short news story, [they] re-word it and don't give credit." We see similar practices at the better-resourced Region C papers. In 2014, one Region C newspaper created a separate position—"re-writers," who combed the internet for content and revised it. The work brought clicks but was poorly paid. The online editor said he did not see this as plagiarism, as "we are making sure news is properly re-written." Lean staffs, heavy work burden and low recompense encourage both sharing and pilfering of online content, and the line between the two can be a fine one. In 2014, a blogger in Region A said reporters frequently asked him to share information "because newspapers are lacking staff these days." A second blogger said a local information agency routinely turned his blog posts into news stories, and neither agency nor newspapers gave credit.

Unethical monitoring of other papers continued through the period of study, but a more socially beneficial practice emerged as well—the practice of identifying important stories outside the region and checking for local relevance. In 2013, a *Private* reporter said their reporters had started "localizing" information found online: "We found out that a boy died from an infected vaccine in one of the regions, [and] we did investigation and found out that [over 100] deadly vaccines were received by our region."

Change Efforts and Obstacles to Change, across the Regions

The ungoverned nature of the internet can encourage professionally deviant behavior, but it may also foster new sanctioned journalistic roles and identities, such as the "digital journalist" who is at the vanguard of journalism (Vos & Ferrucci, 2018).

Yet, there was little evidence in our study that digital journalists saw themselves as leaders of journalistic innovation. As one of the *Government* digital reporters said, they were more likely to view themselves as news deliverers. While there was some evidence of experimentation by news managers, efforts tended to be incremental, reluctant, and protective of the status quo and of those in charge. A few examples of modest efforts follow.

In 2013, the *Government* paper hired a "so-called blogger," as the vice-editor called him. The new staffer was charged with monitoring regional bloggers' activities, but management was unimpressed:

> There is very little info we can use. [Bloggers] have a low intellectual level, and their writing is self-reflection. They don't gather or analyse information. They brag in front of each other.

Asked whether some beats could be outsourced to local bloggers, the *Traditional*'s editor said that although bloggers are "associated with freedom," they are not journalists—and it is not even clear that "they want to be associated with traditional media." According to the Region A bloggers interviewed at this time—both freelancers and full-time reporters—there was some truth in this statement. They tended to view blogging as a form of *sozidanie*, or "creation" outside the machinery of government-driven and commerce-driven journalism. It was a way to escape routine journalism production and write "for intelligent people, for thinkers," as a senior reporter put it. Bloggers perceived themselves as a loose social collective, and for them, the sharing of content was sanctioned by feelings of community. There was a "healthy co-existence" among both freelancers and newspaper journalists according to one blogger, attributing this to the personal familiarity of a small province. Bloggers did not "badmouth" one another, as he said they did in Moscow.

We note that interview participants distinguished this more literary form of blogging from blog posts "made for hire," which was intended to fill holes in newspaper content or boost online traffic. This practice started around 2012–2013. Full-time reporters sometimes produced content for hire in hopes of supplementing their low income, but at their own risk, as promises of payment frequently fell through in the ungoverned online market. A *Private* reporter said she had been writing for an online medium for six months: "They owe me about 50,000 rubles. They are not going to pay."

Also in 2013, the *Government* started exploring more uses of social media. They required reporters to learn to tweet information from iPads during news conferences, giving the editor more control—i.e., the power to "look, change and kill" reporters' content. More important, the editor said, was "the [reporter's] mindset that 'it was published in the print edition and that's enough' has been changed." However, not all agreed this mindset had changed. An online manager said he has seen little social-media initiative from reporters, who still required prompting: "If I ask, they would do." According to the editor, writing for online news is a low bar for reporters, but it is still a hard sell:

> It's difficult to turn "print" reporters toward online news. I am telling them, "If you go to a meeting, come back and write for the site. One more time—I am not requiring you to write a news story while attending the meeting like [our digital and print] reporters do. Come back, write and submit it to online managers."

In 2013, the *Traditional* editor tried to create and register an independent news organization that would focus on engaging audiences. It would stand as a contrast to unpopular state-supported online news agencies:

> We have a number of pro-government news agencies in the city, and people are tired from their propaganda. They might not [even] know the regional government pays [the] agencies. The agencies' information simply doesn't appeal to them.

The editor's idea was to launch a private website that would "appeal to different audiences—gardeners, book lovers, pet lovers, and so forth." He dreamed big, hoping to turn this future online news agency into an online TV channel. Colleagues appreciated the idea but were skeptical. They did not see the project idea as the gold mine that the editor did:

> Traditional journalism is gone; online journalism hasn't been born. Such a mess ... The situation looks like in Alaska in the 18th century—run and grab land. Not sure what will happen next, but the land is rich; most likely, you will be able to dig gold. I have understanding what online journalism is, but I don't have resources. Others have resources, but they don't have understanding.

There was little experimentation at the *Private*, which resisted having a digital issue. The *Private* manager said the paper would not create a website until he knew how to make money from it. This attitude was unsurprising, given the manager's well-known cost-benefit mindset and frugality. A *Private* reporter worked on such an old computer that a technician put a "To morgue," sticker on it, and it sat on the reporter's desk for another year.

In 2018, the *Private* hired a reporter for double duty: writing stories for print and managing a social networking group. According to the editor, the new social media manager was eager to experiment and grow reader engagement. A video-recorded announcement about an upcoming newspaper issue gained 700 views, while another experiment met with less success:

The social media manager even attempted to stream online our direct (phone) lines with officials. It didn't work out—we were getting a lot of rude comments online. And it is boring to watch online an official/expert who sits in an office and speaks on the phone with callers.

The social media manager said that at a national journalism conference, she heard concerns from colleagues across the country about failures to translate online traffic to revenue, and the importance of user engagement. However, she said there had been little time to grow engagement with the social media group. The *Private* editor added that the *Private* would be a profitable, functional online newspaper when a majority of *Private* readers become "digital savvy," but this day seemed far off: "We can't abandon readers who don't have computers; they need a paper issue to read, cut out, and store useful information."

The *Traditional*'s website launched in 2014 as a depository for stories published in the print editions, and no improvements have been made since. The *Traditional* online manager explained that the newspaper lacked resources for a fully functioning website or social media presence:

> To manage a newsfeed, I need to have at least 10 posts every day. We have three reporters who are busy with producing content for a print issue. They are not motivated to write for the website because honorarium is 70 rubles [about $1] for a story. If it's a [rewritten] news release from the internet, it's 40 rubles.

An exception to this halting innovation is the relatively well-funded Region C private newspaper, which has been more aggressive online. Reporters work on special investigative projects for the online space—stories that Region A papers would not address without direction from the government. The online editor mentioned a few examples: "Supervisors' abuse at a juvenile detention centre," and "Shortage of kindergartens in the city." He said these two projects received thousands of likes and reposts on social media. "While re-written news brings clicks, special projects keep the readers interested." In short, the paper's online production runs on two tracks, one that keeps the traffic high on an ongoing basis, and the other that bolsters the paper's legitimacy. "Re-writing" reporters cover breaking news by finding them on other outlets' websites, while "special" reporters, who are better paid, work on "long reads."

Employed by a newspaper with both print and digital copies, the online editor for this Region C paper thought of himself as independent, guided by metrics rather than supervisors: "I don't depend on an army of other people—editors, print and delivery workers—to disseminate news ... I am receiving feedback in the next moment after uploading a story."

Region C papers generally attempted to regulate the online news production process by ensuring at least some stories bring in a certain amount of traffic.

Neither Region A nor Region B had written newsroom policies that formally or strategically tied story selection and production to web metrics. According to the editor of the Region C private newspaper:

> From a professional standpoint, a news story might be valuable, but if the story brings 300 visitors, it's not OK. We sell the number of visitors to advertisers, and the story with 300 visitors would not help ... The task is to produce a news story that assures 2,000 readers and after that work on something that brings lesser traffic. Topics grow, we can't cover all of them—this is why we have rules.

The editor said he occasionally hires a polling company to conduct research on reader preferences, but the data often contradicts their website analytics: "Readers are saying they are tired of чернуха (chernukha, or negative news—e.g., crime, violence), but then we look at traffic and see what kind of news stories evoke interest—"chernukha!" The online editor agreed: People "click on news about car accidents and murder."

The editor said his team worked hard trying to understand the journalism-audience dynamic in an online environment:

> Who forms the news agenda? The audience that dictates it through clicks and shares? Or the media that offer topics and gradually create an interest around them? It is clear that there is a moment of synergy in the process, but who leads in such a game?

Compared to papers in the other regions, Region C had more content variety in its social media. A close reading of Facebook posts showed an emphasis on city news—reconstruction of iconic city buildings (a theater), construction of a new bridge, holiday events and increased popularity of local tourist destinations. However, audience engagement seemed low. It was mainly reporters who "liked" and shared the news, and in fact, posts with the most engagement were related to newsroom activities, like celebrating reporters' birthdays.

Papers in the other two regions are still learning the basics of online news production and are far more comfortable with production and monetization of the print edition. While acknowledging the role of emerging technologies, some participants professed loyalty to print journalism. In 2014, the *Government's* vice-editor called herself a "classical journalist." When production of movies began, she said "some actors moved to the movie industry, and some remained in the theatre." In 2018, the *Government's* editor-in-chief said he has continued to refuse online managers' pressure for resources to manage their online operations, saying his priority is the print edition, which is more relevant: "I can't take better care of an armored train that stands on the side than of people who fight at the forefront."

Inconsistent attention and resources for online processes and training mean the staffs at most papers are at a loss for interpreting online traffic patterns. The

Government's vice-editor said the paper saw a significant increase in weekly traffic from 4,000 or 5,000 in 2015 to 18,000 views in 2019, but they were unsure how to interpret the change. Unable to predict what types of stories will be popular, they aim widely, with unclear strategy. "Often times, online managers say, 'To our surprise, such and such article attracted attention,'" the vice-editor said. "We need diverse articles because we don't always know which story would become popular."

Online production at the Region B newspaper was comparable to the *Government's* online production in terms of updating news feeds and uploading long reads, and the staff was similarly puzzled by users' activities. During a focus group, reporters mentioned their "website had 27,000 visitors yesterday" while the usual number of visitors does not exceed 3,500. Region B reporters had no idea why the change had occurred. One young reporter said the paper's staff was simply out of touch:

> Other newspapers in our region have two staffs—for print and online editions. We don't. Our website editor is not a journalist—she posts stories that were published in print.
>
> Our digital presence is driven by the desire to have a high citation ranking, not to attract readers. We have reporters who don't use computers and refuse to use email … We do need younger reporters because they bring different perspectives.

Region B newspaper's Facebook page attracted little engagement. About 700 people followed the page, which mirrored the website's content, but it was challenging to find a post that was "liked" by at least one person. Newspaper stories shared by the editor on his personal Facebook page were "liked" and shared, suggesting he has supportive friends. Online statistics showed that news stories might have up to 10,000 readers over six months, but readers left no comments. As with other papers in our study, meaningful audience engagement remains out of reach.

Discussion

Many of the obstacles facing online journalism in these regions are identical to those facing online journalism globally: unclear business models and meager revenue, unpredictable audience patterns, work at an unrelenting pace, unauthorized "borrowing" of content, and disconnect from professional value and identity. Yet, some contexts are not as common—notably, a sizable rural segment of the audience with little interest in online media and a cultural allegiance to print, continuing allegiance to print among senior journalists, weak or highly concentrated markets, and not least, an invasive government.

Some of these conditions vary across the regions. Papers in Region C, the wealthiest province of the three, have provided the most sophisticated, meaningful online content, are more hooked in with mobile, and use the most up-to-date analytics-based processes. The poorer Region A has lagged behind the other three, though the *Government* paper has made efforts to ramp up online production. The Region B newspaper has also made such efforts.

Despite sincere efforts by some of the publications, none has really engaged meaningfully with online audiences. Generally, two types of audience predominate in the regions: (1) older and/or rural audiences who are devoted to print, and (2) audiences that skew younger and tend to be better educated and less rural, and are heavy social media users. Seasoned journalists tend to denigrate the second group, calling them "news consumers," a disparaging reference to Western consumerism, rather than "readers."

Digital reporter positions are a consequence of government support: Government finds value in potential capital, and much of this work is apolitical. Digital reporters take up these positions, even finding some cultural capital through story placement in Yandex. Yet, it is not at all clear how much audiences are being engaged or money is being generated, suggesting an institutional orientation, with practices being pursued without clear benefits or goals. There is an ecological quality to these positions as well. These reporters have drifted into the only niche area in the "system" that was available to them. Official news seems of little interest to them or to their readers, and the socio-political journalism of the senior reporters is out of reach.

Senior journalists worry audiences are increasingly losing touch with the meaning of news, mistaking casual social media posts and fabricated sensationalism for news stories. Journalists want to engage with local community, and online media afford a way to do this, but to these journalists, online media also encourage commoditization of audiences, sensationalistic approaches, and confusion about journalism's boundaries. The online space is fluid, and relationships are symbiotic and confusing. As the Region C editor said: "there is a moment of synergy in the process, but who leads in such a game?" Leadership goals at the organizational level is unclear, as news organizations and mass media departments chase elusive audiences, though they know not where. However, at the individual level, we still see ongoing personal interactions between journalists and regional residents, and efforts to reach some shared meaning about local community, and online technology may facilitate these interactions.

Hindering journalists in these processes is their dependence on regional officials. The government has done little to encourage the production of engaging content through the regions' newspapers. They have offered inadequate or uncertain support for audience engagement and for innovative or substantive projects, making it no easier for journalists to bridge the gap between government and citizens. Poor pay, long hours and managers' expectations for high online traffic all undermine quality and pressure digital journalists into ethical violations—e.g., content theft, fabrication and sensationalism. Further, fragmentation and confusion in the online media environment are making it easier for the government to encroach into journalists' "jurisdictional area," though the production of its own websites and social media accounts.

While the online environment in these regions is far from a utopian digital public space, the online network can lead media to connect with one another and with citizens in ways that bypass government: Citizens (though, many are not local) have criticized the governor on social media, while journalists have gained some camaraderie from online communities and have used online networks to share information—a modest boost for journalists' occupational community. But network connections are double-edged, as they also enable stealing of stories, a practice that seems rampant across these regions, and that undermines journalists' occupational community, further obscuring the already unclear boundaries around the local journalism space.

References

Hess, K. & Waller, L. (2017). *Local journalism in a digital world*. London: Palgrave Macmillan.

Kemp, S. (2020). Digital reports: 3.8 billion people use social media. Retrieved August 15, 2020 from https://wearesocial.com/blog/2020/01/digital-2020-3-8-billion-people-use-social-media

Pfanshtil, I. (2019). Pol'zovateli sotssetey v Rossii: statistika i portrety auditoria. Social network users in Russia: statistics and audience portraits. Retrieved May 4, 2020 from https://rusability.ru/internet-marketing/polzovateli-sotssetej-v-rossii-statistika-i-portrety-auditorii/?fbclid=IwAR2YzkcAwtVYU5_nDhzw8lq91u9hXKX_FhzSRSn6TlqGq5RwRD4GmHJuRs4.

Rosstat. (2018). Vyborochnoye federal'noye statisticheskoye nablyudeniye po voprosam ispol'zovaniya naseleniyem informatsionnykh tekhnologiy i informatsionno-telekommunikatsionnykh setey [Selected Federal Statistical Observation on the Use of Information Technologies and Information and Telecommunication Networks by the Population]. Retrieved February 7, 2020 from https://www.gks.ru/free_doc/new_site/business/it/fed_nabl-croc/index.html.

Tendentsii monetizatsii kontenta v Internete. Mediapotrebleniye v Rossii [Trends in monetizing online content. Media consumption in Russia]. (2019). Retrieved February 9, 2020 from https://www2.deloitte.com/ru/ru/pages/technology-media-and-telecommunications/articles/media-consumption-in-russia.html

Vos, T. P., & Ferrucci, P. (2018). Who am I? Perceptions of digital journalists' professional identity, in S. A. Eldridge and B. Franklin (Eds.), *The Routledge Handbook of Developments in Digital Journalism Studies*, pp. 40–52. Abingdon: Routledge.

Zamith, R. (2018). Quantified audiences in news production. *Digital Journalism 6(4)*, 418–435. doi: 10.1080/21670811.2018.1444999

CHAPTER SEVEN

Journalists' Shifting, Versatile Roles

In 2007, a Regional Branch reporter shared a phone conversation he had witnessed at a national journalism conference between a newspaper's editor-in-chief and vice-editor. The vice-editor had called to say that one of their journalists had found compromising material on an oligarch. The oligarchs' PR people had offered to place a $30,000 ad, and the vice-editor asked what to do. Publish the story or the ad? "Many other people knew the journalist worked on the story," the editor-in-chief said, "and this is why the story must be published. As for the money, the oligarch would [keep paying] for [the paper's] friendship anyway." The Regional Branch reporter commented: "A journalist is like a hunting dog. If you kill his desire to go after prey, you would turn him into a lap dog."

In Chapter 3, we noted that a number of logics shape the local Russian journalism space, leading to common roles. Some logics, such as the "moral education" and "literary" logics, are age-old, reproduced through occupational and local community, generation after generation. Others are more consistent with a power-centric approach, with journalists taking positions in accord with, or (less commonly) in opposition to, political and economic power. Power-centric logics, too, are reproduced through journalists' ongoing practice. Practices related to challenging authority diminish not only because the powerful retaliate, but because opposition as a way of thinking—as a familiar, acceptable "logic"—fades, and the "desire is killed," as the editor put it, above. We also argue that journalists and their outlets increasingly follow a "survival" logic, choosing courses of action that help them merely continue on during harsh times. When multiple logics are accessible, opportunities arise for choices and for agency, as the opening anecdote suggests.

We have touched on many of these logics throughout the book. In this chapter, we detail dominant logics and the roles they encourage, discussing evidence for them, their change over time, and possible consequences of their influence.

Perestroika-Era Logic

The era of perestroika and glasnost has been viewed as a "golden age" of Russian journalism (Azhgikhina, 2007). Glasnost, or freedom of speech and publication[1], was, officially, intended to enhance political and economic reforms, or perestroika. Even reporters too young to work during the perestroika era said they perceived it as the "happiest" and "freest" time—a time when reporters were allowed "to practice true journalism" and investigate the powerful. In 2007, a young *Traditional* reporter said she knew well that her older colleagues had been ready to sacrifice personal liberties when they fought the 1991 coup and its goals of extinguishing Gorbachev's reforms. She said it pained her to see perestroika principles betrayed by the region's main types of print outlets—"yellow or pro-governor newspapers, and *никакая* ['neither' by which she meant faceless or worthless] newspapers like the *Traditional*." Ten years later, reflecting on his own perestroika experience, the *Traditional's* editor recalled why investigative journalism became so popular during those years: "Many topics were taboo before perestroika, ... there was a demand for this kind of journalism," and financially independent media could provide it.

During the early years of our research, younger reporters were more likely to express deference to perestroika-era reporters than they were later. Today's younger journalists are more financially pragmatic, as they came of age during the tough economic times of the early 2000s, many in privately owned, digitally oriented outlets (Lowrey & Erzikova, 2013). Older reporters' views of journalism as a professional "mission" to fight for social justice, to seek ways around "government control," and to provide citizens with moral education, clashed with younger journalists' embrace of digital commerce and the idea of journalism as a business and citizens as consumers. Younger digital journalists were increasingly likely to view audiences as commodities and to strive to "beat other online portals with a high reader engagement," as a *Government* digital manager said in 2018. News they gather and share with online readers (e.g., traffic accidents, celebrity gossip) rarely relates to politics or government. As a second *Government* digital manager explained in 2019, older reporters seek political content, but younger reporters avoid "poisoning the news pipeline with official information." These views do not describe the entire sample, as other papers have been slow to adopt and advance digital online practices; however, the appeal of digital commerce is a meaningful marker between the two cohorts.

Financial compensation is a key motivation for ignoring the perestroika-era logic. Perestroika-era journalists have tended to avoid writing stories that contradict professional beliefs—stories that an older *Government* reporter called "clear propaganda stories"—but younger reporters were less picky. In 2015, a beginning *Private* reporter said some reporters at his paper had few scruples about story choices. "If I was told I would get 5,000 rubles [about 100 USD] for a paid story, I would write anything." This motivation is fueled by a need for money, and at some papers, by competition over online metrics. To be fair, younger journalists with their smaller salaries face daunting financial realities. And, pedaling to keep up with a relentless 24/7 news cycle leaves little time for professional self-reflection, which is important for maintaining a perestroika-era sense of mission. Burnout among digital staff is real, according to a *Government* digital manager. "I don't want to come to work," she shared in 2019. "My editor knows that. And I don't see much initiative from reporters."

The professional guard rails of the perestroika era that once discouraged this transactional behavior have worn down. Still, this logic hasn't disappeared—even many younger journalists recognize this as a valued logic. In Chapter 8, we provide numerous examples of journalists still seeking ways to challenge authority, even if by circuitous or latent paths.

Interviews offer some evidence of a budding "digital commerce" logic among journalists and a growing focus on audience numbers, and the apolitical orientation this encourages correlates with regional governments' interests. However, the use of analytics for tracking audiences is uneven and has yet to fully take root: In general, owners, managers and regional government administrators have been slow to explore the full range of digital online practices, though we see them embraced more in Region C than in regions A and B.

Government Service Logic

In Region A, a new and unusual category of professional competition emerged from interviews: the level of dependence on the regional government. *Private* and *Governor* journalists verbally jousted over which paper was more dependent, and in 2010, a *Private* reporter made his claim: "The *Government* reporters say about themselves, 'We are an organ, not a newspaper' [and they say they are] more dependent on the government than we are—we can disagree." But according to *Government* reporters, it's no contest. *Government* reporters say they must attend "*every* event" on long lists of events that officials give them weekly.

A "government service" logic was evident across all three regions. The Region C government encouraged their papers' allegiance through ample funding and close connections between officials and newspaper management. In 2016, a focus-group participant at a privately owned Region C paper put it concisely: "We have only one point of view—the authorities." The publication's editor later said that he "didn't want to jeopardize" his newspaper business by "investigating political figures." Yet, the journalism in Region C was generally more aggressive than regions A or B in covering regional problems, if not officials—for example, the investigation of abuse at juvenile detention centers mentioned in Chapter 6. Region C papers were better compensated by the government and they were on a longer leash, largely because the region was relatively well-off economically, and there was less scrutiny from Moscow. In 2018, the private newspaper in Region C received a large grant, comparable to the considerable subsidies allocated for the *Government* in Region A. The Region C paper kept this news from its readers, but competitors shared it.

Years of dependence on the government have eroded perestroika-era commitment to investigating societal problems. Digging into controversial issues requires a major investment of reporters' time. It means missing opportunities to earn honoraria from writing easy, government-mandated stories. As economic situations in the regions have worsened, reporters have increasingly sought out—or at least they have tolerated—coverage of official events (e.g., news conferences) because such events are "assuredly publishable," as the allocated budget for assigned stories needs to be used, and easy-to-write stories provide easier honoraria.

Too often, when a reporter does commit to doing an investigative story, the government pulls the plug. In 2016, a seasoned *Government* reporter was dissuaded from covering a crumbling apartment building, despite the government's awareness of, and concern about, the problem.

> I went to meet with a group of residents who live in an apartment building that is about to crash. I wanted to write a story, but the editor told me he received a call from government with a request to suspend working on the story, [which] means the article will never be published.

This sporadic interference and on-again, off-again direction creates continuing uncertainty in reporters' minds, weakening motivation to do in-depth work, regardless of a perestroika-era logic or desire to serve the local community.

Dependence on government has also nurtured a naïve allegiance to officials, evident even early in our study. In 2007, a former vice-editor of the *Government* shared an example of the lack of critical thinking among regional journalists that led her to resign. A young reporter had just written a story "about how great the governor was" because he had bought "yellow buses" to transport children from smaller villages to a school in a single larger village. After editing the story, the editor confronted the reporter: "Do you realize the yellow bus is not a symbol of the governor's greatness but [rather] of his inability to rescue dying villages?" The question caught the reporter by surprise. "The reporter did not understand," she said, "that as a journalist he was not supposed to listen to an official who provided him with an 'appropriate' framework for the story, but [should instead] think for himself."

At a 2010 regional journalists' meeting, the *Government*'s managing editor vented her frustration over a "mandatory list" of topics the government gave her to cover. The *Traditional* editor offered a tongue-in-cheek solution: "If you refuse to receive a million rubles a month from the regional budget, the [regional] government would not give you a list of topics." Close reading of the *Government* revealed that at least a fourth of the content of a typical 16-page issue resembled an internal newsletter for regional government officials. "Newspaper stories are akin to an evaluation [from officials' superiors]," said one top *Government* journalist. "Officials do not have other criteria of assessment of their efforts."

Over the years and across all regions we studied, political and economic pressures strengthened, and the government-service logic gained strength as well. Journalists acquiesced to government demands with increasing passivity, assuming these demands fit the natural order. There were fewer flare-ups over limitations on independence or over reporters' lack of critical thinking. Journalists did not always acquiesce quietly; however, their protests often took the form of grumbling over burdensome work, meagre pay and scarcity of time rather than outrage over encroachment into professional autonomy. During a focus group in 2016, one *Government* journalist complained that resources were inadequate to meet the regional government's demands:

> I've seen so many times the vice editor desperately running around to find an available reporter. The [regional] government requires us to attend all events, even not significant ones that can be covered by using a news release. The goal is to imitate [actual] activities. It will be TV coverage, and after that people will tell you, "I saw you on TV." Cheap popularity. [But] we can't be everywhere. If we attend all news conferences, we would not have time to write stories. More financial support is needed if the government wants us to work for them.

However, some journalists have found cultural capital in working for a government-backed newspaper. In a role that recalls Communist-era journalism, *Government* journalists said they felt empowered to keep officials accountable because a published story could encourage officials to respond to newspaper inquiries about problems in the province. "To disregard us means to disregard the governor," said a *Government* vice-editor in 2010. In Chapter 8, we further discuss the strategy of "preventive journalism," in which the threat of publication may spur government action.

Some journalists drew solace from the frequent overlap between the government and journalists' agendas. In 2015, Region B reporters said it was common for a reporter to go on a "press tour" to write about a ribbon-cutting event. While the governor wanted the media coverage, the event might still be newsworthy.

> We would write about the new sports center anyway, but not through the governor—through the facts. All these new buildings—centers, schools—they are for our readers, we would inform them. Simply, we need to pull the blanket a little bit [i.e., give the governor attention because the paper has a contract to cover his activities]. Overall, it will be regular information, with just one last sentence about the governor.

The Region B newspaper editor said he was sure the government's PR service "would not invite reporters on a 'rotten' object," and he noted the coverage also gave exposure to the organization the governor visited: "Opening a new campus at a well-respected university is not just PR for the governor—[the coverage] advances the university, too." Government-mandated stories can do social good, according to a senior *Government* reporter in 2016:

> We don't need to do obvious propaganda. The government requests [our] covering topics that should be covered—social responsibility of business, problem of drug addiction. Some topics we cover even without government recommendations [e.g., tourism, protecting the environment]. It's just official events that drive us crazy.

A *Government* vice-editor, who replaced a less compromising editor at the beginning of our research, provided a complex account of the wide range of obligations regional journalists face. In a 2015 interview, he said he sees no problem in conveying government PR, as it often serves the local people.

> Much of what the government does is for people. Not everything done is against people, right? We explain to people what the government does for them. For example, the government gives grants for farmers. How would they know about them? Not everyone uses the internet, unfortunately. And farmers are busy. We tell about what politics the government leads toward agriculture. We don't serve the interests of one person. We serve the interests of the regional government and Russian government. We tell farmers to apply for the grants. What's wrong with that? Other departments in the

government also share information with us—for example, how a new ambulance system works. We start discussion [usually on Facebook]: Is the system good or bad? We are not a submissive paper. We have normal relationships. They are our founders, they give money. Why did they launch the paper and spend money? For us to write about which dress a celebrity was wearing at a podium? No!

The vice-editor also noted that they couple this reporting with stories about the communities, its people, and everyday life:

We had a meeting with a Russian journalism icon recently—he said short [hard] news stories are losing popularity. Stories about people are replacing news. But we have never stopped writing about [common] people. We were so far behind that we became far ahead. We are so primitive and yet we are alive [as a newspaper]. We keep telling stories about "Uncle Ivan and his goats."

This vice-editor's statement reflects the two historical strains of Russian local journalism: information from the government and the accounts or "chronicles" of everyday people. "Despite our obligations before the government," said one seasoned *Government* reporter in 2015, "we still try to write about ordinary people." The reporter said they did this on their own, without direction from the regional government. Yet, despite the persistence of the two strains, they tend to remain separate, and accounts of the lives of everyday people rarely, if ever, mix in the same stories with state-directed information about policy. The division of the *Government* paper into a section for government and a section "for the people" illustrates this.

The logic of journalistic service to government was disrupted toward the end of our research period, when a new press team for the governor took over in Region A. Confusion in the government-media relationship undermined the government-service logic and disrupted the journalists' "newsletter" role, wherein journalists report to officials about officials. For unexplained reasons, respondents said, the press team restricted access to governmental information. "Now we are told 'you are journalists so find information that you need!'" said a *Government* reporter in a 2019 focus group. "No press releases … but [then] after we went through many obstacles to get news, they would not let us publish it."

A former member of the regional government interviewed in 2019 said the problem is not government control, but rather the government's inexperience in controlling, or overseeing, the media. He gave his explanation for the media-government confusion. Ignorance and apathy play a role, and he said the media, which have become overly passive, share the blame.

The local government does not care about the press. It's a burden for bureaucrats, who simply don't know what to do with all these newspapers. Education is needed—for all of them: reporters, editors, and government officials. As for right now, the government doesn't know how to rule the media except commanding them to publish ten stories per issue about the governor, while the media are not capable of offering alternatives. There is no dialogue between the power and journalists.

Anti-Western Logic

Across the years of data gathering, Region A participants frequently communicated anti-Western sentiments. Animosity toward the West fluctuated, dipping between 2011 and 2014, but rising between 2014 and 2019. We include animosity toward Moscow in this section as well, given the tendency to view Moscow skeptically, as a Western-facing city. Across our participants generally, Western influence was seen as undermining traditional Russian journalism. Moscow was also viewed negatively—in the strident words of one *Traditional* reporter, as a "goddamn place that absorbs everything that contradicts the Russian essence."

A *Private* reporter in 2007 characterized Western journalism in one word: "yellow." The same year, a beginning *Traditional* reporter said she did not think that Western journalistic practices had strongly shaped local Russian journalism: "Western layout of some regional newspapers is the only Western influence I noticed." She had no wish to see Western journalistic influences, which she "associated with a low-taste entertainment." Even the *Regional Branch*, which other local journalists perceived as a "yellow pro-Western" paper, distanced itself from perceived Western-style reporting, as its editor explained in 2010:

> We [Russian journalists] have always been unique, and thank God, now we want to resemble or mimic the West less and less. We have always had a special mentality and journalism, and [there's] nothing wrong with it. Let us be us.

During a 2009 focus group, *Regional Branch* reporters said they believed in "subjectivity with a human face," defined in opposition to their perception of a fact-driven Western journalism. The reporter's task, according to one reporter, was to "immerse yourself in the situation" and evoke warm feelings in readers. The reporter said the paper's most popular article in 2009 told the story of a family of seven children, two of whom were adopted:

> Imagine, a woman gives birth to a fifth child, while her roommate at hospital abandons her twins. A father stands in front of a hospital window, and his wife appears holding three new-borns. She starts crying. He cries too and yells, "Of course, of course!" Do you think it's the end of the story? No! Children grow up, parents work day and night, providing for the kids. Finances are tight ... From time to time the father takes up an accordion and all nine sing, not to feel hunger ...

In contrast, impersonal, neutral reporting was associated with Western journalism. It was perceived as having no news value, as oppositional to the interpretive act that is central to traditional Russian journalism, and as useless for addressing social problems. The *Traditional* editor said he confronted his staff writers every time he found them "hiding behind facts" for the sake of "Western objectivity." Whether you "support or undermine the government," he said, "you cannot be cold-minded like Westerners."

Western journalism is also linked with a sensationalism that serves the commercial aims of private owners and that many participants felt poisoned the social environment during the early post-perestroika years. In 2015, the *Government* vice-editor shared her past experience working for a publication headquartered in Moscow, which openly positioned itself as pro-Western:

> I worked for a while for a private yellow newspaper. I was able to avoid the yellowness. I decided to work for the paper to research the phenomenon of its popularity. Well ... It was serving a private interest. The owner had, I would say, necrophilia—he demanded blood and death [in the stories]. When you work for a state paper, you are protected from this kind of crap. I am from the Soviet Union, and I stick to a socio-political newspaper.

The Region B newspaper also distanced itself from Western-like reporting, largely perceived as driven by sensationalism. During a focus group, a reporter contrasted sensationalism with the journalistic role of educating the public:

> Of course, sensational stories sell the paper. But what kind of education will we offer if we publish yellow info? We will raise a generation that is not capable to think—just to consume. Our strength is our ability to connect and analyse facts and offer serious publications. People value analytical journalism.

For some reporters, negative attitudes toward Western journalism went hand in hand with hostile feelings toward the West. In 2019, a seasoned *Private* reporter said that "it is not only the Russian government that is anti-West—we are all anti-West." He explained:

> Look at history, look how the West has tried not to let Russia develop into a strong country. We especially dislike Americans. Russia helped so many countries to achieve independence—Poland, Czechoslovakia and other—and they all betrayed us many times. The older the person becomes, the more skeptical he would be about the West.

Another reporter perceived strong anti-American sentiment among the regions' population, but thought many journalists rejected the sentiment.

> A majority [of residents] are patriots here ... They believe that [the West] wants to conquer us, and we are the best country in the world. The local authorities speak

publicly about [the West] wanting to turn us into slaves, but I haven't seen or heard it in the media reporting. It means that regional reporters have common sense.

A few reporters said they had no negative attitudes toward the West. In 2015, one declined to participate in newsroom conversations about the 2014 Crimea's annexation, not wanting to reveal disagreement. Another reporter preferred not to "advertise" personal feelings about the West because of the "anti-West climate in the paper and beyond," a climate that sometimes influences reporter's decision-making about stories:

> My internal censor has been turned on. For example, I am asking a person about her achievements and she is mentioning the Soros fund. I know I will not mention it [in the story] because attitudes toward America are quite complicated now.

However, anti-Moscow sentiments were a strong uniting factor among regional journalists. The Russian capital—"a greedy, selfish city" as a *Traditional* reporter put it in 2008— was contrasted with the heartland and its hardworking people, suffering humbly from Moscow-driven injustices. Early in our study an official blamed Moscow for the regions' poor journalism labor pool: "Moscow has been sucking up the best provincial professionals for more than 15 years." Journalists echoed this opinion throughout the study. "Moscow lives at the expense of provinces," according to a *Traditional* reporter in 2012, and according to a *Regional Branch* reporter in 2013, "a reporter has to move to Moscow if he wants to build a career."

Adverse feelings toward Moscow even led local journalists to distance themselves from their fellow journalists in Moscow. In June 2019, a Russian investigative reporter, Ivan Golunov, was arrested in Moscow on fabricated drug charges that were later dropped, and thousands of Russian reporters signed a petition supporting Golunov. *Meduza*, the independent outlet he reported for, encouraged other media to reprint Golunov's anti-corruption stories. Asked if any newspaper in Region A would answer the call and disseminate his work, our participants gave a definitive "no." A manager for the *Government* explained that it would be difficult to evoke support for "a reporter from Moscow" among regional reporters: "Capital reporters have high salaries, and [no capital reporters] sympathize with us when we are eating bread without salt." Her colleague shared more evidence of a capital-regional gap:

> As a winner of an all-Russia journalistic competition, I went to Moscow to pick up the prize. One of the organizers said, "I understand that it's difficult for regional reporters to live on 30,000–40,000 rubles a month." What?! We get 15,000 at best!

A seasoned reporter explained that local journalists view the Golunov case as only tangentially relevant to regional journalists because the journalist involved falls outside the occupational community of regional journalists.

All regional journalists followed the Golunov case, [but only] some people are very active and followed the case very closely. Some were indifferent. It's his personal story. It's not an 'all Russia war.' It's a war of certain circles.

One reporter spoke of oppositional media (which Golunov worked for) as something "other": "It's not clear for whom they work and who pays them."

Social Mission Logics

Throughout the book, we've argued that local Russian journalism is historically grounded in two very different traditions: (1) institutional accounts that reflect the powerful, usually in passive or supportive ways but sometimes in opposition, and (2) accounts of everyday people. The perception that journalism is, first and foremost, a social mission that works with everyday people developed centuries ago and was reinforced in Soviet times (Azhgikhina, 2007; Esin, 2000). The educational purposes of the Soviet-era worker-peasant correspondents (*rabselkory*) are a good example (Hopkins, 1970). We found several logics to be consistent with this "social mission" idea—a logic of moral education, a literary logic, and a "life-hacking" logic that focuses on people's everyday problems—and we discuss these below. We note that these logics are largely apolitical, encouraging content that frames the region's people in the context of their personal and "everyday life" (Hanitzsch & Vos, 2018), as opposed to framing them as a "public" in the context of civic life, in the Western democratic tradition.

Moral Education Logic

The moral education logic is consistent with Dzyaloshinsky's "journalism of compassion" for ordinary people (cited in Strovsky [2004]), focusing journalists on content that encourages virtuous, unprofane and uplifting qualities of people's lives. Practicing journalists have reproduced this age-old logic across time. It is generally encouraged by the state, and it continues to contour local journalism practices.

As we've argued in previous studies (e.g., Erzikova & Lowrey, 2010), many regional journalists have considered themselves moral educators, or "spiritual and practical advisers to ordinary people." They have "sought to lift spirits through 'stories that make [readers] better' and 'stories that evoke emotions'" (p. 8). One *Traditional* reporter said in 2019 that she wanted to focus on a "different, better world" in her writing—one that "helps people become purer, better."

The role of journalist as moral educator is evident in interviews throughout the data-gathering period. In 2007, a manager for the *Traditional* said journalists must bypass authorities who "do not allow telling [political] truth" by finding a politics-free niche in which to practice truth-telling in a community-service context. According to a *Traditional* senior reporter in 2007, the newspaper could assist the church with its mission.

> Americans go to church and listen to a priest who talks about morals. In Russia, mainly old women go to church. A newspaper fills this vacuum—talks about morals. If the newspaper abandons its moral education mission, it would be a catastrophe. People would be deprived from having access to a spiritual source.

A *Private* reporter said she practiced "mass psychotherapy" by "writing about families with successful parents and happy children":

> Some reporters are fueled by criticism ... Not me. I don't use criticism unless it's a quote from people whom I interview. It's my credo. I want to bring "reasonable, good, eternal" [сеять разумное, доброе, вечное - a quote from a poem] to the newspaper page. When I write a feature story about a family, I will write about a good family—not about a family with hungry children. To finish all stories positively is important in every situation.

A senior reporter for the *Government* in 2013 also viewed herself as a "mass psychotherapist" and, somewhat bemusedly, she viewed the local paper as enacting a tired yet somehow reaffirming ritual that provides people with ongoing reassurance:

> Do we function as society's psychotherapists by giving readers моральные костыли (moral crutches)? Maybe. I guess we provide a sense of stability. A reader opens the *Government* and immerses himself into unbridled enthusiasm. We publish the same crap year after year. The same minister of agriculture, the same eternal fight for harvest ... [But] even I want to live after reading our paper.

In 2015, an award-winning reporter for the *Government* newspaper discussed a routine for writing uplifting stories about exemplary ordinary people. "It's a skillfully crafted morale: a story's impoverished and unselfish character dedicated to helping others carries a classical interpretation of the good and the bad." The routine is effective—so effective, the reporter said, that the stories may also inspire journalists: "We ourselves read the stories and think we should follow the character's example."

For some journalists, the papers' "uplifting" and reaffirming content comes more from a sense of obligation to both everyday readers and to the state than from journalists' own beliefs. The *Government* senior reporter continues:

This sense of the "moral crutches:" People in remote villages do read the paper, and they take it seriously. In a village, I met with our readers who started a conversation by saying, "You wrote about patriotism …" I was about to cry. I felt that we deceive these people. We write it because we know we are obligated to cover this kind of topic, but they think it's coming from our hearts!

"Uplift" takes the form of cultural education as well. According to the *Government's* editor, art education can "elevate" the reader. A *Traditional* manager sees cultural education as lifting a person "above routine."

We cover not only utilitarian news (crime, utility bills), but also write about theatre, history, Christianity … Topics that might expand a person's horizon, educate him and touch his soul. Educational function is important.

Five focus group participants in Region B in 2015 were united in their perceptions of a newspaper as a moral educator and readers who want to be emotionally moved. "We are responsible before our readers" one reporter said. "We want to help them educate their children and grandchildren as individuals with morals." Said another, "Indeed, our newspaper has been моральный камертон [a moral tuning fork] for a few generations." And said a third: "When we meet with our readers, especially in rural areas, they thank us for publishing stories that make them think, [for] stories that touch them and make them reconsider their deeds."

However, moral education does not seem as strong a priority in Region C. A Region C editor said he had doubts that a "moral educator" approach was appropriate in economic hard times, though he respected the "normativity of moral upbringing." He said that someone "hanging on a cleft fighting for his life" is not likely to be interested in "moral talk." Rather, "he needs a hand." One of the paper's senior reporters added that because "moral education" can be emotionally depressing, she has found that readers may avoid these stories in tough times, to prevent "душевная боль (heartache)."

Literary Logic

To sustain the tradition of Russian journalism as moral and spiritual uplift, said an accomplished *Government* reporter in 2012, journalists must "be gifted writers who are able to 'глаголом жечь сердца людей' [burn people's hearts with words] to inspire the people to become better." A literary logic is grounded in Russia's proud literary history and the important place of journalism in this history. According to Solganik (2017), the language of mass media should "cultivate and maintain a high level of speech culture in society" and must be "flexible, in order to express all the subtleties and innovations of the cultural process" (p. 20). Klushina (2017) argued that mass media should outline "the contours of a new humanism, understood as the search for spirituality, harmony and aesthetics of human existence in the information age" (p. 27). A mass media language that reaches for these heights is worthy of serving as "the shared language of the nation" (Konrad cited in Solganik, 2017, p. 18).

Traditionally, Russian journalism has been a literature-centric journalism, with commenting/reasoning and facts being equally important to a story (Vartanova & Azhgikhina, 2011), and a typical journalism education features the study of world literature and discursive analysis of journalistic writing (Lukina & Vartanova, 2017). However, rapid changes in all spheres of life during perestroika brought new developments into the journalism profession, including admiration of a less literary Western-style reporting. The adoption of facts without comments, shorn of malleable interpretation, was one effort to overcome the Soviet propagandistic heritage: Artful language is a more easily manipulated language, and the powerful have the resources to drive the manipulation and shape interpretation. But the pendulum swung too far, according to Vartanova & Azhgikhina (2011). Russian journalism "lost a lot," they said, "when it adopted the American model "as an absolute ideal"—particularly its requirements that "a fact should not be commented in a broader context by journalists" (p. 74).

Interviews suggest literary journalism has been slowly re-establishing itself in regional newsrooms—if not always in practice then at least as an aspiration. This resurgence seems attributable to old-guard journalists who started their careers before perestroika and act as carriers of traditional journalism culture. The gift of being a newspaper writer rather than a news transmitter is cultural capital among regional journalists in ours study, and when discussing inherent qualities of facts, journalists tend to emphasize their "dryness" more than their "accuracy." Praise of literary writing was commonly heard across newsrooms and across the years, among both senior and junior staff, even if it was not practiced by all. In 2007, a young *Traditional* reporter said that during her internship at another newspaper, she was repeatedly reminded, "everyone can put together a few sentences of a news story but only one of thousands becomes a journalist." In 2009, a *Regional Branch* manager said she could guess "who authored a story just looking at very first lines." To her, "a style of writing is not less important than content."

Literary writing in newsrooms tends to be typified as feature writing in the newspaper newsrooms—colorful narratives of individuals facing challenges, infused with moral lessons. Even some digital reporters who have never published a story, and who scoffed at artful language, gave grudging respect to "print" journalists who wrote literary features. A digital reporter in one newsroom called feature writers "journalists from God" (Erzikova & Lowrey, 2020). Region B newspaper managers made every attempt to assure each issue had a feature story that would "bring a family together to discuss it," as an editor said in 2015. While he said "no significant news should be missed," it's the feature story that "makes a newspaper stand out among hundreds of others."

While praise for literary journalism was common across the years, concerns increased that literary journalism and the journalistic essay were a dying art. Growing government demands, journalist's need for financial survival, and changing values, practices, technologies and forms among newer generations of journalists were hindrances. While a Region C reporter said in 2016 that she embraced the idea that "journalism is storytelling, not fact sharing," she feared that the literary form was waning. "Those who were able to set the tone," she said, "either left journalism for PR or write 'fast-food' articles to earn money." The Region C editor shared his bleak perspective. Asked about literary journalism, he shot back, "Какие, блин, очерки! [What damn essays!], we don't [even] have time to fill pages with breaking news!" The internet, he said, was a "huge-huge dumpster [that is] killing journalism and especially literary journalism."

These concerns were also heard earlier in our research, though they were not as common. In 2007, a *Traditional* editor bemoaned the loss of literary writing. He had tired of "articles written like справка [a 'reference']." Reminded of his 2007 quote in 2019, the editor said he "knew journalism would be in crisis," but he did not expect that the "most acute problem would be a shortage of writers, not censorship."

Life-Hacking Logic

With economic conditions worsening in the 1990s, regional reporters who came of age during perestroika became more cautious about challenging authorities, as lawsuits bankrupted news outlets, advertisers stayed away, sensationalism lured many readers, and public-issue news lured few. Journalists increasingly felt the need to grow audiences while avoiding confrontation with political-economic elite. Many journalists also felt the pull to help the many people in their communities who suffered from the economic fallout while caught in the slow grind of government bureaucracy.

The region's people needed help with everyday, practical problems: advice about car repair, gardening, home finance, new government regulations and paperwork, health and safety. These problems opened a niche for journalists in the local ecology. This "life-hacking" niche, as journalists called it, involved researching of problems and providing people information, often on demand. "Life-hacking" brought journalists closer to the people and fostered trust.

Life-hacking aims at personal, individual-level problems. It generally falls outside the public sphere, as it has traditionally addressed no macro-level, societal issues. Many reporters have seen little difference between micro and macro, however. Stories about "personal finances and family budget," said a *Private* reporter in 2015, "is no less important than to talk about an economic situation in the country."

Generally, reporters at Region A papers—the *Traditional, Private, Regional Branch* and to a lesser extent, the *Government*—took pride in prioritizing the ordinary interests of ordinary people. The *Private* and *Traditional* were especially active in this area. Early in our study, they saw themselves as "on a mission" to provide librarian-like assistance for readers (Erzikova & Lowrey, 2010). Reporters regularly published advice found in books for handymen and housewives, insisting their readers had no access to these sources. They said publishing this advice also helped the papers commercially, as it attracted readers. The *Traditional* became, in the words of one reporter, a "factory of useful tips" through stories focused on medical advice and self-treatment, and a gardening supplement that included gardening tips, cost-cutting strategies, and recipes from affordable ingredients. The *Private* produced an "assembly line" of mundane tips, bus schedules, moon calendars, addresses of retail stores selling seeds, and more.

The *Government* also provided "life-hacking" tips, though managers and staff did not see this practice as part of the paper's core mission. Providing "down-to-earth" tips—for example, "how to make cottage cheese at home"—was "a divergence from the paper's goals" of providing (government-produced) socio-political information, a senior reporter said in 2011. In 2015, journalists at the Region B paper, also traditionally a socio-political paper, shared a similar attitude in a 2015 focus group. "Our role is to inform and analyse," a reporter said, "and not to provide shallow information."

The "life-hacking" approach became a way for some journalists to lower the volume on government propaganda, or to counterbalance government PR, as a Region C reporter said. This content also provided citizens with practical mechanisms for dealing with the government. In 2007, two *Regional Branch* reporters shared their approach for turning government-ordered stories into content that ordinary people could actually use. "Instead of praising the officials for organizing the City Day," one said, "we published the event schedule." According to the *Private* editor in 2015, use of officials' quotes served multiple purposes: Publishing their quotes made officials happy, and by focusing on the quote's practical content, journalists could provide daily help to readers while avoiding officials' self-aggrandizement.

People, especially during a financial crisis, don't care about politicians. They think of themselves, families, living conditions and kopeks. Of course, we would cite an official saying that the cost of a bus ticket for retirees went down, but the emphasis would be on the price, not the official.

We note that many of our research participants have seen "life-hacking" tips as genuinely helpful for readers while also viewing the practice as something less than journalism. A sense of humor helped to deal with the dissonance. During a focus group, *Private* reporters noted that during slow times, they have to "think outside the box" for life-hacking advice: "For example," a reporter said, "if you crossbreed a rooster and a pig, you will have not only pork but also eggs."

By 2010, the *Private* had graduated from simply re-typing useful tips from books to providing instructions on how to protect rights while dealing with bureaucrats. Their "self-help" information was starting to encompass more problems related to public life, according to the paper's publisher.

> We realized that people were tired of simplified utilitarian articles like how to grow dill in the kitchen. We moved to another niche. Now we arm ordinary people with documents to allow them to protect their rights.

According to *Private* journalists, this approach improved their relationship with the community. In 2015, a reporter recalled a conversation with a grateful villager.

> A few years ago, I went to a remote village. An older man looked at me and said, "I know you! Thank you for the advice on how to get benefits for schoolteachers you published a few years ago. I followed your instruction and won." And he asked if I didn't mind to take a picture with him.

In 2019, *Private* focus group participants said they published life-hacking information to save people money, educating people about opportunities that are hidden, intentionally or not. Close reading of *Private* issues revealed that at least a quarter of all published stories in an issue provided life-hacking information. In one issue, information was published on how to check accuracy of utility bills, obtain free medication, reduce monthly spending, protect skin from the sun, and rescue a drowning person. The *Private* also puts readers in touch with officials through a "direct line," where an official comes to the newsroom and takes phone calls—for example, a reader having trouble scheduling surgery was able to talk directly with a health official.

Interviews suggested journalists were further encroaching into the work of government bureaucrats, as the region's bureaucratic processes could seem dysfunctional and opaque to local residents, requiring work-arounds and readable instructions. Reporters increasingly helped citizens negotiate governmental red tape. Midway through our research, journalists, particularly at the *Private*, began publicizing people's struggles, interpreting government regulations, and navigating work-arounds in the system. The "life-hacking" role grew and continued to encroach into the governmental space over the study period—partly a consequence of people's economic struggles and a lumbering bureaucracy.

Survival Logic

An ecological framework allows us to look beyond professional goals as we shed light on these journalists' behaviors. The dire economic and political situation within which regional journalists work warrants a logic of a mere adaptive survival for these journalists—a framework that can constrain or redirect the influences of other logics. Increasingly over the years, this logic has colored the decisions of all journalists in our sample, but it has been most evident in Region A.

Each year, without prompting, journalists brought up the topic of low salaries. "[Region A] is the worst region in Russia based on salaries," said a *Traditional* reporter in 2015. "Even TV reporters complain." Papers in the two other regions have also suffered, if somewhat less than Region A media. These regions also have recently been working in "survival mode," as the Region B editor said, as a result of economic and political pressure, social apathy, and fragmentation of the journalism workforce. In 2016, a Region C reporter said that "like everyone in Russia, we [journalists] are periodically forced to survive … surviving is ingrained in us."

In 2019, the *Government* editor painted a bleak picture of the overall financial situation for regional newspapers. This picture would not seem unfamiliar to many newspaper managers in other countries—e.g., scant ad revenue, high newsprint costs.

> I am networking with colleagues from different regions. Same picture is everywhere. Paper and printing prices go up. The main source of advertising—small and medium size business—go down. Where to get money? Newspapers have to cut the number of pages and staff positions—the quality goes down. Four to five years ago, *raionki* [small newspapers in rural areas] attracted staffers with degrees in education and social work because salaries were higher in newspapers. Now these staffers go back because salaries grow in education and social work. We have grown our earnings, but our spending grew faster. Prices on printing paper kill us. It's unimaginable.

Editors try to distribute pay fairly, but the pay is paltry, and managers and staff struggle, regardless of how it is distributed. "I feel like I am at the level of a cleaning lady—morally and financially," said the *Government*'s managing editor, a mother of two children. "Half of my salary goes to utilities bill."

In 2015, the *Traditional's* managing editor explained the government's lack of support for his paper.

> They know that even if our salaries will be cut five times, we will still show up for work. Because we need to go to do something every day. It's like in the early post-Soviet times—plant/factory workers were not paid for months, but they were still coming to work, hoping the situation would be changed for the better tomorrow.

Amid tough times, competition for space to produce stories for honoraria has grown, and attention to quality has waned. As a *Traditional* reporter said in response to her editor's plea for quality, she preferred "quick and easy money over the endless creative torture" of writing competition-winning stories (Lowrey & Erzikova, 2010). In 2012, a seasoned *Government* reporter admitted that she—like others in her newsroom—met a reporter's resignation with joy: "More space for my stories," which would mean higher monthly honoraria. To prevent tension over scarce space, *Private* managers divided newspaper issues among its reporters and let them police the "trespassers" on their own. Conflicts still arose. In 2011, a young reporter complained that a senior reporter had demanded that she give her back "a quarter of the page." The older reporter explained that the beginning reporter submitted a half-page story instead of the budgeted quarter-page story. "My honorarium suffered."

The logic of mere survival altered practices in various ways, as journalists adapted to tough times. Journalists value working from home, which has allowed them to earn more honoraria for stories. In 2015, *Private* reporters complained that management required them to be physically present to participate in meetings and receive assignments; however, reporters earned only 150 rubles (~$2) an hour during "office" hours, and their story-writing productivity suffered from distractions. Journalists have adopted a pace of constant work, as most hold jobs on the side—another trend that is familiar to local journalists in other countries. Working from home is also popular because it makes it easier to write for other publications and earn money working side jobs, away from managers' eyes. A senior reporter said in 2019 that she had no days off: "As a managing editor for a 'side' paper, I work during weekends." An editor added that "everyone has a job on the side," and not all are journalism-related:

> One of our reporters spends her vacation working as a teacher at a children's summer camp because she doesn't have any other opportunity to take her own children out of the dusty city. If she had money to pay for her children's camp, she would not work during her vacation.

Mentioned in Chapter 5, tight resources across the regions, while sparking some competition, has also fostered occupational community in latent ways among regional journalists, who covertly share opportunities for freelance work.

Across papers in Region A, the need to survive has eroded perestroika-era logic and the will to fight for journalists' autonomy. An award-winning *Government* reporter pinned regional journalists' lack of support for Moscow journalist Ivan Golunov on local journalists' meager salaries: "Nobody is ready to risk for an idea," he said. "Everyone has obligations to relatives, a fear to lose money."

In 2019, *Traditional* focus group participants agreed that, in principle, journalism "is not serfdom" and that it is important to criticize power. But they were not able to recall examples of criticism. In defense, a reporter said, government criticism "is stupid" in the current climate. They did not want to "bite a hand that gives them bread." Another reporter shouted, "What bread? A piece of crust!"

Discussion

A number of logics are shaping local Russian journalism, ranging from the politically oriented to the community oriented, and this repertoire of multiple logics provides choices and unexpected directions for action.

The logic of the perestroika era is still evident among older journalists, and it is still respected, if not followed, by most younger journalists. However, a budding logic of digital commerce is rising alongside the perestroika-era logic, framing readers as countable units rather than as citizens or local residents.

A government-service logic is age-old—one of the original "strains" in local Russian journalism. The logic is strongly reproduced through daily practice, and it is reinforced through a variety of government practices. Mandated attendance at government events— particularly for papers that officially represent the government, like Region A's *Government*—robs journalists of time for reporting and writing. Low salaries coupled with honoraria encourage production of easy-to-write government-mandated stories. Pay-per-story honoraria also discourage in-depth, investigative work (particularly in Region A). Economic conditions have increased dependence on government support, e.g., through paid government contracts that determine or constrain coverage. Yet, some journalists found cultural capital in reporting the "socio-political" information required in government-backed papers. This was common at papers like the *Government*, that were close to the regional government administratively and financially, suggesting a translation of economic capital to cultural capital. The *Government's* socio-political tradition is also a factor, as it is at the Region B paper. "Socio-political" content was viewed as far preferable to "Western" sensationalism, and many journalists have come to define this content as consistent with the regions' social needs.

A growing anti-Western/anti-Moscow logic encourages and sanctions the move away from "fact-based" journalism, which is viewed as devoid of compassion and interpretive meaning. This logic has complex consequences. It reinforces both the moral education logic and government service logics, neither of which encourages investigation of public issues. It encourages an embrace of traditional provincial life, unsullied by big-city, Western influences, consistent with Putin's claims that true patriotism lies in the heartland. To the degree that journalists embrace this idea (not all do), it can bind journalists more closely with local residents but distance them from the wider national journalistic profession.

Both moral education and literary logics encourage a focus on lifting the spirits and moral character of local residents. The emphasis is apolitical and community-oriented—the focus is on improving individual-level character rather than on improving society. The aesthetics and inspiration of literary writing are put in the service of these aims, bolstered by the cultural capital that excellent writing brings the journalist. These logics are age-old, they are reproduced in school, and both moral education and literary forms have been heralded across they study period. However, according to participants, the literary logic has not been consistently reproduced in practice, suggesting this logic may be waning. Yet, both logics offer a unique "safe haven" in the ecosystem—a rare position allowing journalists to serve the people in a way that does not challenge the government.

The life-hacking logic is also community-oriented. While it is mostly apolitical, the service to readers that this logic encourages has edged toward subtle judgment of government actions, offering a possible back door to criticism of officials, particularly at the *Private*.

Finally, the logic of mere survival colors and stains all of the roles and practices that journalists pursue. Strategies for survival lead to unexpected practices—i.e., working from home away from managers' eyes, and sharing of "side job" opportunities among journalists, both of which can encourage occupational community. As they seek to adapt, journalists continue to try to straddle service to government with service to the people while maintaining some occupational legitimacy. Life-hacking journalism seems to hold some promise for journalists, at least in the short term, though more purely socio-political journalists deride these kinds of stories. Life-hacking allows journalists to both dutifully report government information and help stressed citizens with practical problems, while it may provide an opening for critique of government policies and actions, if only implicitly.

Note

1. We note the point that glasnost is not "synonymous with freedom of the press," as party authorities were able to limit freedoms when threatened (Rulyova, 2010, p. 232).

References

Azhgikhina, N. (2007).The struggle for press freedom in Russia: Reflections of a Russian journalism. *Europe-Asia Studies, 59*, 1245–1262.

Erzikova, E., & Lowrey, W. (2010). Seeking safe ground: Russian regional journalists' withdrawal from civic service journalism. *Journalism Studies, 11(3)*, 343–358.

Erzikova, E., & Lowrey, W. (2020). Poverty and morality: A field theory analysis of Russia's struggling provincial journalism. *Demokratizatsiya, 28*(3), 345–366.

Esin, B. I. (2000). *History of Russian Journalism*. Moscow: Nauka.

Hanitzsch, T. & Vos, T.P. (2018). Journalism beyond democracy: A new look into journalistic roles in political and everyday life. *Journalism 192*(2), 146–164.

Hopkins, M. W. (1970). *Mass media in the Soviet Union*. New York: Pegasus.

Lowrey, W., & Erzikova, E. (2013). One profession, multiple identities: Russian regional reporters' perceptions of the professional community. *Mass Communication and Society, 16*(5), 639–660.

Lukina, M. & Vartanova, E. (2017). Journalism education in Russia: How the academy and media collide, cooperate, and coexist. In R. S. Goodman and E. Steyn (Eds.), *Global journalism education in the 21st century: Challenges and innovations*, pp. 155–174. Knight Center for Journalism in the Americas, Austin: University of Texas at Austin.

Rulyova, N. (2010). Television news and its satirical interpretation in Medvedev's Russia: Is glasnost back? *Russian Journal of Communication, 3*(3–4): 229–248.

Solganik, G. Ya. (2017). Yazyk SMI i kul'tura [Media language and culture]. *Aktual'nyye Problemy Stilistiki, 13*, 13–25.

Klushina, N. I. (2017). Gumanisticheskaya kontseptsiya sovremennykh massmedia [The humanistic concept of modern mass media], *Aktual'nyye Problemy Stilistiki, 13*, 26–29.

Vartanova, E., & Azhgikhina, N. (2011). *Dialogi o zhurnalistike [Dialogs about journalism]*. IREX Russia and Moscow: MGU.

CHAPTER EIGHT

Cracks in the System: Journalists' Pursuit of Autonomy

One evening in summer 2019, a group of concerned citizens blocked a federal highway to protest foreign companies buying enterprises in their town. The group interrupted busy traffic after local officials refused to discuss the issue. Police rushed to the area. A few activists were detained, enflaming the situation, and social media exploded with rumors about protesters' injuries and deaths. The following morning, the Government newspaper was in turmoil as reporters unsuccessfully tried to gather information about the night before. Governor and police press services ignored inquiries, so a reporter called the town administration. An official unexperienced in dealing with media provided a truthful comment. Within a few minutes, a news story had been uploaded to the Government website, and the regional government had called the newspaper. A bureaucrat yelled at the reporter, accusing her of undermining regional authority and insisting the headline, "Government will attempt to resolve the conflict," be changed to "Government will resolve the conflict." The headline was edited, but a social media manager had already shared the story with the original headline through her fake social network accounts. She knew the web story would be heavily edited. "Nobody would come to read this news on the website," she said. "All the people are on social media."

Local Russian journalists, constrained by an oppressive political and economic environment, still pursue opportunities to challenge officials, inform communities and help solve residents' problems. Opportunities emerge as narrow and sometimes unexpected cracks in the system. These "cracks" are situations in the political-economic landscape that the elite find difficult to control, choose to overlook, or are blind to. They may arise because of fissures or inconsistencies between layers of government—between national and regional, or between regional and municipal. They may arise because government control has not caught up with new technologies and social change, or because of a gap in communication and understanding between local officials and local citizens, which journalists can help bridge.

Journalists in this study have challenged the powerful on behalf of citizens in only modest ways. Journalists do not typically assert themselves with "the strength of grass," in the words of a *Government* newspaper reporter—powerfully and up from the roots, breaking through pavement above. While some challenges have involved direct opposition, more often, challenges have involved adaptation to cracks of opportunity, which have been afforded by the multiple logics that contour the space.

Fissures between Layers of Government

Complex relationships between regional governments and the federal government have shaped news production in Region A. Local officials, dependent on and submissive to Moscow authorities, have worked to control the regional government's image in the regional media. To summarize what research participants have said over the years: Moscow expects the governor and regional administration to monitor the competence of the local bureaucracy and the welfare of the region, and national officials scrutinize regional officials' success or failure. Region A local papers are expected to help regional officials by collecting information on local problems and either publishing the information or, more likely, showing it to officials before publication. The governor and other officials may then act on the problems, and they may be seen in the media as acting on the problems (Erzikova & Lowrey, 2014).

It's not clear how effective this has been as a PR strategy for Region A officials. *Government* reporters said the Kremlin tracks the regional governor's *media rating* as determined monthly by the Russian media monitoring company Medialogia, based on the number of mentions in the media. "The governor's visibility is important for the Kremlin," said one reporter. "If the media cover him, it means residents know he is working." The press service insisted that news about the governor be published on the cover or second page of the *Government* and the *Traditional* to signal importance to readers. A look through a typical *Government* and *Traditional* issue shows that around a fifth of the stories (roughly five of 25 stories) relate to the governor and his ministers, and these stories are prominently placed: stories about government meetings, about the governors' comments on social media, about United Russia's good deeds, and reports from regional ministers such as the Ministry of Agriculture's harvest prognosis—all take an optimistic, business-like tone, reminiscent of the Soviet era.

This prominent placement suggests readers are eager for news about the governor. But in reality, the *Government* reporter said, regional citizens are "irritated" by the "intensive coverage of the governor because the coverage does not match the reality." Another reporter pointed out that many of the regions' residents do not use the "rated" mainstream government-supported media—less than half do, based on recent statistics. The reporter thought it was fairly common for residents' "digitally savvy relatives" to share information from "alternative information sources"—for example, from Russian opposition leader Alexei Navalnyi's YouTube channel.

Journalists do not always jump when Moscow calls. National politicians have commonly sought publicity in the regional media, to the annoyance of journalists, and during this study, several calls were observed at the *Government* paper. In 2008, a *Government* vice-editor angrily dropped the phone after a conversation with a Moscow politician's PR manager. The vice-editor said she would appeal to the regional government to stop "all these Moscow politicians who want to litter the *Government* with their nonsense." Business leaders headquartered in the regions have been less likely to seek publicity in the regions we studied: They assume regional newspapers are seeking paid content, and they worry that the wrong kind of publicity may incur Moscow's wrath. This suggested the newspaper is "still a power," as one *Government* reporter said, "if [business leaders] are afraid we can write something that will upset Moscow."

Region B and C participants did not appear to be as concerned about Moscow-regional government relationships. Though these relationships were not entirely stable, a Region C editor said they generally had shifted in his province from "thorny and complicated to relatively calm" during the years of data gathering. The editor said he has "stayed away from political games in principle." The Region B editor was more concerned about the daily work and the challenges of having "a huge volume of information to process."

There can also be a disconnect between municipal and regional governments. City mayors may be aligned with powerful Moscow politicians who undermine the regional governor, or mayors and governors may be aligned with different political-business groups within the same region, leading to tension. This was the case in Region A, prior to our period of study. The *Traditional* newspaper was owned by the city's mayor, who was at odds with the region's governor. Resulting tensions between the *Traditional* and *Government* papers provided more opportunity for reporting of conflict in the region. The mayor lost power, leaving the *Traditional* underfunded and toothless, and marking the end of serious regional/municipal fissures within Region A. However, the mere fact that municipal and regional governments function separately can present "cracks" in the governing system that lead to opportunities for journalists. An example is the village official in the chapter's opening anecdote who shared information about the protest when regional officials would not.

Preventive Journalism

Despite tensions with the national level, most regional journalists saw little value in revealing the region's problems if it led to reduced funding from Moscow. Even in the early years of our research, Region A journalists generally considered investigative reporting of political corruption and economic crime to be self-destructive. To do so could jeopardize the government's financial support and risk claims of legal violations that could bankrupt a paper. It could also result in less revenue for the region. Very few participants across all regions showed much interest in practicing or discussing watchdog reporting during the 13 years of data gathering. As a young reporter for the *Traditional* said in 2010, "As journalists, we have so many problems to solve, besides going after the government." While Region C papers were more likely to investigate broad regional problems, they avoided direct criticism of the administration such as accusations of corruption.

However, there were less overt, less direct methods for holding officials accountable, and tensions between Region A and Moscow provided one. In 2009–2010, *Government* journalists realized they could take advantage of the regional government's need to avoid negative coverage. They even coined a term for this method: "preventive journalism." Preventive journalism was the practice of disclosing citizens' problems to regional officials so officials could act on the problems before they could become public and reach Moscow officials. Justice could then be served for the individual citizen, and the root problem might even be addressed, benefiting local citizens generally (Erzikova & Lowrey, 2014). *Government* newspaper journalists said this practice ended with the advent of the region's most recent administration, though as discussed below, *Private* reporters continued to practice a variation of it.

Journalists did not seem to view "preventive journalism" as a consequence of government pressure or manipulation. By all accounts, journalists perceived they were in the same boat with the regional government and it was in their interests to work with local officials to protect the region. Reporters said they knew Moscow monitored provincial media (through Medialogia) and used stories attacking local officials as a rationale for depriving the region of federal financial assistance. Doubtless, preventive journalism is self-censorship, and it undermines journalists' professional autonomy. Yet, turning the prism, it can also be seen as a strategic adaptation that puts journalists in the rare position of pushing the government to help people, if only in modest ways.

From the regional administrative perspective, officials knew that portraying the region as "too good to be true" could undermine the credibility of the regional government and the local media. When a news publication appeared to have some autonomy in its reporting, it strengthened its credibility, boosting the legitimacy of the publication and the local institutions it covers. And so, at times over the last 13 years, the region's governor encouraged local media to go after public officials. Some reporters, especially those who came of age after perestroika, were hesitant, fearing they may accidentally criticize "sacred cows." However, many took advantage of these emerging opportunities to act on behalf of regional citizens.

The *Government* and *Private* were most active in producing preventive journalism, but the *Traditional* engaged in these practices as well, early in our research. At that time, the *Traditional's* vice-editor (soon to become the *Government* editor) said he viewed "preventive journalism" as important for avoiding "a social explosion" in the form of protests. "We make agreements with the government," he said, "and change the situation for the better." In 2010, the *Traditional* drafted a critical piece on local town officials that was designed to force them to help a World War II veteran fix his house, but the paper withdrew the story because, after some newsroom conversations, it was decided it would "hurt the region if the story gets into the internet," the vice-editor said. The *Traditional* was not subsidized by the regional government at that time, but editors said they were concerned about Kremlin support for the region's people. Instead of publishing, the paper informed the regional government about the problem, and ultimately, the regional government put pressure on the town government to help the veteran.

Preventive journalism could also take the form of co-optation of reporters' expertise and knowledge. A veteran *Private* reporter said in 2012 that journalists become experts in the areas they cover and "know much more than some bureaucrats." Journalists' analyses, intended for news stories, were sometimes incorporated into the government's reports, growing the government's stock of knowledge. Officials came to rely on these seasoned journalists. However, journalists' expert analyses can create political problems if they imply too much dysfunction, and so officials have prevented publication, instead using the analyses to inform their governance. In 2007, a *Government* reporter's comprehensive analysis of agriculture in the region was prohibited from publication—the analysis suggested poor management by the regional government. Yet, officials recognized its value, gave the journalist an honorarium, and repurposed the analysis "as an educational handout for officials and specialists."

One female staffer, who was especially successful as an investigative reporter for the *Government* paper, had previously worked as a press secretary for a law enforcement agency, and this experience informed her investigations. But very few of her investigations were published. During one month in 2010, six of her stories "went down the sink," she said. As a rule, officials would resolve the issue after her intervention, and government would ask her not to publish the article. The officials' rationale: "Why inform readers about something that is not a concern anymore?" The reporter joked that she was mainly a *решала* (slang for "problem-solver"). Given that the problems she investigated reflected wider social concerns such as corruption and lawlessness, it is a small wonder that officials kept asking her to kill stories. Her death from illness in 2015 marked the end of (largely unpublished) investigative reporting at the *Government*.

In 2009, *Private* reporters began practicing their own form of preventive journalism. For these reporters, sharing people's problems with officials was inspired less by allegiance to the region and worries about Moscow, and more by individual citizens' needs and by the adulation reporters received from addressing needs. Their arrangements also tended to be with individual government agencies at both regional and municipal levels rather than with the governor's office. A *Private* reporter explained the process. "We critique the city administration on an agreed-upon issue, and the administration then uses it as a public relations strategy, [saying] 'The *Private* slammed us officials, and we responded to criticism by improving the situation.'" As a result, the *Private* produces a supervised and somewhat choreographed version of watchdog reporting that can bridge citizen needs to government resources. The *Private* has acquired a reputation as the people's defender—a senior reporter said she receives three to four phone calls a day from readers about problems and injustices. Officials are "intimidated and quick to respond," according to a *Private* reporter in 2018.

We note that in this type of preventive journalism, only the need of the individual is addressed—not the larger systemic problem. In 2012, a *Private* senior reporter shared an example of an intervention on behalf of citizens. In this case, an old man came to the newsroom and told her that 100 people had been fired from his workplace without pay. She declined to write about the situation, but she contacted officials.

> I called the court authorities; they said that the situation was not difficult; the man should have brought his paperwork to them and that was it. I told him to do it. He left in a good mood.

She said the layoff of 100 people without pay was "an ordinary situation," not worthy of publication and a situation that she felt publication could not help. "A majority of cases are not publishable," she said, "since it's ridiculous to write stories about every leaking roof in the city." But, she said, reporters do contact officials in order to "fix the hole through which stars are seen." "Preventive actions," she said, whether large or small, take time but pay off for the paper because people spread the word about the paper's efforts on their behalf. "For many of our readers, the paper is the last resort."

Another *Private* reporter said in 2012 that her colleague acted on behalf of a reader reaching out to a bureaucrat who was in charge of scheduling individual meetings with the governor:

> The bureaucrat was rude. He attempted to grab the [reporter's] ID and called reporters "yellow jackals." My colleague told him to wait for a newspaper story about the situation. Next day, the bureaucrat came to the newsroom and almost cried, begging [us] not to publish the story. [He said] if the governor knows, he would fire him immediately. The bureaucrat was ready to fall on his knees.

Near the end of the research period, the practice of preventive journalism was becoming extinct across all papers in Region A, largely due to the disconnect between the new administration and the news media. Interviewed in 2019, the *Government* editor said his opinion about collaboration with government had changed since the new governor was elected. Now, he said "the [region's] powerful don't care about people's problems," even when journalists explain the benefits. "We show the power—'do this and this [and] how you would benefit from this.' But the power doesn't react." According to the editor, both journalists and officials feared but respected the previous governor, "a quite charismatic person."

> [The former governor] directed newspapers to go after officials. He would say, "Help me clean up this region." Bureaucrats knew he started his day with reading newspapers, and if there was criticism toward them in that issue, they would be called on the carpet.

The *Government* editor said the current governor thinks he can ignore local papers because he has an Instagram account and "can have a direct conversation with people." However, when local residents leave posts about alleged misdeeds of their bosses, the governor "starts screaming and sending the press to write criticism." The governor "doesn't understand that a simple fact-check is needed" on such information before he sends reporters out on false trails. He also doesn't understand that "his Instagram harms his reputation," the editor said. "[The account is] managed unprofessionally and people laugh at him." As mentioned in Chapter 6, a look at comments on the governor's social media accounts suggests the strategy of portraying the governor as open and approachable is backfiring.

Asked whether journalists now help prevent political crises, a journalist in a *Private* focus group said that under the new regime, the work of reporters and officials "do not cross."

> The previous governor started his day with reading our paper. Not sure if the current governor does. But they are still fearful. They call and ask us not to write, for example, about the [political] opposition's meeting. Not everyone has a computer at home, and so they hope if the *Private* doesn't report, people would not know.

Regions B and C reporters did not mention a "preventive journalism" practice. First, none of the outlets in these two regions was a government organ. Second, the stronger economic conditions of these regions led to smoother relationships with Moscow. Third, it appeared that both regional governments were more sophisticated and nuanced in their work with regional publications. Governments allowed the media more day-to-day autonomy, urging no united front against Moscow (about which there was less concern), and requiring less media cheerleading, which the governments knew was likely to backfire. As a Region C senior reporter said in 2016, "The power knows people are angry and the power would not require us to write stories that would make people angrier [via obvious PR]." The relationships between officials and newspapers in both regions were not as close as in Region A, and this distance reduced tension between officials and publications. As a Region C editor said in 2020, "No drama, just business."

Subterfuge and Other Small Acts of Defiance

Evidence of direct defiance and confrontation was rare, increasingly so across the years of our research. However, there have been incidents, particularly early on. During the first year, 2007, a previous *Government* editor said she refused to accommodate a last-minute request from a government official to redo a newspaper issue in order to add official documents. "It's our newspaper," the official yelled, "and we do what we want with it!" She yelled back: "If it's yours, go ahead and work on it—but my staff go home!" Also early in the research, a seasoned *Government* reporter said she was able to slip a story into publication that highlighted a nationally award-winning teacher and revealed facts about poverty in Russia. The story mentioned the woman had to sweep streets in the summer to make ends meet, which brought outrage from officials, but only after publication. The *Government's* editor from this period is long gone, but the spirit of disobedience lingers in the hallways, and there have been incidents of dissent since. One example, mentioned in Chapter 4: The *Government's* award-winning top feature writer has refused to serve political candidates during election campaigns.

In 2007, the *Regional Branch* editor monitored the regional government's website and found incorrect information about the governor's decision to combine all vocational schools into one unit. In reality, the plan was to merge only two neighboring schools. Rather than alerting the press secretary to her mistake, the editor published the incorrect information on the newspaper's website, causing distress among teachers and students. A manager of the *Regional Branch* said that a government official called the paper and "орал как потерпевший" (screamed like a victim). The manager admitted they were "happy on that day," as they had "aggravated the government." They had acted, he said, like "a newspaper with teeth." Yet, other regional journalists saw this move as sensationalism rather than accountability journalism. While discussing *Regional Branch* methods, a senior *Government* reporter said in 2007, "We do respect them [reporters] as individuals, but we don't respect what they do."

Over the years of data gathering, *Private* reporters talked about confronting officials more often than did journalists from other publications. The *Private* reporters proudly called themselves the "most professional and most independent newspaper in the region." In 2012, a staffer shared that the *Private* was the only outlet that advocated for a high school teacher fired by authorities after his student sent a letter to President Putin questioning the quality of a textbook. These reporters were not above using deception to gain information from officials. One young *Private* reporter was praised for her savvy by a senior reporter: "She meets with an official and if she feels resistance, she starts crying, saying the editor would fire her if she doesn't collect information for the story."

Interviewed in summer 2015, both *Private* and *Government* reporters said their newspapers addressed the topic of high prices, a consequence of a plunging Russian ruble. Their approaches differed. The *Government's* report was superficial, minimizing the problem, an approach that was consistent with the official line. *Private* reporters also monitored the prices, but they used it to reveal actual prices and thereby dispute officials' claims. "We quote an official who said buckwheat costs 25 rubles," said a senior reporter, "and we comment by saying we went to different stores and found out that the price is much higher in all of them."

In 2012, a senior *Private* reporter said the newspaper regularly published phone numbers of bureaucrats who provided false comments "to let readers yell at them." They did this, the reporter said, to "educate officials on what comment is acceptable and what is not." Since 2007, the *Private* has also conducted so-called direct lines or phone conversations between public officials and readers, a practice devised during perestroika. This practice allows the paper to outsource to the readers the journalistic task of asking officials tough questions. The *Regional Branch* also published content from a "direct line," and the *Government* used a round-table format in which journalists asked officials' questions that were relevant to readers. Over time, however, these formats slipped from their perestroika-era purposes, as the round table became a promotional forum for officials, who edited the text, and the *Regional Branch*'s direct line became a list of paid promotional stories.

Most investigations of problems were left unpublished, but they were more likely to see publication if framed as problems that officials were actively addressing. In 2012, a *Government* reporter's story "about desperate schoolteachers who lost jobs because the only (rural) school was closed down" was not published. The reporter explained that her "story contradicted the Party's line"—a government policy encouraging citizens to become entrepreneurs. Two other reporters offered her advice: "You should have used the Aesop language," said one. "You should have framed the situation in such a way that people were in trouble, but the governor came and helped them," said the other. "Then it would have been published."

Journalists sometimes used online and social media as a way to bypass official control. The opening anecdote for this chapter offers one example: A social media manager shared the news of protests over foreign companies on her own social media accounts. "All people are on social media," she said. The complex, challenging ecosystem of online news urges journalists toward this kind of dissent. Social-media managers of the regions' established newspapers are expected to publish "news from officials" while also growing audience traffic, and this puts them in a very difficult situation—"between two fires," as one digital reporter put it. Users post derisive comments about the newspapers' dry online content while informed regional citizens post about real problems and even break news, but the paper's journalists are anchored to the use of an official press service that is in no hurry to comment on events. "The press service that manages his [social media] account talks about him participating in a ribbon-cutting event," said a *Government* digital manager, "while ordinary people's comments talk about a broken bridge, unjustifiably high cost of trash collection, a poisoned river, and lack of doctors at a local hospital."

As these social-media managers wait, competitors flood news streams with unverified information, including content from private media competitors who produce online portals with eye-catching, sensationalist content, often based on rumors. "Our attempt to shape a news story based only on what the power has provided us with is met with laughter and sarcasm [by social media users]," said a *Government* digital reporter. "Readers know we are cover-ups for the power; they don't come to read our news—they visit us to spew on us."

The pulls and pushes of this difficult environment urge this social-media manager and others toward nonconformity. In her posts, she connects the dots of problems in the region by using information from the social media accounts of knowledgeable citizens. For example, she monitors a local page of "Подслушано" (Overheard), a VK-based social media community (https://vk.com/overhear). Community members share eyewitness information and supply photos and videos. She analyzes information from various citizen sources to make sense of what's happening, and she then balances citizen rumors with official information. The result can often be subtly subversive. She does not directly and openly confront authorities, but opposition emerges in latent ways, through the positioning of standard government news releases near citizens' information and comments, which can show the ineffectiveness of the government releases.

Since around 2016, newspapers' digital managers themselves have produced dissenting comments in online forums that accompany news stories. Scrutiny of social media posts show that after sharing "feel good stories" about the regional government on newspapers' official social media pages, managers have posted sarcastic comments using their private accounts.

Beyond the online environment, journalists have found other cracks to slip subversive messages through. A *Private* reporter, who had earned a reputation as a "people's defender," used a sanctioned Q&A story format to undermine a fraudulent business scheme presented in the form of paid content. Most reporters will not go after an organization without clearing it with their paper's ad department, but this older, experienced reporter moved ahead without checking.

> Even if I work on a paid story and write not what I think but what I am supposed to write, I still find a way to let readers know what I think, through subtext, undertone …. For example, I wrote a paid story (advertisement) about a company that asked people to give up their apartments now and get two apartments in five years. They were crooked. I realized that. Yet, our ad department insisted on the story. I used an interview format—questions and answers—to let readers know the company was a bunch of crooks. The crooks read the story before it was published. But they were stupid and couldn't read between the lines. The Prosecutor Office started investigating them after the story was published.

Both Region B and C newspapers also use subversive tactics to report news that spotlight regional problems, but they have been more likely to do so through interviews with famous people and experts. A reading of newspaper issues showed that the Region B paper was more likely to use local experts, while Region C publications used more nationally known experts. For example, in 2015, the Region B newspaper addressed a long-term plan for the region's economic development (proposed by the governor) through an interview with a professor of economics at a local university, while a Region C newspaper published comments by a world-renowned Russian political scientist living in Europe to discuss the impact of Western sanctions. In 2015, the Region B editor said this approach helped shield his newspaper from government wrath: "It's not us, it's the expert."

These small acts of defiance and subterfuge are noteworthy and have shown bravery. But, while commenting on some successful attempts by regional journalists to assert dissent, a seasoned *Government* reporter revealed her scepticism. She said relations between journalists and the powerful sometimes may be described as "Не сила травинки, а слабость асфальта"—"not the strength of grass but the weakness of the asphalt." Journalists benefit from the weakness of government oversight—poor-quality asphalt—that allow reporters' stories to be published. "The grass grows through the asphalt," she said. Journalists' acts of disobedience do not usually shoot up organically from firmly planted roots; rather, "the government lets it happen intentionally or simply doesn't care."

Facades of Serious Journalism

In the first decade of data gathering, the idea of preventive journalism coexisted with a "pinch but don't punch" approach in Region A. The previous governor realized that portraying the region as having no problems could raise suspicions. Giving a green light to reporters to criticize public officials, the governor helped the media appear somewhat independent and more legitimate, in the eyes of the people and Moscow officials. The media, in fact, had little independence, and the "green light" gave the go-ahead mostly to superficial dissent. We gave the example in Chapter 4 of officials insincerely urging journalists to "make a bomb!" and expose societal problems—but, as the *Government* reporter said, it is "a bomb that will not touch anyone."

In institutional theory, the term "decoupling" describes this kind of behavior, in which an aspiration and the corresponding action are at a remove from one another (Boxenbaum & Jonsson, 2008; Lowrey & Erzikova, 2010): A tough-sounding investigation focuses on an insubstantial issue; reporting on officials' malfeasance is pre-approved by the government; or an investigation of criminal activities is softened because, as a *Government* reporter said, it could lead to discoveries of high-level corruption "no one was prepared to make." Such "decoupled" behavior shores up an organization's legitimacy by helping it stay in accord with aspirational societal norms (local journalism *should* investigate administrative problems to help local people) while allowing for business as usual (government protects itself by controlling local journalism). Of course, the newspapers have had motivations for decoupling as well, mostly related to their fundamental financial dependence on the government.

Yet, if this "green-lighted" investigative work has been small-scale or not truly oppositional, neither has it been negligible. Contemporary regional Russia has been described as an "adaptive society," in which everyday people tend to adjust to unfair, unlawful situations, and make changes at the individual level to accommodate and survive, rather than systemic changes at a societal level (Gudkov, Dubin, & Levinson, 2009, p. 32). We saw evidence of this adaptive tendency, consistent with an ecological perspective.

In 2010, a *Private* reporter said that critique of the city administration was typically based on agreed-upon issues, and the administration used their response to the criticism as public relations. Through this performance, the city administration appeared to be responding to criticism and seeking to improve their performance. The paper was able to maintain the government's financial support while giving a boost to the paper's professional legitimacy by appearing as a "watchdog." This strategy has waned in recent years.

A seasoned *Government* reporter shared an anecdote from 2007 in which the government orchestrated the newspaper's "watchdog" criticism of officials.

> We received заказ (an order) to write about two officials from one particular district. One person had a store that was burned down. He didn't remove debris, and he even didn't fence the territory. Another official had a closed-down store that was overgrown with weeds. Both men violated a beautification law. Authorities called and warned them, but these two didn't react. I wrote a story. The authorities requested to wait until elections and publish then to take these two officials down.

Interview data from 2009–2010 showed that, under an earlier regional administration, *Government* journalists viewed themselves as the freest newspaper in the region, claiming they could "investigate and fire appointed officials." However, the list of bureaucrats who lost positions following newspaper criticism was pre-approved by the government. While the information about officials' malfeasance gave citizens a glimpse behind the curtain, the newspaper's role in exposing the malfeasance was mostly window-dressing, as the bureaucrats' fate had been sealed. The regional government needed stories that "exposed wrong-doings" so officials appeared to be fighting corruption and striving to work for the region's people. Journalists also benefited from this practice. It appeared they were fighting the authority, and this helped them justify their dependence on the regional budget and boosted their professional self-esteem. "Desperate people have a little bit of hope that something that resembles justice exists," the vice-editor of the *Government* said in 2009. At some point, *Government* reporters began to confuse the window dressing for actual independence, believing they were free to criticize bureaucrats without approval from the regional government. In 2010, a story that attacked one of the governor's favorites cost the *Government*'s editor her position. The editor was one of the governor's closest aides, and the firing sent a strong message to the entire journalistic community. "It was a chilling effect," said a *Regional Branch* manager. "A reminder to stay within the defined boundaries."

Over the years, the idea that journalists can help restore justice almost disappeared from interviews with *Government* journalists. It seems the current government feels no need to publicly legitimate the firing of bureaucrats who lost favor. In 2015, a seasoned *Government* reporter said she thought the region's people still cared about the role of officials' malfeasance in the region's problems, but the paper no longer touches these issues.

> People will be interested in publications about corruption in the utilities and housing department. But we are not able to do it because we don't have internal resources. A reporter needs to be a winner, to have a history of victories to take on this kind of project. But if the reporter is constantly held off [prevented from reporting], the reporter feels discouraged. There is no enthusiasm. I believe that money is not important if a reporter has an internal call [to do investigative reporting]. But reporters unfortunately think it's meaningless.

There is still evidence that *Private* reporters try to challenge the government, but with diminishing results. In 2015, three *Private* reporters in a focus group talked about journalists' mission to interpret socially important events and trends, and not merely to disseminate information. "But we don't analyze," the reporters said, and close reading of *Private* issues supported this statement: In the past nine years, an overwhelming majority of stories have been relatively short —around 500 words or less—and situational, covering recent events (a new public transportation fare; renovation of a local history museum; and property tax increase). Analytical stories, expected from a weekly legacy newspaper, were not evident. Nevertheless, as one reporter said, their reporters persist in seeking information, and following the letter of the law in requesting it, even if efforts are futile—another "decoupling" of journalists' actions from consequences:

> We ask uncomfortable interview questions, according to public officials ... We ask them to comment, for example, on the economic situation in the region. We act according to the law of the mass media. They might not want to give us statistics about crime in the region, but we still write requests. They don't want to share the stats, but we insist.

Reporters and editors from regions B and C focused less on negotiating with or challenging their governments than did Region A newspapers, at least during the years when these regions were included in the study. They reported on problems in the region, but watchdog reporting that focused on politicians' corruption was seen as unnecessary "drama." "The idea is to create solid content for readers," said a Region C reporter in 2016, "and not to fight government." Such fights risk losing government and business advertisers. She said she believed "people still remember information wars of the 1990s, and every subversive story is met with a suspicious question: 'Who is behind [the story's accusation]?'" She said she thought "people know better than reporters about corruption" and that journalists did not need to report on this topic.

Alternative Avenues of Expression

Across the data gathering period and across papers, we witnessed alternative means of expression by journalists such as local civic activism, online blogs and social media posts, and collective online projects. Online expression, in particular, grew increasingly noticeable.

Early in our study, a prominent *Traditional* reporter inspired by perestroika turned into a local activist. Her main mission was to protect greenery and historic buildings in the regional capital. A fearless fighter, she challenged authorities with straightforward questions. In the aftermath of terrorist attacks in Russia in 2004–2005, the entrances to both city and regional government buildings were guarded by police, and, she said, police were instructed to bar the reporter-activist from entering. However, she found her way in, and she said that in 2007, she once found her way in through a back door, physically moved a secretary out of the way, and demanded that the mayor stop cutting trees in a children's park.

> I didn't have a choice but to storm the mayor's office. The company that planned to build a shopping mall on the park's territory didn't want bad publicity. They called the printing house and stopped printing the *Traditional* with my article the night before. They called the editor and offered to place an ad instead of my article. Editor said it's up to me. I said 'no.' They called again and tripled the price. I said 'no' again. The issue with my article was printed [but] they bought the entire circulation of the *Traditional*. The mayor said he wasn't involved in this tree cutting situation, and he didn't sign any paperwork. I went to the park with a group of activists, and we blocked traffic near the park. Bureaucrats were furious, but they hesitated to use force against older women.

The reporter-activist lost her battle to the authorities. Almost 1,000 trees were cut, and a shopping mall was erected despite mass protests of local residents. So-called точечная застройка (urban planning infill) continues in the city, but without protests.

Activism in online forms became increasingly common. The *Government* and *Private* each had a staff writer who was a member of a group of regional bloggers who spent considerable time together offline, sometimes socializing but often organizing work on community projects—for example, cleaning up parks. For these two staffers, blogging was a way to bypass editorial control and re-engage with the idea of journalism as social mission. "I live when I blog, one of them said in 2016. "I merely exist while writing stories for the newspaper."

According to a *Government* reporter, the papers' online portals may also allow journalists to connect directly with readers in efforts that bypass authorities—in searching for missing persons, for example.

> Readers want to know who has gone missing. We have a team of volunteers in the region that does searches. The team is so well-known that some people call them instead of the police. People are missing often because of psychiatric diseases … We cover the team activities—our small contribution.

Journalists also express themselves individually online, in ways that may or may not relate to their journalistic work, but which make routine daily chores more bearable. One editor in Region C was highly vocal about situations he encountered in everyday life, such as medical visits or interaction with law enforcement representatives. A number of *Government* and *Private* reporters have become social media micro-influencers, posting both journalistic and personal content several times a day. A *Government* reporter turned herself into a fantasy writer online, supplementing her pay with honoraria, and bringing much needed relief from the dry "news delivery" of her newspaper job.

Armies of One

Finally, we note that the news outlets' most creative, forceful efforts to champion the people and challenge authorities often involved strong, experienced individual reporters who channeled both the logics of perestroika and moral education. These rare journalists made their own "cracks" in the system. During the data collection, we witnessed several examples in which a newspaper's role as a people's defender faded when a specific reporter, a champion of the effort, left the paper. The *Government* and the *Traditional* lost their reporters-activists to illness, and a long-time staffer at the *Private* left for another outlet. These three reporters earned respect from colleagues as well as some modest degree of autonomy from the government, sometimes finding success in quests to find solutions for local problems and bring justice for local citizens suffering problems. Just one example: In 2012, a senior *Private* reporter successfully fought against the closing of a local flea market, a small but important source of income for retired people. Her clout in the region was important to her ability to stand up for these citizens:

> Old poor women complained. The paper published a story and photos. The city district authorities listened to us. A week later, I went to the flea market to check the situation. The women ran to me to thank me. They said the authorities left them alone after the photographer and I showed up to take pictures and talk. I mean they left the sellers alone before the story was published.

The Russian saying "и один в поле воин" (one can be an army) applies to these journalists and their efforts, whether efforts were successful, as with the *Private* reporter saving a flea market, or frustrated, as with the *Traditional* reporter's futile battle over the children's park.

Discussion

In the early years of our data collection, there were small signs that Region A papers were seeking ways to maintain professional boundaries. The *Private* engaged in creative approaches for questioning authority that shielded the paper from authorities' wrath—letting readers ask tough questions directly during phone conversations between officials and readers, for example. *Government* journalists also felt air under their wings, writing stories that took officials to task. The *Regional Branch* occasionally rattled cages, emboldened by its Moscow owners, though these efforts could be more sensationalistic than community-minded. And a few senior, committed reporters, sprinkled across the papers, tried to keep up the fight.

But this task has proved overwhelming in Russia's regions, where the political and economic environment has become increasingly hostile to media freedom. The *Regional Branch*'s reporters were burdened by a lack of freedom from the paper's owner, who saddled them with long hours, low pay and unethical practices, hindering their professional growth and obstructing service to local readers. The paper eventually became an advertising vehicle. The *Government* lost its assertive editor, and its reporters have been increasingly burdened by their financial dependence on the regional government, and the workload that officials assign their staff. The *Traditional* has been an independent but desperately poor publication, and the absence of dependency on an owner is more of a burden than a blessing, as the paper seeks mere survival. Through neglect, the paper lacks the resources to act on independence.

While the *Private* found creative ways to distance themselves from authorities throughout the period of study, *Private* journalists have still felt much frustration over the limits of their autonomy and their inability to satisfy their frustrated readers. In 2013, a vice-editor of the *Private* tried to explain the cultural and social passivity of the region:

> Our people are unique. Their genetic memory is so strong that they can endure anything, tolerate any government to avoid bloodshed. When a generation that doesn't remember the time of repressions grows, something will be changed in Russia.

Direct acts of defiance were rare across the period of study, and they have become almost unheard of in recent years. Yet as the chapter details, journalists have continued to pursue subtle and indirect ways of challenging officials and helping citizens, taking advantage of "cracks in the system." These opportunities have encouraged infrequent nonconformist actions, but such actions have lacked "the strength of grass," which is found in the roots—they have done little to change the underlying system. They do not seem to rise to the level of "oppositional position-taking" from field theory, as in most cases, nonconformity does not break publicly with the powers that be, and the "stakes of the struggle" remain low. Preventive journalism could fix individual problems and isolated situations but, typically, it did not touch the deeper system. Superficial ("decoupled") watchdog efforts provided some information to citizens, provided journalists some professional motivation, and encouraged citizens to view journalists as being "on their side"—but these efforts have been controlled and shallow.

Recent changes in Region A are discouraging. The new government lacks an understanding of how to work with local journalists, and local news outlets keep losing quality and expertise. If the expectations are a journalism with clearly defined professional boundaries that actively and publicly stands ready to confront political and economic power, local Russian journalism falls woefully short. But, if the expectations are a journalism that continues to seek ways, through the cracks, to help everyday people while surviving day-to-day in hostile conditions, then the results are more commendable. As Josephi (2013) noted, a fully functioning democracy is not a requirement for the practice of journalism.

Mere survival and adaptation cannot be called sufficient. The ability to "endure anything" provides patience to persist into better days, but (turn the prism) it is also a habitus that affords and reinforces docility and passivity. Yet, small victories have been hard-won, and there are journalists in these news organizations who continue the struggle.

References

Boxenbaum, E. & Jonsson, S. (2008). Isomorphism, diffusion and decoupling. In R. Greenwood, C. Olver, K. Sahlin & R. Suddaby, *The Sage Handbook of Organizational Institutionalism*, pp. 78–98. London: Sage Publications.

Erzikova, E., & Lowrey, W. (2014). Preventive journalism as a means of controlling regional media in Russia. *Global Media and Communication, 10(1),* 35–52.

Gudkov, L. D., Dubin, B. V., & Levinson, A. G. (2009). Fotorobot rossiiskogo obuvatelya [A sketch of the Russian everyman]. *Mir Rossii, 2,* 22–33.

Josephi, B. (2013). How much democracy does journalism need? *Journalism, 14*(4), 474–489.

Lowrey, W. & Erzikova, E. (2010). Institutional legitimacy and Russian news: Case studies of four regional newspapers. *Political Communication, 27(3),* 275–288.

CHAPTER NINE

Conclusions: Daunting Challenges and Ways Forward

In 2009, a senior Traditional reporter recalled an incident during her years at the Government newspaper when she became acting editor during the editor's vacation. "The government press service called me: 'Such and such event is today at 14:00 – which of your reporters is coming?' I said, 'Wait a minute, what event? Why is it important?' and they said, 'because the governor will be there.'" The senior reporter responded in frustration: "The presence of the governor does not constitute newsworthiness!" She hung up. Rumor had it, according to the reporter, that the press service complained to a government bureaucrat, but the bureaucrat said the press service should "not mess with her." They were to wait until the editor came back.

At times, journalists in the regions we studied have stood their ground in opposition to the government and persevered. But these moments have been rare and fleeting, and often they have relied on government acquiescence—in the anecdote above, a tactical retreat "until the editor came back." Typically, challenges by journalists have been part of a "dance" between government and media that allows some give and take for the sake of appearances. However, challenges rarely have amounted to substantial opposition.

From a bird's-eye view across the regions and across all 13 years of study, we see an increasingly conformist local journalism, with increasingly conformist journalists reporting on increasingly powerless regions. Rhetoric from Moscow glorifies the nation's regions as the "heartland," the wellspring of Russian virtue, but as

Moscow consolidated power and resources through the policy of the "power vertical," the authority of the regions declined, as did the relative autonomy of the news outlets and journalists we studied. The "rules of the game" became less forgiving and more taken-for-granted by journalists, who were increasingly hemmed in and coerced by shrinking salaries and staffs and a mounting workload. This is the broad view, and it's also what we see when looking through the commonly used liberal democratic lens, with its focus on self-governance and political independence.

If we move in on this view, the broad patterns for regional context and journalists' autonomy look more complex and uneven across the years. Economic patterns and political relationships have played out differently across the different regions and papers. Social domains such as the digital online space and generational spaces emerged, challenging old logics and suggesting new ones. Administrations, officials and news managers came and went, with varying policies and levels of media expertise. Reporters also came and went, resulting in shifting, though often declining, levels of experience and commitment over the years.

The view also changes when we switch between the meso-level approaches of fields and social ecologies. The more critical field approach focuses our attention on power and how it compels and affords the positioning of journalists. It also focuses our attention on journalists' opposition to power, on the availability of capital for claiming and maintaining positions, and on the relative definitiveness of the local journalism field's boundaries. The ecological approach and its emphasis on long-term equilibrium rather than power (Abbott, 1988) focuses us on the diverse ways journalists interact, compete, and adapt in a system that offers unpredictable, informal opportunities, day to day. Actors in both ecologies and fields seek survival and advantage, but ecology approaches emphasize surviving, and field approaches emphasize winning.

We look through both lenses to draw conclusions about the state of local journalism in these regions, its most important contexts, and possible paths forward. We need look no farther than the COVID-19 pandemic for evidence of the importance of local journalism. The pandemic, which is spreading worldwide as we complete this book, is putting additional stresses on the regions' citizens and systems, including an already strained regional media. The ability of journalists to adapt to power and unpredictable circumstances and to report relevant truths has rarely been more critical.

Throughout the chapters, we have explored a wide variety of contexts that have shaped local journalists' efforts to help citizens, to challenge officials, to hang together as an occupational community, and to simply endure. In this final chapter, we aggregate and make sense of findings about these contexts and their influence.

- Political and economic contexts: How are they structured, how have they changed, and what is their relevance to local journalists' roles, decisions and practices?
- The governing logics of local journalism spaces: Which logics are most relevant and how have they shaped the roles, decisions and practices of local Russian journalism across the regions studied and across the period of study?
- The journalism occupational community: What is the changing nature of this community, and how has it shaped roles, decisions and practices?
- The local community: What have been journalists' perceptions of local community and their connections with citizens? How have these shaped roles, decisions and practices across the period of study?

We have also made the case that many challenges facing local Russian journalism are found in local communities everywhere, as local journalism struggles worldwide. In this chapter, we draw conclusions about the relevance of these broader struggles to the regional journalism we studied.

Political-Economic Structures and Regional Journalism

- *What are the defining political-economic structures of journalism's social space in these regions? How have they changed or remained unchanged over time?*

Findings reveal faint and fading boundaries around a journalism space that is increasingly hard to distinguish within the context of political and economic power. While some journalists have challenged limitations and while there are some differences across regions and papers, journalists generally are coming to take these limitations and constraints for granted, viewing their deepening dependency on government as regrettable and frustrating, but normal.

Over the years, uncertainty about funding added to the problems of dependency, especially for Region A publications. Financial support through direct subsidies from the regional government's budget decreased dramatically following the 2007–2008 recession, and over time, revenue was tied more tightly to specific reporting topics and tasks, and stories more closely reflected officials' wishes. These trends accelerated under the new governor's administration, which started during the research period. Funding programs have tied newspaper production to the government's agenda more tightly, and though the term "contract" suggests negotiability, the lack of alternative resources has made contracts with the government a critical and non-negotiable source of revenue. Links have also been tightened between managers and individual journalists in the form of honoraria, or payment per story, on which underpaid journalists depend increasingly. Reporters have had to choose story quantity over story quality in order to survive. Reporters have also had to pursue work on the side to make ends meet. Survival rather than journalistic quality has become the more salient goal.

Direct dissent and push-back by media against the government was never strident or strong during our research, and "watchdog journalism" was almost never discussed, much less practiced. We also saw a decline over the years in the value of professional recognition, especially by younger reporters. Awards put no food on the table. However, early on, Region A journalists would challenge the administration about public issues and object to news policies they saw as unfair. This was most common around 2007–2009, especially prior to the Great Recession, and was at least occasionally evident until the new regional administration took over. Early on, the *Regional Branch* (with its Moscow headquarters) and the *Government* were more likely to publish information that challenged officials. But the *Regional Branch* converted to an advertising vehicle, and the *Government* was stunned into submission when the governor fired its popular editor.

Generally, up until the most recent regional administration, some Region A publications pursued choreographed investigations of local problems, in cooperation with the regional government—a sort of crack in the system. The regional administration, seeking to stay in Moscow's good graces, saw value in the media bringing regional problems to its attention so problems could be addressed, though in a way the regional administration could control. During the most recent years of our study, even these orchestrated efforts dwindled. The new media administration's lack of interest and experience in dealing with the media has led to a flood of meaningless PR tasks for journalists, robbing them of time needed to investigate regional problems, which could benefit citizens and the administration.

Comparing the three regions, we see some similarities in relationships between government and media, but we also see differences due to disparities in regional wealth. The administration in the relatively poorer Region A urged the papers it subsidized to seek private ad revenue in order to supplement subsidies. The government had little concern that alternative sources of revenue might support efforts at independence: Private ad revenue was scarce, and journalists at these papers, who have been more interested in surviving than striving for independence, were reluctant to seek advertising anyway, viewing it as a lot of work for little payoff. Region C was relatively wealthier than regions A and B; however, private money was concentrated in large energy industries, which had little need of newspaper ads. Region C newspapers were fairly well fed by the government, and newspaper managers knew where their next "meal" was coming from. They generally did not seek private ads, finding them unpredictable and unreliable.

The Region C government also gave Region C papers a relatively long leash, as the regional administration was not overly concerned about Moscow, according to editors and reporters. Region C journalists were among the most experienced and well-educated across the papers we studied, and they produced more investigative work than papers in other regions; however, interviewed journalists had no wish to confront authorities, and were no more insistent on journalistic independence than were journalists in the other two regions. Generally, across the regions and across time, Region A's *Private* and the Region B paper showed the strongest urge for autonomy, and it was no coincidence that these two newspapers chose to be less reliant on government funding, though the government still subsidized them. Region B actually had the healthiest ad market for part of the study, and up to this point it has kept its dependence on the Region B government relatively low, though there are signs that this may be ending.

The Logics of the Local Russian Journalism Space

- *How are journalists' role conceptions and practices shaped by the various structures and logics of the social space?*

According to meso-level approaches, structures shape but do not determine social action. A repertoire of multiple logics also guide social action, opening possibilities for journalists' agency, even in the regions' oppressive contexts. Several logics relevant to power and conflict emerged: an age-old government-service logic; a perestroika-era logic, which encourages oppositional assumptions and behaviors; and a provincial anti-Western logic, which tends to support the government-service logic and undermine the perestroika logic.

Government service logic. The government-service logic most deeply contours the social space, and contours deepened during the research period. This logic has not guided journalists toward blind contentment with officials. Rather, it has led journalists to a more latent form of obedience, in which they grumble about burdens of daily work, and government tolerates the grumbling, but many journalists—especially true in later years—have tended not to question their fundamental subservience. In Region A, journalists complained about the unofficial role of producing a sort of internal newsletter for bureaucrats: Like newsletter articles, their news stories conveyed information about officials to officials, and to officials' evaluating superiors. Journalists also complained about long lists of mandatory government events. But, they largely accepted these roles as a fait accompli, and many (but not all) considered the news releases the government fed them to be legitimate socio-political information, in comparison to what they increasingly saw as Western-inspired sensationalism in other papers. Besides, some journalists reasoned, this was information their newspaper would have reported anyway.

Late in our research, the government service logic in Region A was disrupted by a new media administration—one "that does not care about the press," in the words of a former official. Journalists have said the long lists of mandated stories about bureaucratic events do not interest local citizens (the target audience is Moscow), and they take time and energy from reporting on local problems. However, shared antipathy toward the administration has sparked some feelings of community among journalists across the region, as discussed below.

Perestroika-era logic. The perestroika-era logic has been evident across the newsrooms we studied, but its vitality faded over time amid economic crises and political constraints. Senior journalists and even some younger journalists still speak of perestroika with reverence, but the lessons for journalism from this era are mixed. Stories from older journalists demonstrate that the freedom to run one's own newspaper and aggressively question officials is possible, rendering journalistic independence conceivable. However, the rancor and chaos with which the perestroika era ended left bad memories in the minds of many journalists, who now tend to question the value of aggressive reporting.

Many seasoned journalists still feel the urge to challenge authorities, and they point to perestroika for motivation. However, actually realizing the urge depends on "cracks in the system"— oversight, accident or official permission that provide opportunities to report on real problems in the province. Opportunities may emerge from inconsistencies between levels of government or from the longer leash given to media in a wealthier, more confident region (as in Region C). We discussed numerous examples in Chapter 8. These are not the stuff of rebellion, but they suggest a perestroika flame still flickers.

Anti-Western logic. Anti-Western sentiments among regional residents, officials and journalists have been on the rise during the research period, and regional residents' disdain for wealthy, Western-oriented Muscovites has always been high. Our research participants—even those who have worked for Western style media—generally associated Western journalism with bleak neutrality and commercial sensationalism. The moral education and literary logics have been antidotes to what they see as a soulless, fact-based journalism. Reporters have also pointed to the consumerist quality of Western journalism to justify their reporting of trivial government events. At least, journalists have said, we're working on "serious" rather than "yellow" journalism.

Local journalists' antipathy toward a Western-facing Moscow dampened their support for national-level journalists who challenged authority, and this weakened journalistic community at the national level. "It's not our war," a *Traditional* reporter said, referring both to the relevance of the issue and to the "war" between national elites who "pay Moscow journalists well to fight for them." Resentment toward "the capitals" is long-held in Russia's regions, and many of the journalists interviewed were sympathetic to the Kremlin-promoted view that true Russian patriotism is found in the regions, Russia's "heartland." This local populism is the problematic underside of strong identification with local community. It can run counter to the idea that journalism should serve "a general 'public interest' transcending particular interests'" (Hallin & Mancini, 2004, p. 56), and it seems to undermine national-level occupational community for Russian journalists.

Moral education logic. Other logics were less directly related to questions of journalists' autonomy, though they related tangentially. The moral education, literary and life-hacking logics offered ways through "the cracks" to serve the region and its citizens without running afoul of political-economic power. Journalists' roles may transcend "expectations of the Western standard model" and find paths to meaningful journalism through the "private" and personal, as well as the public (Hanitzsch & Vos, 2018, p. 150).

The journalists we interviewed pursued two main ways to lift the spirits of beleaguered citizens during economically dire and politically repressive times. One path is to offer solutions for practical problems—what some of our participants called "life-hacking." The other is to provide moral support in the form of spiritual uplift and moral lessons. Even the more cynical journalists we interviewed took it for granted that moral education in some form, whether spiritual or cultural, is appropriate. This logic is not always consistent with government aims. Time-consuming, thoughtful essays and stories take time away from government PR tasks. But neither does it run directly afoul of the government. The moral education logic is mostly apolitical, with its emphasis on individual-level needs and aspirations rather than policy problems. The anti-Western role and moral education roles support one another, as dispassionate reporting of facts does little to serve the needs of the human spirit.

Literary logic. The literary logic is also long-established in Russian journalism. Literary feature writing is still revered across the newsrooms we studied, but it is increasingly viewed as a luxury. Many, old and young, see this as regrettable. For some of the younger and more digitally savvy reporters we interviewed, it is high time, as they view literary essays and artful language as dated and unsuited for new digital audiences. But among seasoned print journalists, literary feature writing carries significant cultural capital. What is less clear is that this cultural capital still translates into significant economic capital.

The literary logic intertwines with other logics. It supports the moral education logic and the production of meaningful, thoughtful content. The literary and anti-Western logics are somewhat consistent with one another and with the idea that Western fact-based writing is "dry" and "soulless," though literary writing can encourage nuance of thought that may not be consistent with dutiful nationalism.

Life-hacking logic. An intriguing ecological development in the local Russian journalism space is the organic growth of the life-hacking logic. Early in our research, we observed journalists engaged in "librarian-like" assistance for their local readers, providing tips for everyday mundane activities—car repair, gardening, personal healthcare and finance. These tips were published in stories, but they were also provided in interactions with readers who called, wrote or came by the office to ask for help. Not all outlets and journalists embraced the practice, and while journalists who practiced it saw benefits in terms of engaging readers and helping struggling citizens, some—particularly socio-political reporters at the *Government* and the Region B paper—distanced themselves from this role, perceiving it as something less than serious journalistic work.

However, at several publications this role has evolved. Focusing on "life-hacking" content is one way to reframe government PR. Rather than emphasizing the self-promoting comments of officials, journalists may focus on the practical, actionable information officials provide for citizens. Further, a story in which officials try to spin a problem for the province as a positive can be re-spun: Journalists may use the story as an opportunity to emphasize practical steps citizens can take to get around the problem—but in doing so, they highlight the problem's existence.

Survival logic. The *Private*'s vice-editor described the region's people as unique because they could "endure anything, tolerate any government." Findings are full of references to daily challenges for journalists and the overriding need to carry on and endure. Journalists in Region A talked about finding a "hub," a port in the storm where they could merely continue on, seeking to adapt rather than staking out positions. We have proposed "mere survival" as a logic because we noticed journalists referring to the need to survive when rationalizing their actions. The idea that there is only so much one can do serves as a framework that channels journalists' daily decisions and practices, and we note a similarity between the "survival logic" and the "fatalism" that has run through Russian culture "for many centuries" (Goodwin et al., 2002, p. 1167). The survival logic contributes to the adoption of other logics— government service, especially, but also the mostly apolitical logics of moral education and life-hacking.

A (budding) digital commerce logic. We found some evidence of a "digital commerce" logic or role, but this was limited to particular papers and journalists, as online platforms and production are relatively undeveloped across many of the papers we studied. Numerous readers in rural areas still have little interest in online platforms, though interest is growing. The fact that the wealthier Region C papers have been the most willing to embrace and strategize about the online environment shows the importance of resources.

Boundaries around the local journalism space are vague in the regions we studied, and digital online practices and platforms are blurring them further. Journalists worry that the ease of online publishing, the popularity of trivial and sensationalized social media posts, and the allure of accumulating visitors and followers are luring non-journalists— particularly officials and advertisers— into journalists' space and nudging journalists out. Journalists also worry that "even educated readers," as one journalist said, are no longer distinguishing "Instagram posts" from journalistic accounts. We note that this challenge is not unique to Russian regions, as journalists around the world are struggling with similar boundary challenges.

The budding digital commerce role runs parallel to increasing ethical challenges to journalism in these regions. The appeal of audience traffic, the 24/7 pace, understaffed and underpaid newsrooms, the link between story quantity and reporters' pay, and the "scopic" view of other content that online media provide (Boczkowski, 2010, p. 79)—these all have encouraged journalists to deviate from traditional Russian journalism logics, roles and values. "Borrowing" content from other outlets is rampant, among both legacy and fledgling outlets.

Still, most journalists recognize the ethical problems, and these problems further decrease the respect senior journalists have for online work. This split between older and younger journalists obstructs the emergence of digital commerce as a taken-for-granted logic in the local journalism space. Yet, we see evidence of this logic/role on the horizon. Younger journalists seek recognition, legitimacy and cultural capital beyond traditional professional recognition. The niche of producing viral content seems to be all that is left to them as a way of gaining cultural standing. We also note that the budding logic of digital commerce seems likely to become more and more accessible: Social media use among regional residents is high, even in rural areas, and administrators in all three regions are devoting more resources to support it.

Occupational Community of Local Russian Journalists

- *What is the nature of the occupational community of these local Russian journalists, and how and why has it changed or remained unchanged?*

Journalists' roles and practices are shaped not only by institutional contexts and political-economic elite, but also by interaction within various social collectives, including the news organization, the occupational community, and the local community.

At the organizational level, most newsroom staffs showed collegiality. Shared experiences strengthened bonds, and so did hard times, as colleagues drew on one another for support. Collective identity was fortified by aversion to "out groups," whether rival papers, government administrators, Muscovites, or insistent readers. While organizational cohesion was the dominant trend, the generational and print/digital divides were countercurrents.

Across the regions' papers, there was moderately weak evidence of "occupational community"—a cross-organizational collective of journalists who share norms and values that apply to daily work and beyond work, "and whose social relationships meld work and leisure" (Van Maanen & Barley, 1984, p. 287). Across time, occupational community has generally weakened, but recent frustration in Region A over new media administrators has kindled a sense of shared goals and values across newsrooms.

At times, journalists from different outlets have come together—when a well-known journalist has suffered a personal loss, for example. Generally, however, journalists were much more likely to embrace the norms, values, identities and practices of their individual news organizations. News outlets' competition over government contracts strengthened internal organizational bonds and undermined occupational community, and as we noted earlier, anti-Western/anti-Moscow sentiment hindered nationwide journalistic unity. The pronounced generation gap between perestroika-era journalists and the most recent generation of journalists, particularly during the first 7–8 years of our study, also eroded occupational community. These two groups traveled distinct trajectories that launched from different origins. Senior journalists viewed younger journalists as a "lost generation," obsessed with consumerism, lacking commitment to the craft, and as overly deferential to officials. Younger journalists viewed older journalists as weak and out of touch. Younger journalists' dependence on honoraria, coupled with the ease of churning out online stories helped trap these younger journalists in tasks that stunted professional growth. Most had started off at a disadvantage, as the formal system for journalism education had eroded, particularly in Region A, according to both journalists and regional officials. Many left the field, and few senior journalists shed tears over these departures. Still, senior journalists and managers showed concern about the labor pool and pipeline into the field.

A few contexts and factors fostered occupational community. Throughout their careers, journalists have moved across news outlets within their own regions, and so journalists know journalists at other papers. While tough economic times encouraged competition for government revenue, they also encouraged informal, hidden agreements among individual journalists at different outlets, as journalists wrote stories for rivals or subbed for one another on government assignments. This was fairly common, given increasing government demands, shrinking news staffs, and the need for extra income. Most managers empathized with their staff's financial struggles and turned a blind eye to these policy transgressions, which widened the door to relationships across rival news outlets.

The online environment both fostered and frustrated occupational-level interaction. A collective of regional bloggers, starting around 2010, which included journalists and non-journalist citizens, both published content that fell outside the realm of government-sanctioned content, and shared their work. Online interaction among journalists and bloggers sometimes became hostile, but criticism could be constructive, with journalists challenging one another professionally. However, the growing prominence of digital online news in everyday news work is having divisive effects, spurring 24/7 competition with a growing number of outlets, encouraging ethical violations and distrust between outlets, and fragmenting journalists' understanding of audiences, practices and goals.

In sum, evidence for occupational community was fairly weak. The local journalism union was inactive, and journalists identified most strongly with their organizations. Government funding policies encouraged competition and resentment between journalists and between news outlets. Yet, some informal dynamics encouraged tenuous interaction across newsrooms, a loose and informal network, with, as yet, unrealized potential.

Journalists and Local Community

- *What is the nature of journalists' connections with their local community, and how and why has this changed or remained unchanged?*
- *To what degree are local journalists bridging local citizens' needs with official responses, and in what ways?*

The two age-old threads of local Russian journalism—service to governing elite and service to the region's people—have remained apart more than they have intertwined. The format of the *Government's* paper represents this continuing disconnection: one section for government reports and another "for people," as reporters called it. More recently, news managers have discouraged posting of government information through social media, believing it will drive away online users who seek engaging, entertaining content.

Local journalists have found it extremely difficult to address the problems of their communities and citizens beyond the level of the individual. Regional policy has been largely inaccessible to journalists and citizens during our study, and historically, there has been no meaningful public sphere in Russia's regions, as some scholars have argued (e.g., Kiriya & Kachkaeva, 2011). From a critical perspective, the ongoing distinction between "journalism for the elite" and "journalism for the common people" has supported social control by political-economic elite—control that could be challenged by a public sphere with integrated discourse among regional leaders, journalists and citizens. In fact, many journalists, especially in Region A, do not even think of service to the regions' residents as a societal-level task. Problems that are framed as public, societal or collective are trouble for the regional government, and, particularly in Region A, regional officials have focused on putting out individual fires before they grow large enough to catch attention beyond the region. What little focus there was on large-scale public-level problems in Region A early in the study narrowed to nearly nothing over the years. Economic dependence has played an important role in this trend—the continuing publication of investigative projects in the wealthier Region C seems evidence of this. But it is also true that the logics that might channel journalists toward a societal-level service have faded. The perestroika-era desire to draw back the curtain on the governing elite has weakened across the years of study, and moral education stories are framed as individual-level problems and challenges.

While the "life-hacking" logic takes an individual-level orientation, these stories hold some promise in terms of journalists' ability to represent people's problems to the government. Some stories have approached system-level criticism. Life-hacking journalists dutifully report government information, but they may also critique government implicitly, through the reporting of practical steps to deal with problems. This is very subtle criticism, however, and life-hacking journalism has limited appeal to journalists who value more interpretive socio-political journalism, even if they are rarely able to practice it.

Efforts to intertwine the threads of government and citizens—through life-hacking stories and personal assistance to readers, as well as through moral education stories—are limited. These seem to be niches left open in an underdeveloped ecology more than oppositional positions that journalists are taking in a competitive field. However, these efforts hold some promise for preserving the connective social tissue and shared trust between journalists and citizens, and mere maintenance of these connections keeps hope alive for collective action later. This maintenance may be a consequence of journalists carrying on and adapting from day to day, more than their staking out positions in opposition.

A few other trends in relationships between journalists and citizens were observed, mostly in Region A. Greene (2009) noted that paternalism toward citizens —"we know what's good for you"—was a core feature of some local Russian papers. We saw evidence of paternalism, but it did not seem a core characteristic of the regions' journalism. In fact, as newspaper staffs became more depleted and citizens' personal requests and complaints grew alongside increasing shortages and governmental red tape, a strained sense of obligation began to erode journalists' "calling" to help citizens. A Region C reporter noted that citizens were "angry," and at the *Government* paper, some journalists viewed readers as fed up with pointless coverage of government events. Journalists' patience with the region's demanding and sometimes hostile residents wore thin, and journalists became increasingly preoccupied with their own subsistence. They channeled the survival logic. Dealing with their own daily challenges drained away time and patience needed to attend to needy residents, and reporter burnout was a problem.

Digital online practices have been changing the journalist-citizen relationship in some ways, though dynamics differ across generations and work roles. Online technology enables journalists to connect with residents and even mobilize small-scale collective aid projects. Senior reporters have been most likely to use it to learn about residents' individual problems and stories. Younger journalists have appeared to be more comfortable in the online environment, but the call to engage interpersonally with local citizens and community has been fainter for these journalists, who came of age in a less high-minded time—after the ideological Soviet era and after the "freest" period of perestroika.

Most news outlets in our study have not tracked their online traffic in consistent, systematic ways, with the exception of some Region C papers. Most journalists and managers don't have a clear shared vision of the region's residents from their metrics, and few papers have conducted readership research. Instead, journalists have developed various shared constructions of "imagined" readers, a routine common to journalism across media systems (Sumpter, 2000), and these differed across papers. Examples: the reader in need, the non-urban reader who leads a "real life and not a virtual life," the hostile reader, the backward provincial, and in recent years, journalists have discussed readers in commodified ways, as consumers of print or online. One emerging typification of the reader is causing concern: the confused social media user—i.e., the reader who is losing touch with journalism and its meanings. Journalists worried that citizens were mistaking uninformed and sensationalized social media posts for journalistic work. "Journalism and social media do not overlap," as the *Traditional* reporter said.

Local Journalists: Autonomy or Survival?

- *To what degree are journalists' pursuing autonomy relative to local power, and to what degree are they mostly trying to adapt and survive?*

Field approaches assume social actors take oppositional positions against dominant positions, and the stakes of these struggles define the field, its boundaries, and who is or is not a player. Certainly, we need to understand the positions journalists take in a social space, and the influence of power and capital distribution in shaping these positions, when we analyze local Russian journalism. Yet, contemporary regional Russia has been called an "adaptive society" (Gudkov, Dubin and Levinson (2009), p. 32). Everyday people adjust to ongoing unfair, unlawful situations, and make changes informally (Ledeneva, 2006), at the individual level, to accommodate and survive rather than seek societal changes. Throughout our research, we have seen evidence of both field theory's opposition and ecological adaptation. Journalists seek some modest measure of professional autonomy, but they also seek to live to fight another day, or just to survive another day.

Whether seeking to win or to merely survive, local journalists engage in struggle. Findings suggest that struggles and their outcomes are shaped by constraining but shifting political-economic structures, by varying availability of logics and practices, and by emerging opportunities or cracks in the system. These varied constraints, channels and openings have led to creative acts of criticism and dissent, both meaningful and superficial. And often they have led to conformity.

Region A case studies offer helpful examples of these various struggles. Region A journalists have taken jabs at those encroaching on the boundaries, especially in the initial few years of our research, but these jabs became increasingly rare as the economy worsened after the recession and dependency on the government grew. When a new regional administration came to power, opportunities for journalists to assert themselves dwindled further. Prior to the new administration, journalists' assertions had already begun to take on a more controlled form. Reporting that urged authorities to address the region's problems was increasingly brought "in house," within the bounds of the bureaucracy. These took various forms: (1) telling officials about problems in lieu of publication—so-called preventive journalism, with roots in the Soviet era (Roudakova, 2017); (2) serving as a channel for transmitting residents' problems to officials; (3) producing in-depth analyses of issues that were appropriated as information for officials rather than published; and (4) giving citizens practical work-arounds and solutions for problems, some of which helped with bureaucratic red tape and unclear policy. Though these efforts have been largely state-controlled or skin-deep, they are examples of journalists asserting themselves and/or having influence: Preventive journalism allowed reporting on problems, for example, and sometimes led to government action. Journalists have found other cracks to exploit, leading to creative forms of subterfuge: using citizens to pose hard questions to officials; incorporating criticism or pointed questions from experts; and posting critical online commentary next to officially approved news stories.

Overall, our study revealed shrinking autonomy for journalists, but erosion of independence has not been linear, and the fact that journalists have managed to adjust and adapt as they continue to seek professional purpose and motivation is important.

Russian Local Journalism from a Global Perspective

- *What is local Russian journalism's place within the global context of local journalism, and what do our findings tell us about the contexts, purposes and practices of local journalism, generally?*

Pressures from local government and local business are not unique to Russian local journalism. Smaller social spaces everywhere (towns, cities, provinces) tend to have fewer power centers and are more likely to be governed by an elite who work together than are larger societal spaces, and this makes reporting of conflict less likely. In comparison to national-level outlets, local news outlets tend to have lower levels of resources and expertise, and stronger, more personal bonds between journalists and audience, both of which also can discourage reporting of conflict and revelation of problems (Nah & Armstrong, 2011; Hatcher & Haavik, 2014; Nielsen, 2015; Tichenor, Donohue & Olien, 1980). We saw similar mechanisms at work in our findings. For example, regional news outlets struggled with scarce revenue, small staffs and uneven expertise, and they tended to support the region, its people and its leaders from perceived external threats. Though the challenges of small social scale are relevant, their effects are secondary to the oppressive effects of the power vertical, the lack of meaningful legal support for the press, the strong financial dependence on government and lack of alternative sources of revenue, and an elusive public sphere. Even in Region C, as a reporter said, journalists feel they "have only one point of view—the authorities."

The fact that some practices and processes in local Russian journalism are found in other media systems place these practices and processes in a different light. An example is the increasing use of contracts and grants as funding mechanisms. In Russia's regions, it is not hard to see the mechanisms of control behind the funding. Yet, these contractual arrangements still have a veneer of openness, equality and voluntariness, which enhance their outward legitimacy. Interestingly, we are seeing grants from foundations and large tech companies, and in some countries from governments, play an increasingly important role in supporting financially troubled local news operations around the world. Journalists and scholars in liberal and social democratic media systems have voiced concerns about the influence of foundations, large tech companies and government on news content decisions, given their typically narrow missions (Benson, 2018; Hess & Waller, 2017; Nielsen & Ganter, 2018). The control that follows from dependence on these resources in Russia provides a cautionary tale, though, of course, the important differences across political-economic contexts must be taken into account. A phenomenon we did not see in our regions is collaboration among outlets on grant projects, which is increasingly popular in the West (Collaborative Journalism Database, 2020). The competition for contracts and grants in Russia is instead fragmenting the local journalistic community, partly a consequence of these competitions not being truly open and equal.

The growing neglect and irrelevance of traditional local news media seen in Russia's regions is also seen in other countries. In recent years, neglect has become an unusual mechanism of control, seen most clearly in Region A under its new media administration. Region A's *Traditional* newspaper is a poster child for the effects of neglect. The paper has no controlling ownership, and while weak ownership would seem to offer independence, it brings mostly economic hardship for the paper and saps journalists' motivation, which are their own kinds of shackles. One consequence of insufficient resources, a problem experienced across many papers, is a growing disconnect between the regions' newspapers and citizens. Judging from journalists' comments and readers' posts, many readers are tiring of content they see as irrelevant and uninteresting. Again, though these situation in Russia are severe, they are not entirely unique to Russia's regions. Local news publications around the world are suffering from neglect, and some newspapers have turned into severely understaffed and under-resourced "ghost papers," continuing to inhabit the media ecosystem but with little animated purpose (Abernathy, 2018). This literature often frames these problems as economic rather than political, though some recent scholarship has discussed political motivations and implications (e.g., Ali, 2017). Also, there have been problems with "superficial and deferential" reporting in local journalism around the world and a growing worry that these news outlets are "no longer an integral part of community life" (Nielsen, 2015, p. 18).

The Strength of Grass

Our account of journalists' work in three Russian regions describes a complex and changing social space that is experiencing eroding autonomy as well as some creative adaptation. The future looks grim, though it is not a certain future or one without possibilities. Findings here focus on journalists' perceptions. Logical next research steps involve analysis of regional residents' perceptions of local news and a deeper exploration of news content (with care taken for anonymity). Our claims in this study are limited solely to the journalists, papers and regions we studied, but findings should inform other scholars' work. The regions we studied have similarities with others, while the differences across time and regions that our findings do reveal also suggest value in additional comparative study.

The way forward for these regional journalists and their news outlets looks bleak, and in the midst of the COVID-19 crisis, we must say that things look bleaker. We have no illusions that journalists in the regions we studied will soon find themselves interacting in a dynamic local public sphere, united as a strong journalistic community, or that they will find the authority to right their regions' wrongs in the face of power.

We have focused on small and modest victories throughout the text, not because they have mobilized social action or led to impressive change, but because small and modest victories are what are available and evident. Yet, we find the efforts that led to these victories to be remarkable. Many of these journalists—especially those who came of age before or during perestroika—have kept the faith, continuing to care about their regions and their citizens and the roles they still play in shaping these.

These journalists have a double burden—the burdens inherent to local journalism generally, and the burdens inherent to journalists working within a quasi-authoritarian system. Under these pressures, these journalists have bent the knee to the powerful, squabbled with their colleagues, and stepped over ethical lines. It would be a miracle if they hadn't. Yet, in a way, even these actions show ingenuity, common sense and commitment. When they capitulate to power, they have found latent ways to parry; when they squabble with colleagues, they testify to their passion for their work; when they violate an ethical principle, they know why and they regret it, with an eye on better days. By continuing on and keeping the faith, they have shown the "strength of grass," struggling upward toward the small opportunities that constitute hope in the heartland.

References

Abbot, A. (1988). *System of professions: An essay on the division of expert labor*. Chicago: The University of Chicago Press.

Abernathy, P. M. (2018). The expanding news desert. UNC School of Media and Journalism. https://www.usnewsdeserts.com/

Ali, C. (2017). *Media localism: The policies of place.* Urbana: University of Illinois Press.

Benson, R. (2018). Can foundations solve the journalism crisis? *Journalism, 19*(8), 1059–1077.

Boczkowski, P.J. (2010). *News at work: Imitation in an age of information abundance.* Chicago: University of Chicago Press.

Collaborative Journalism Database (2020). https://collaborativejournalism.org/database-search-sort-learn-collaborative-projects-around-world/

Goodwin, R., Allen, P., Nizharadze, G., Emelyanova, T., Dedkova, N., Saenko, Y., & Bugrova, I. (2002). Fatalism, social support, and mental health in four former Soviet cultures. *Personality and Social Psychology Bulletin, 28,* 1166–1171.

Greene, S. A. (2009). Shifting media and the failure of political communication in Russia. In B. Beumers, S. Hutchings & N. Rulyova (Eds.), *The post-Soviet Russian media: Conflicting signals* (pp. 56–70). London: Routledge.

Gudkov, L. D., Dubin, B. V., & Levinson, A G. (2009). Fotorobot rossiiskogo obuvatelya [A sketch of the Russian everyman]. *Mir Rossii, 2,* 22–33.

Hallin, D. C., & Mancini, P. (2004). *Comparing media systems: Three models of media and politics.* Cambridge: Cambridge University Press.

Hanitzsch, T. & Vos, T.P. (2018). Journalism beyond democracy: A new look into journalistic roles in political and everyday life. *Journalism, 192*(2), 146–164. https://doi.org/10.1177/1464884916673386

Hatcher, J., & Haavik, E. (2014). We write with our hearts. *Journalism Practice, 8*(2), 149–163. https://doi.org/10.1080/17512786.2013.859828

Hess, K., & Waller, L. (2017). *Local journalism in a digital world.* London: Palgrave Macmillan.

Kiriya, I., & Kachkaeva, A. (2011). Economical forms of state pressure in Russian regional media. *Romanian Journal of Journalism and Communication, 6*(2), 5–11.

Ledeneva, A.V. (2006). *How Russia really works: The informal practices that shaped post-Soviet politics and business.* Ithaca: Cornell University Press.

Nah, S., & Armstrong, C. L. (2011). Structural pluralism in journalism and media studies: A concept explication and theory construction. *Mass Communication and Society, 14*(6), 857–878. doi:10.1080/15205436.2011.615446

Nielsen, R. K. (2015). Introduction: The uncertain future of local journalism. In R. K. Nielsen (Ed.), *Local journalism: The decline of newspapers and the rise of digital media* (pp. 1–25). I. B. Tauris & Co.

Nielsen, R. K. & Ganter, S. A. (2018). Dealing with digital intermediaries: A case study of the relations between publishers and platforms. *New Media & Society, 20*(4), 1600–1617.

Roudakova, N. (2017). *Losing Pravda: Ethics and the press in post-truth Russia.* Cambridge: Cambridge University Press.

Sumpter, R. (2000). Daily newspaper editors' audience construction routines: A case study. *Critical Studies in Mass Communication, 17*(3), 334–336.

Tichenor, P. J., Donohue, G. A., & Olien, C. N. (1980). *Community conflict & the press.* Beverly Hills: Sage.

Van Maanen, J., & Barley, S. R. (1984). Occupational communities: Culture and control in organizations. *Research in Organizational Behavior, 6,* 287–365.

APPENDIX

Methodology

This research is based on the qualitative study of local journalism practices and contexts in three Russian provinces. Overall, 124 individuals participated in the study. Qualitative data have been collected each summer from 2007 to 2019, resulting in 104 weeks of data across 13 years, averaging eight weeks per year. Between summers, participants were followed on social media and through stories on news outlets' websites. Email interaction and Skype conversations with key participants took place each year during months between summers.

Research participants. Over the years, a number of public officials at different levels—from heads of city districts to the State Duma deputies—shared additional insights into the news production process in the three regions. Regional leaders of the Russian Union of Journalists in regions A and C and five leaders of the Russian Union of Journalists in Moscow were interviewed. 18 public relations practitioners employed by state and private enterprises in the three regions were also interviewed. Some of the PR practitioners were former journalists who participated in our study as newspaper staffers and later moved to PR.

24 of 56 Region A participants interviewed in 2007 remained respondents throughout the study. Many were interviewed multiple times each year. Three Region A participants were hired by mainstream publications in Moscow at some point during data collection. Four became press secretaries for business organizations in the region's capital. Nine retired, and three were fired (for performance

Table 1. Number of in-person interview participants by job responsibilities.

	Region A 2007–2019	Region B 2012 and 2015	Region C 2013 and 2016	Moscow 2012	Total
Editors	9	1	2		12
Publishers	1				1
Reporters	43	7	11		61
Digital/Social media	3	1	5		9
Photographers	3				3
Proofreaders (copy editors)	5				5
PR private, including agency	7	5	6		18
PR government	2				2
Government officials	5				5
The Russian Journalism Union leaders	2		1	5	8
Total	80	14	25	5	124

Table 2. Number of interviews each year (2007–2019).

s	Region A	Region B	Region C	Moscow	Total
2007	56				56
2008	42				42
2009	45				45
2010	40				40
2011	32				32
2012	32	14		5	51
2013	34		20		54
2014	36				36
2015	34	7			41
2016	32		13		45
2017	34				34
2018	37				37
2019	41				41
Total	495	21	33	5	554 unique and repeated participants
Average	38.08				42.61

reasons). One nationally recognized journalist from Region A left the profession to start a successful business enterprise. He continued to follow the region's media and offered an outsider/insider view. A few others who left the field also continued to provide information. Five participants were lost to cancer.

Respondents' length of professional experiences varied, from three months to 40 years, averaging around 12 years. Previous experience varied, from rural newspapers to urban mainstream publications. Most staffers (about 80%) were between the ages of 30 and 50, but there were outliers at each newspaper, with some staffers in their 60s (about 10%) and some in their 20s (about 10%). All respondents had university diplomas, though not required for employment. Roughly a quarter had journalism degrees, and others majored in Russian language and literature, history, engineering, law, finance and public relations. The majority (60%) of respondents were women. At least 90% of participants were born and raised in the region in which they worked. Some additional characteristics of these newspaper staffs are provided in Chapter 5.

Data gathering. An average of around 40 interviews and 8 focus groups were conducted each year. Interviews and focus group sessions were audio-recorded after informed consent was obtained. Only one of the authors, Dr. Elina Erzikova, engaged in data collection.

The average interview lasted approximately 70 minutes. One interview lasted five hours, an outlier—a conversation with an experienced newspaper editor who had an urge to share insights on journalism's past, present and future. (In Russian culture, it is considered rude to try to control the time spent on conversation.) 15- to 20-minute interviews often followed lengthier interviews, in order to expand on and clarify points. Interviews were in-depth and semi-structured. Some questions were pre-planned, informed by research questions and theoretical perspectives, but many non-scripted questions emerged organically during interviews, and interviews allowed for follow-up questions during and after. Newspaper issues (offline and online) and particular news stories were used during interviews to ground discussion in actual lived situations.

Focus groups were conducted to shed light on group dynamics within newsrooms, to shed additional light on individual interview responses, and to triangulate, serving as a trustworthiness check on interviews. The average focus group lasted approximately 50 minutes. Typically, two focus groups were conducted at each paper in Region A during each summer of the research period. Two focus groups were conducted in Region B in both 2012 and 2015, and two focus groups were conducted in Region C in both 2013 and 2016. Focus-group size ranged from three to seven, and the researcher served as the focus-group moderator. Most focus-group questions were semi-structured and pre-planned, but unscripted follow-up questions were also asked, for clarification or to pursue productive lines of discussion. Most questions were similar to interview questions, but some questions were added if prior interviews suggested they would be productive.

Assuming that researchers "come to the field with presuppositions, questions and frameworks" (Burawoy, 1998) and "theoretical backgrounds" (Timmerman & Tavory, 2012), the coding process was both deductive and inductive. Codes—i.e., types of logics and roles, and strategies for challenging authority—emerged from interview and focus-group findings and were informed by theory and previous research on Russian journalism and local journalism. Two researchers analyzed content from transcripts, noting differences in emerging codes and interpretations (Cresswell, 2014; Guba, 1981).

Newsroom observations (direct rather than participant) were conducted primarily for triangulation purposes, to shed light on points and themes that emerged from the interviews and focus groups and to strengthen the trustworthiness of the study's findings and conclusions. On average, the researcher spent approximately 10 hours per week at each newspaper that was included in a particular year's sample for a given summer, and approximately eight hours were dedicated to interviews, focus groups, informal conversations and observations. During "quiet times" (when reporters were busy with tasks), the researcher wrote notes on observations and reflections to be looked over later for analysis, and jotted down preliminary thoughts about conclusions.

Observations included participation in weekly formal and informal meetings. Respondents' informal interaction with one another and with management and government officials were also observed. Readers and reporters' friends visited newsrooms to chat and drink tea—occurrences that were more part of the routine than they were interruptions—and these were observed.

Some participants preferred to meet for interviews at a workplace, and others preferred to meet at informal settings such as coffee shops. About three-fourth of interviews were conducted at newspaper locations, either in small meeting areas (with reporters) or personal offices (with editors and managers), behind closed doors. Precautions were taken to ensure interviews were not overheard by colleagues. The focus groups with reporters were held without the presence of the management team. Occasionally, informal meetings outside of newsrooms were observed, for context—e.g., birthday celebrations and other special occasions. These provided insights into reporters' lives outside of work, which is relevant to the concept of occupational community.

Each summer, at the end of data collection, brief private meetings were held in participating newspapers to review and discuss major results, adding trustworthiness to findings. Participants were able to check accuracy of the findings, comment and expand on them. Changes seen as appropriate were made.

In the coding, analysis and write-up, pseudonyms were used for names of newspapers and regions to protect reporters' confidentiality, promised to them in informed consent. Individuals were identified only by roles, level of experience or general age (e.g., a vice-editor, a senior reporter, a new editor, a media department official) and gender. Because regions B and C are mentioned less frequently than Region A, neither names nor pseudonyms were provided for region B and C papers. While we provided relevant information on each region, we avoided detailed information because of journalists' potentially tenuous employment situations and the sometimes fraught political environments. The identities of specific regions and papers are not at issue, as the research focus is largely on research participants' perceptions of political, financial, social and cultural contexts and factors, and how these vary across types of regions and across time.

Cases: newspapers and regions. We identified three regions for study: Region A, the primary case study region and the only region studied across all 13 years, from 2007 to 2019; Region B, which was added in 2012 (and studied in-person in 2012 and 2015); and Region C, added in 2013 (and studied in person in 2013 and 2016). These three were selected because of variation in population size and national resource levels. Region A is the poorest and the smallest in population, Region C is the wealthiest and largest, and Region B falls between A and C on both resource level and population size. For the purposes of this study, the terms "regional," "provincial," and "local" are used interchangeably. More characteristics about each region, in comparison to national characteristics, are provided in Chapter 2.

The study launched in 2007 with a sample of four legacy newspapers from Region A. When selected, these papers met six criteria: (a) they were regional in scope (produced and distributed in an administrative area outside the capitals, and focused on local-level issues, events, places and people); (b) they were socio-political or "quality" publications, meaning they addressed public issues (and were not just advertising vehicles); (c) they had circulations of at least 10,000 copies a week; (d) they were published regularly; (e) they had operated in the local media market for at least 10 years prior to selection for study; and (f) type of ownership varied across the four papers. One newspaper, the *Regional Branch*, was dropped from the study in 2013 because reporters were replaced by advertising managers, and the paper became an advertising vehicle.

Below we provide general information on paper size, circulation and staff sizes for papers, across the period of study. We note that none of the newspapers' circulations has been audited, and there was some evidence, based on interviews, that Region A circulation numbers were overstated.

The *Government* is the oldest newspaper in Region A. As the official organ of the regional government, the paper is supported with subsidies from the regional government's budget. At the beginning of the study, in 2007, the *Government* was a 24-page bi-weekly (twice a week) with circulation of around 20,000-25,000 copies/week. By the end of the study period, following economic challenges, both the number of pages and weekly circulation numbers had dropped by around a third. The *Government* has had a regularly maintained website, managed by two to three reporters, 24/7, who also managed three social-media platforms. The paper had several advertising managers throughout the data collection.

The *Private* has been owned by a local business owner with other media holdings. The newspaper has an advertising department with a salaried head and a few freelance managers, and the department has targeted local businesses with some success. The paper's managers have also regularly obtained information contracts with the regional government that have ensured ongoing access to government information. The paper has had free advertising from the owner's other media, which increased newspaper copy sales. As with the *Government*, the *Private* was forced to reduce the number of pages in each issue by a third during the Great Recession. The *Private*'s circulation fluctuated during the data collection, from 20,000-30,000 copies a week in 2007 to less than 20,000 in 2009–2013 and back up slightly in 2014–2019. The *Private* does not have a website. The *Private* was fairly stable in the number of staffers—around five reporters worked for the paper each year in 2007–2019.

The *Traditional*, a weekly publication, was launched by the city administration and mayor during perestroika to counterbalance the regional media controlled by the governor. The mayor was eventually defeated, and his resignation started years of financial struggle for the *Traditional*. As a result of the Great Recession, the paper laid off staffers and reduced the number of pages by a third. In 2007, the publication had more than 10 reporters and its circulation was over 10,000 copies a week. In 2019, the newspaper could afford fewer than five reporters, and its circulation dropped by around half. For several years, the regional government has been supporting the *Traditional* through paid "state assignments," but the subsidies are tiny. The paper has survived mainly due to the revenue earned by a low-cost supplement for gardeners. The *Traditional* has a website that has been updated once a week after publication of each print copy. The *Traditional*'s advertising department decreased from five managers in 2007 to two in 2019.

The fourth newspaper, the *Regional Branch*, was a regional branch paper of a mainstream publication headquartered in Moscow. The *Regional Branch* received both private advertising revenue and government funding, and it was the only paper in Region A that made a sizeable profit in 2007–2010. The paper published an ad/classified supplement to support main newspaper operations. Colleagues from other publications called the *Regional Branch* a "sweat shop" due to a high productivity demand—at least 20 stories a day. Reporters produced stories for a website with a 24/7 newsfeed and a print publication. The *Regional Branch* had a circulation of 10,000-20,000 copies a week in 2007. Circulation declined to less than 5,000 copies a week in 2013. The number of reporters declined from more than 10 in 2007 to zero in 2013. Because advertising managers curated news content found on other regional news outlets' websites, the decision was made to exclude the *Regional Branch* from the study in 2013.

None of the interviewed reporters in Region A knew the exact sources of revenue in their newspapers, and none of the Region A managers were willing to discuss the topic. However, we provide estimates here.[1] 90% of the *Government* revenue came from state subsidies and 10% from advertising and subscriptions. Importantly, the subsidies included "government ads" or payment for printing regional government decisions and regional Duma's legislations, a key revenue source for regional publications. The Region B participant benefited from publishing government documents from the early `90s to the mid 2000s, when this task and the revenue were transferred to an organ of the regional government. Recently, Region B newspaper management began working on giving up private ownership and becoming a state-owned newspaper to assure steady financial support.

The *Private* revenue breakdown was approximately 50% from newsstand sales, 25% from adverting sales and 25% from "state assignments" (contracts with regional government departments). The largest source of revenue for the *Traditional*—up to 70%—was subscriptions and newsstand sales of its weekly supplement for gardeners; approximately 20% came from advertising sales and subscriptions for the *Traditional* itself (separately from its supplement) and 10% came from paid state assignments.

The Region B paper, added in 2012, is a longtime newspaper in the region with a weekly circulation of 15,000-25,000 (as mentioned, pseudonyms were not used for region B and C papers). This is a privately owned newspaper, owned by a group of reporters. The paper's website, launched in 2001, is updated on a 24/7 basis, and the paper also has regularly managed social-media accounts. The paper's main revenue sources are subscriptions, newsstand sales and private advertising, and the paper has an advertising sales staff. The newspaper also has obtained government contracts to cover activities of the city administration and regional government. In 2019, 50% of the paper's earnings came from advertising, 25% from contracts and

25% from subscription, according to the editor. (Newspaper managers in other regions avoided speaking about revenue sources.)

In 2013, three newspapers were recruited from Region C. As with regions A and B, the papers were socio-political legacy publications that had operated in the Region C market for more than 10 years. As with the Region B paper and Region A's *Government*, the first Region C paper was a longtime paper in the region, and the paper is comparable with the Region B paper and the *Government* in terms of history and professional culture (adhering to Russian traditional journalistic approaches such as, for example, valuing feature stories over neutral breaking news stories). The newspaper has both print and digital versions, and offers paid access to a PDF version of a print edition. The paper's circulation was less than 15,000 copies a week in 2019.

The second Region C paper is part of a private holding that includes a magazine and weekend edition, and each of these three outlets has its own website. Among all newspapers in the three regions, this paper would generally be considered number one in quality of design, writing and printing. Twelve reporters worked for the holding in 2013, and only seven in 2019. The majority of staffers have journalism degrees, and they tend to be young and ambitious. They produce what they call a "capital quality" (i.e., Moscow quality) product, but content is primarily native advertising, or paid content. The editor said that 70% of all revenue was "state and municipal contracts," that "advertising (comes) only from large companies" and that his paper receives contracts for doing "corporate PR." In 2019, the second Region C's paper circulation was under 10,000 copies a week, while its weekend supplement had circulation of over 100,000 copies a week.

The third Region C paper was launched by an energetic recent journalism school graduate as a print publication in the early 2000s, and it expanded to the digital space within its first year. The newspaper offers business news, city events, and analysis of socially important trends. Ad revenue comes primarily from respected business owners. In 2019, around 70% of profit came from advertising sales, and 30% came from contracts to cover regional and city government activities. Subscriptions bring little (circulation was under 10,000 copies a week in 2019). Between 2013 and 2016, a team of around five reporters was strengthened by a digital editor and digital analyst.

Note

1. Based on circulation and subscription numbers, analysis of newspaper content including advertisements, and conversations with journalists.

References

Burawoy, M. (1998). The extended case method. *Sociological Theory, 16(1)*, 4–33.
Creswell, J. W. (2014). *Research Design: Qualitative, Quantitative and Mixed Methods Approaches (4th ed.)*. Thousand Oaks, CA: Sage.
Guba, E. G. (1981). Criteria for Assessing the Trustworthiness of Naturalistic Inquiries. *Educational Communication and Technology: A Journal of Theory, Research, and Development, 29(2)*, 75–91.
Timmermans, S., & Tavory, I. (2012). Theory construction in qualitative research: From grounded theory to abductive analysis. *Sociological Theory, 30(3)*, 167–186.

Index

A

Abbott, A. 48, 50, 52, 174
Advertising 31, 36, 72–75, 87, 196–98
　ad revenue 31, 32, 72–75, 87, 176, 198
　hidden advertising 72, 80
　paid content 72, 155, 163, 198
Alexeev, M. 25
Ali, C. 53, 188
Anderson, C.W. 5, 52, 53, 57
Anikina, M. 12, 33
Audience 38–39, 83–86
　online 83, 110, 111–114, 119, 125, 126–28
　offline 83
Autonomy 8–9, 47–48, 50–53, 153–170, 174, 186–87
Azhgikhina 71, 100, 132, 141, 144

B

Barley, S. R. 95, 182
Becker, H.S. 52

Benson, R. 48, 51, 53, 99, 188
Beumers, B. 6, 13, 27, 36, 40
Bourdieu, P. 15, 51–52, 95, 99

C

Camaraderie 92–94, 128
Capital
　cultural capital 51, 115, 127, 136, 144, 150–51, 179, 181
　economic capital 51, 72–75, 79, 90–2, 95, 150, 179
　symbolic capital 91, 99
Carlson, M.C. 52, 57
Censorship 5, 11, 39, 76–77, 156–60
Cold War 101
Community journalism 53–58, 187–188
Community citizens 3–4, 12–13, 39–40, 49–50, 57–8, 83–86
Competition 36, 86, 95, 97, 106, 117, 133, 149, 182, 183, 188
Contracts 37–38, 72, 176, 187–88, 196–98
Corruption 27, 156, 164–67

D

Defiance 75, 86, 160–64, 170
  Aesop language 162
  armies of one 168
  subversive tactics 163, 167
Demographics 30
  participants 90
Dependence on government 75, 133–38
Donohue, G.A. 5, 54, 55, 187
Dovbysh, O.S. 32, 36–38
Dunn, J.A. 27, 33, 34, 36, 55
Dzyaloshinsky, I.M. 33, 34, 36, 141

E

Ecological perspectives 52, 53, 57–59, 186–87
Education and training 103–06
Erzikova, E. 36, 50, 75, 100, 132, 141, 146
Ethics violation 12, 120–121.

F

Federalism 7
Field perspectives 50–52, 58–59
Fligstein, N. 48, 51
Fragmentation
  and newsroom generation gap 99–103
  of occupational community 94–99
Friedland, L. 49, 50, 53, 57

G

Gel'man, V. 8, 9, 10–11
Goszakaz 85, 117
Government
  agencies 79, 158
  assistance 71, 157
  control 11, 36–8, 54–56
  government service logic 133, 178
  Mass Communication Department 70–71, 77
  Moscow-regional government relationships 154–58
  oversight 76–7, 164
  press service 79, 154, 162, 173
  regional government 70–80
  (state) assignments 77–78, 183, 196, 197
  subsidies 55–56, 71–75.
Grants 36–38, 71, 72, 187–88
Gratis press 31, 80
Greene, S.A. 38, 39, 185

H

Hallin, D. 35, 54, 179
Hanitzsch, T. 12, 33, 39, 47, 141, 179
Hatcher, J. 6, 53, 54, 57, 187
Hess, K. 53, 55, 56, 57, 58, 109, 188
Honoraria 91, 97–8, 106, 119, 134, 149, 150, 168, 176, 182
Hutchings, S. 6, 13, 27, 36, 40

I

Institutional "decoupling" 35, 165
Internal newsletter 79, 135, 137, 177

J

Job hopping 97, 182–83
Journalism
  fact-based 100, 138–39, 144–45, 178–80
  investigative 36, 106, 124, 132–33, 134, 150, 156, 158, 164–67, 177, 184
  as a mission 8, 84–5, 106, 132, 133, 141–43, 167–68
Journalists' Union 94, 97

K

Kachkaeva, A. 9, 27, 32, 36, 37, 38, 184
Kasyutin, V.L. 11, 13
Kiriya, I. 9, 27, 32, 34, 35, 36–37, 38, 56, 184
Kobak, D. 29
Koltsova, O. 33, 35
Kordonsky, S.G. 27, 29
Kynev, A. 30

L

Ledeneva, A.V. 8, 10, 50, 186
Liu, S. 15, 48, 50
Logics
    anti-western logic 138–41, 178
    digital commerce logic 133, 150, 180, 181
    government service logic 133–38, 177–78
    moral education logic 141–43, 179
    life-hacking logic 145–48, 180
    literary logic 143–45, 179–80
    perestroika-era logic 132–34
    survival logic 148–50, 180
Lounsbury, M. 49, 51
Lowrey, W. 36, 50, 75, 100, 132, 141, 146

M

McAdam D. 48, 51
Managed democracy 27
Mancini, P. 35, 54, 179
Marx, K. 15
Matveeva, L.V. 38
Methodology
    data gathering 193–95
    newspapers and regions 195–98
    research participants 191–93
Mentorship 99, 105, 106
Meso-level approaches 48–50

Molyarenko, O.A. 27, 29
Moscow 7, 26–27, 28, 140, 154–56, 179

N

Neo-liberalism 32, 36, 56.
News content 33, 57, 72, 84–85, 87, 197
Newsroom culture 92–94
Nielsen, R.K. 50, 52, 53, 54, 56, 57, 187, 188
Nygren, G. 12, 56, 57, 58

O

Oates, S. 5, 38, 39
Ocasio, W. 49, 51
Occupational community 50, 94–99, 106, 181–83
    cohesiveness 95–96, 100, 182–83
    identity 81, 95, 126
Olien, C.N. 5, 54, 55, 187
Online presence 110–28, 168
    analytics and online traffic 112–14, 117, 124–126, 127, 133, 162, 181, 185
    blogging 121–22, 168
    chatrooms 98
    comments 116, 118, 155, 162–64
    "digital only" reporters 116, 117–19
    engagement 117, 123–126, 128
    governor's blog 116
    plagiarism 120–21
    Yandex 117, 127
    паблики ("publiki—social media forums) 119
    сайтовики ("saitoviki"—digital reporters) 119
Orthodox Church 30, 85

P

Pasti, S. 5, 33, 99
Perestroika 8–10, 26, 81–82, 100, 132–33
    logic *see perestroika-era logic*

Petilainen, J. 5
Post-perestroika 10–12
Poverty (personal financial struggle) 9, 90–92, 176
Preventive journalism 136, 156–160, 164, 170, 186
Pshenichnikov, M.S. 29

R

Reader, B. 54
Regions
   characteristics 25–31
   definition 3–4, 18
   history 6–12
Relationships between reporters and
   local elites *see Logics (government service logic)*
   managers 80–82, 86, 87
   readers 83–87
   reporters *see newsroom* culture
Robinson, S. 51, 53, 54, 57
Romanovich, N.A. 5
Ross, C. 29, 9, 10–11
Roudakova, N. 5, 8, 10, 38, 39, 49, 186
Rulyova, N. 6, 13, 27, 151

S

Sensationalism 99–100, 114, 127–28, 139, 161, 178
   chernukha 125
   online 114, 127
Scott, W.R. 15, 48, 51, 52
Shpilkin, S. 29
Slavtcheva-Petkova, V. 5, 12, 34
Smyth, R. 38, 39
Social media 98, 110, 111–14, 115–16, 117–19
   Facebook 110, 112, 116–118, 125, 126, 137
   Odnoklassniki.ru 112, 113, 116, 117
   vKontakte (VK) 112, 116, 117, 163
Socialization to profession 101–105, 119

Supplements 85, 111, 146, 196, 197
   weekend supplement 80, 197, 198
Sustainability 36–38, 57–58, 72–75, 90–92, 111–112, 175–76

T

Thornton, P.H. 49, 51
Tichenor, P.J. 5, 54, 55, 187
Trajectories 99, 182

U

User-generated content 58

V

Van Maanen, J. 95, 182
Vartanova, E. 12, 71, 100, 144
Vorobyev, D. 27, 29
Vos, T.P. 39, 47, 121, 141, 179

W

Waller, L. 53, 55, 56, 57, 58, 109, 188
Weber, M. 49
West
   Anti-Americanism 139
   Anti-Westernism 40, 101, 138–141, 150–51, 177–180, 182
Westernization 100

Y

Yurchak, A. 39–40

Z

Zubarevich, N. 10–11, 26, 28–29, 40, 41